Organization Design

Jeroen van Bree

Organization Design

Frameworks, Principles, and Approaches

palgrave
macmillan

Jeroen van Bree
Berenschot, Utrecht, The Netherlands

ISBN 978-3-030-78678-6 ISBN 978-3-030-78679-3 (eBook)
https://doi.org/10.1007/978-3-030-78679-3

Cover illustration: eStudioCalamar

This Palgrave Macmillan imprint is published by the registered company Springer Nature Switzerland AG.
The registered company address is: Gewerbestrasse 11, 6330 Cham, Switzerland

To Lisa
for your unconditional support

Acknowledgments

Since publishing my first book in 2014,[1] my ideas about organization design have evolved extensively. This has been due to the influence of three communities that I would like to acknowledge here. The first is the European Organisation Design Forum. My first book proved to be my ticket into this wonderful group of people, who are passionate about the field and generous in sharing their knowledge. Paul Tolchinsky and Mark LaScola in particular deserve special mention, because they have shaped the way I look at our profession and at how it should be framed and approached. The second community is that of Berenschot, the consulting firm that I joined at the end of 2014. With my colleagues of the organization design team, we exchanged experiences, challenged each other, and worked on a joint approach. Rutger Verbeet and Christiaan Gort deserve special mention, for the space they offered me to develop myself professionally. Berenschot gave me the opportunity to work on organization design projects for a wide variety of clients, facing many fascinating challenges. Some of the most interesting project examples have found their way into this book, always disguised to protect the innocent. The final community I want to acknowledge is that of the University of Amsterdam, where I started teaching in 2018. Developing two master's courses in organization design challenged me to structure my thinking, back it up with evidence, and keep up to date on research output with a relevance for our field. But most of all, working with my students—sometimes in small, face-to-face settings, lately in large groups mediated by technology—has shown me fresh directions and alternative perspectives on some of the key aspects of organization design.

Lastly, there are a number of people I want to thank in particular, for taking the time to review draft versions of individual chapters: Nick Richmond, Peter Kuiperij, Hans Lekkerkerk, Jodie Goulden, Paul Tolchinsky, Peter Turgoose, and Ime Hüsken. I have tried to do justice to your comments, but any faults that remain are entirely my own.

[1] Game Based Organization Design, Palgrave Macmillan.

Contents

List of Figures

List of Tables

Introduction

1

Abstract

This book is intended to be relevant to both students and practitioners of organization design. It describes the frameworks, principles, and approaches that are helpful in designing organizations, based on the premise that there is value in seeing this activity as a deliberate effort. The first part of the book covers the 'what' of organization design: an organization design as the end product of a design process. The second part covers the 'how' of organization design: organization design as a process to produce that end product.

Keywords

Organization design

This book was conceived and written during what may turn out to be the most remarkable period my generation will live through: the COVID-19 pandemic. The idea to write a book such as this one had been percolating for some time, and the first lockdown in the Spring of 2020 prompted me to start developing it into a proposal. By the time I handed in the manuscript one year later, vaccinations were being rolled out across the world. But even though an unparalleled pandemic formed the backdrop for my writing, COVID-19 barely made it into the book.[1] It is of course possible that I am vastly underestimating the long-term impact the pandemic will have, but from my current vantage point, I do not see major shifts in the frameworks, principles, and approaches that form the field of organization design, other than those that were already taking place. The reason why I could not see any major

[1] It is only mentioned in the context of 'linking mechanisms' (Chap. 8).

J. van Bree, *Organization Design*, https://doi.org/10.1007/978-3-030-78679-3_1

new shifts may have to do with the fact that this book is intended more as a toolbox for designing organizations than as a description or prescription of how to organize. It rarely talks about specific solutions[2] but mostly about ways to design these solutions. And because some of the tools in this toolbox have stood the test of time—some even dating back several decades—I feel confident that their relevance will outlive COVID-19.

1.1 This Book's Purpose and Target Audience

This book's—admittedly rather ambitious—intent is to be relevant to both students and practitioners of organization design. It is an attempt to write a work that is relevant to managers while being anchored in rigorous academic research. There are several reasons why combining these two target audiences is hard. Chief among them is the issue of language. The abstract language of an academic journal article is often far removed from the practical language of a popular business publication. In this book, I have tried to strike a balance.

If you would ask me to choose between these two audiences, I would say that the book is first and foremost a textbook, intended for students in an MBA, master's, or executive masters' program. It was conceived as such, as I was teaching a course at the University of Amsterdam and could not find a textbook that offered a broad enough overview of the field of organization design for my purposes. Where at all possible, this book builds on previous research and on the documented wisdom of practitioners. My ambition was to offer a complete overview of the work that was done in our field over the past decades. Whether you think I succeeded largely depends on how you define organization design. That definition will be the subject of the next chapter. And I should add that some authors and schools of thought receive more attention than others, based on my personal preferences and my design philosophy (more about that philosophy later).

But, in all fairness, I am first and foremost a practitioner. I have kept the practitioner perspective in mind—be it that of a business leader, manager, consultant, coach, or HR professional—with everything I wrote. This means I have added examples where I saw fit, have described subjects in a manner that makes practical application possible, and have tried to build a logic into the book that makes it easy for a practitioner to navigate through the entire toolbox that organization design has to offer. But I realize that the references and the intermittent surges of abstract language will scare off a part of my intended practitioner audience. I am targeting those of you who are looking for evidence-based guidance in the practice of organization design.

[2] With the exception of Chap. 5, which is completely dedicated to examples from the field.

1.2 This Book's Design Philosophy

Before you embark on reading this book, it is important to be aware of the design philosophy from which it was written, because that philosophy necessarily comes with its assumptions and limitations. Some of the elements of this design philosophy are clearly stated along the way, but we need to address a few of them upfront. First of all, I see value in organization design as a deliberate effort. I acknowledge that an organization design can sometimes simply emerge, but that is not the perspective I am taking in this book. Working from that starting point, I describe in this book the frameworks, principles, and approaches that I consider to be helpful in that deliberate design effort. A second element of my design philosophy is a blank slate approach. Designing or redesigning an organization does not mean copying existing models, templates, examples, or best practices, but producing a solution that is specifically geared toward the issues and context that the organization in question is facing. However, a blank slate does not mean you can just start doodling. There is an order to things, and there are frameworks and principles that can be helpful. This leads me to the third element of my design philosophy: I try to be as impartial as possible toward the final product of an organization design process. It is not for me to say whether an organization design is good or bad. That is determined by the fit the design has with the context in question. The tools presented in this book will help you determine and achieve that fit. The end result may just as well be a fairly traditional management hierarchy, as it can be a radically decentralized way of organizing using autonomous teams. Finally, I have chosen in this book to focus purely on the core organization design work. That means only limited attention is paid to implementing a new organization design and to the people processes involved in that transition. Luckily, a wealth of resources on change management, project management, human resource management, and organization development is at the disposal of the reader.[3]

1.3 How This Book Is Organized

This book is organized along two themes. The first four chapters cover the 'what' of organization design: an organization design as the end product of a design process. The last four chapters talk about the 'how' of organization design: organization design as a process to produce that end product. By its nature, the second part of the book is more practical, describing a step-by-step approach for an organization design project. As such, it could be read independently, although it assumes knowledge of the frameworks and principles covered in the first part of the book.

[3] Some of which I will point the reader toward, particularly in Chap. 9

1.3.1 The What of Organization Design: Chaps. 2, 3, 4 and 5

Chapter 2, **"What Is Organization Design?"**, lays the foundation for discussing organization design by introducing a common language and a number of frameworks, which will be used throughout the book. It also contrasts organization design to neighboring fields such as organization development.

Chapter 3, **"What Are the Triggers for Organization Design?"**, discusses the reasons why organizations choose to revise their design. It also talks about the forces that can hold an organization back from embarking on a redesign, even though there is a clear rationale to do so.

Chapter 4, **"What Makes for a Well-Designed Organization?"**, is the part of the book that is most prescriptive in nature. It introduces a number of design principles, based on the work of various scholars and practitioners. The principles are offered as ways to avoid common pitfalls when designing organizations, such as creating too many interdependencies.

Chapter 5, **"What Do New Ways of Organizing Look Like?"**, is the final chapter of the first part of the book and aims to show how the principles of Chap. 4 are visible in a number of contemporary organizations, most of which can be considered pioneering in their way of organizing. The common elements visible in their organization designs are discussed, which acts as a precursor to the approach covered in the second half of the book.

1.3.2 The How of Organization Design: Chaps. 6, 7, 8 and 9

Chapter 6, **"How to Approach an Organization Design Project"**, discusses the modes of intervention that are available to the organization designer. It then goes on to describe the typical stages of an organization design project, which are covered in more detail in the subsequent chapters. The approach proposed in this chapter is a collaborative one, and the central role of the design team is explained.

Chapter 7, **"How to Group the Tasks of an Organization"**, starts with a description of the first step in an organization design project: the discovery stage, in which the current context is explored and the desired future state is described. The discovery stage sets the boundaries and conditions for the core design work of logically grouping the tasks of the organization. With the help of a running practical example, this chapter explains the steps to go through in this grouping stage, which results in a design of the structure of the organization.

Once grouping has been completed, linking needs to start, which is the subject of **Chap.** 8, **"How to Link the Efforts of an Organization**". Linking refers to designing the mechanisms needed to integrate the various units of the organization. The chapter starts off by explaining the concept of interdependence and the various types of interdependence that can occur. It then goes on to describe the array of linking mechanisms that are available to the organization designer and gives guidelines about which linking mechanism to choose for which type of interdependence.

Chapter 9, "How to Prepare for the Transition", deals with the work that remains after the strategic design has been completed. Conducting an impact assessment is described, as well as the decision-making that needs to happen based on the assessment results. The final stage of the design approach described in this book is the 'prepare transition' stage, with the operational design and transition plan as the major deliverables. The chapter and book close with a reflection on the concept of continuous design.

1.3.3 How Each Chapter Is Organized

Each chapter contains a number of pedagogical features that are helpful for any reader, but particularly geared toward students and their instructors:

- Each chapter starts with an abstract, which gives an overview of the topics that will be covered.
- Following the abstract, there is a list of learning objectives, which readers can use to test whether they are grasping the main points of the chapter.
- There are practical examples throughout the text, the more extensive ones highlighted.
- There are tables, figures, and highlighted key points throughout the text, to summarize the most important information.
- Each chapter ends with a list of review questions; these can be used as homework assignments or as a jumping-off point for a discussion, in class or in other settings.
- Finally, each chapter ends with a list of the references used; some of these will be specifically highlighted in the text, but all of them offer interesting further reading.

2 What Is Organization Design?

Abstract

Organization design is a relatively young field with close relations to its neighboring fields of professional endeavor and academic inquiry, such as organization development. One of the aspects that set organization design apart is its focus on formalizable elements such as structures, processes, and roles and a claim that we can design or redesign those elements to achieve intended outcomes. Organization design is about much more than just the structure of the organization. Jay Galbraith's Star model is a framework that shows the other elements that need to be taken into consideration, such as tasks and decision processes. It also shows that these elements interact and need to be aligned. The four fundamental problems of organizing introduced by Puranam et al. provide another framework for analyzing organizations and their design. It identifies two interlinked problems of organizing: the division of labor and the integration of effort. Both Galbraith's and Puranam's frameworks offer useful vocabulary for organization designers with regard to the elements that can be designed or the questions that need to be answered.

Keywords

Organization design • Organization development • Star model • Fundamental problems of organizing • Division of labor • Integration of effort • Organizational structure

J. van Bree, *Organization Design*, https://doi.org/10.1007/978-3-030-78679-3_2

Learning Objectives

- Describe what organization design is.
- Compare organization design to organization development.
- Relate organization design to concepts such as operating models.
- Employ a framework to describe the relevant design elements of an organization.

Organization design[1] is a concept that means many things to many people. I have attended every annual conference of the European Organisation Design Forum[2] (EODF) since 2013, and the variety of people who associate themselves with this topic has always amazed me (Fig. 2.1). It ranges from business unit managers and strategists to HR professionals and leadership coaches, from people interested in Agile practices to those involved in implementing remote working, and from professionals using the latest data-driven tools for designing an organization to those focusing on engaging groups in large-scale sessions. For EODF, this array of people and interests is part of what makes the community so vibrant. That is why the

Fig. 2.1 The market of ideas at an annual conference of EODF (Photo: Organisation Design Institute)

[1] Sometimes referred to as 'organizational design'; for the purposes of this book, the two terms can be considered interchangeable.

[2] The professional association of organization design practitioners based in Europe; find them online at https://eodf.eu.

organization has always been hesitant in drawing too fine a line between what is and what is not organization design. What seems to unite this community is a drive to make organizations, and the people in them, thrive. There are many roads that can lead to this goal, which makes for very rich and expansive conversations at EODF's events. For the purposes of this book, I fear we will need to be a bit less inclusive.

Being less inclusive in this book does not imply that a connection is not needed between organization design and related fields. However, to do our topic justice in this one volume, we will need to limit ourselves. As we will see throughout this chapter and the rest of the book, there are vital connections between organization design and other fields such as organization development. It is not a question of one being more important or more effective than the other in improving organizations. Rather, one cannot go without the other. However, the issues that are explored and addressed, and the competencies required of those exploring and addressing them, can be quite different. This means that both from an academic and from a practitioner standpoint, it makes sense to make a distinction between organization design and related fields.

Let us start with the field that organization design is most commonly linked with, which is the field of organization development. The confusion often starts with the fact that both can be abbreviated as OD.[3] I will try to demarcate organization design in more detail later on in this chapter, but let us start here by saying a few words about its nearest neighbor: organization development.

2.1 Organization Development and Organization Design

In my experience of talking to people in both fields, those that associate themselves most closely with organization development like to talk about topics such as behavior, culture, and change. Those that associate themselves most closely with organization design will most likely talk more about structures, processes, and roles. Obviously, these groups of topics are symbiotic. But it is also evident that they may require very different approaches and perhaps very different types of professionals. To use somewhat of a caricature: organization development professionals think organization designers are too technocratic, too much focused on the rational, formalized view of an organization. On the other hand, organization designers find the field of organization development too esoteric, too much about things you cannot observe, measure, or design.

In a sense, organization design is a more specialized field of enquiry and professional endeavor. It looks at intervening in a number of very specific aspects of the organization (which we will discuss later on in this chapter), whereas organization development looks more broadly at the process for intervening effectively in organizations to achieve change,[4] which may include intervening in some of these design elements. More often than not, the focus of organization development is on

[3] Experienced practitioners always ask what the speaker means when they say OD, so as not to be at cross purposes.

[4] Using the perspective that one of the most prominent textbooks on organization development takes, by Thomas Cummings and Christopher Worley (2015).

- Structure: these are the basic choices about how certain activities—or activities for certain markets or for certain customers—are allocated to units in the organization: to teams, departments, and divisions.
- Information and decision processes: this encompasses a wide range of processes that are essential for tying the organizational structure together and making it work; this entails both vertical processes (prioritizing, planning, budgeting, reporting) and lateral processes (coordinating, aligning, liaising, integrating).
- Reward systems: systems that aim to align the efforts and performance of individuals and teams in the organization with the organization's goals; closely tied to this are the metrics that are used to measure individual and team performance.
- People processes: the HR practices of hiring, developing, and promoting the right talent to successfully run the organizational model that was chosen.

We will return to these elements of the Star model often in this book, as we cover them in much greater depth. The Star model comes with three core messages, which have endured since its inception over 40 years ago:

- Different strategies lead to different organization designs.
- Organization design is more than just structure.
- The elements of the model should be aligned.

Different Strategies Lead to Different Organization Designs

This message of the Star model can be traced back to the fact that Jay Galbraith, in one of his earliest publications (1973), places himself explicitly in the tradition of contingency theory. Galbraith—in his own admission—was heavily influenced by the work of Herbert Simon, James Thompson, and Paul Lawrence and Jay Lorsch. Contingency theory is the idea that organizations adapt their design to fit their context. The theory is summarized by Galbraith in the form of two conclusions it draws from empirical work: "1. There is no one best way to organize. 2. Any way of organizing is not equally effective" (Galbraith, 1973, p. 2). We will return to the ideas of contingency theory in the next chapter, because they remain very relevant 50 years later. A tendency to emulate the latest and greatest organizational model without regard for the context in which it is being applied is still a widespread practice. The contextual factor which gets a prominent place in the Star model is strategy. In the ur-version shown above, it becomes clear that strategy works through the element of 'task'. A firm's strategy determines what it needs to do well and which activities are necessary. This is the starting point for determining the fitting organization design. Producing commodity goods in a mature market should lead to a different design than introducing a new technology in an emerging market.

Organization Design Is More Than Just Structure

To illuminate this point, it is important to bring in a framework similar to the Star model that was developed around the same time and has become at least as influential: the 7-S framework (Fig. 2.4). When it was introduced by Robert Waterman et al. (1980)—all working at McKinsey at the time, the management consulting firm still closely associated with the framework—the authors presented 7-S as a way to think beyond structure in an organization's design. The 1960s and 1970s had seen several fashions with regard to new organizational structures in corporations, the multidivisional form, and the matrix organization being chief among them. But the inevitable disappointment had also set in, especially with regard to matrix structures. It had become obvious that the blunt instrument of structure had lost its power to further improve organizational effectiveness. This meant the time was right to broaden the thinking about organization design with frameworks such as Galbraith's Star model as well as 7-S.

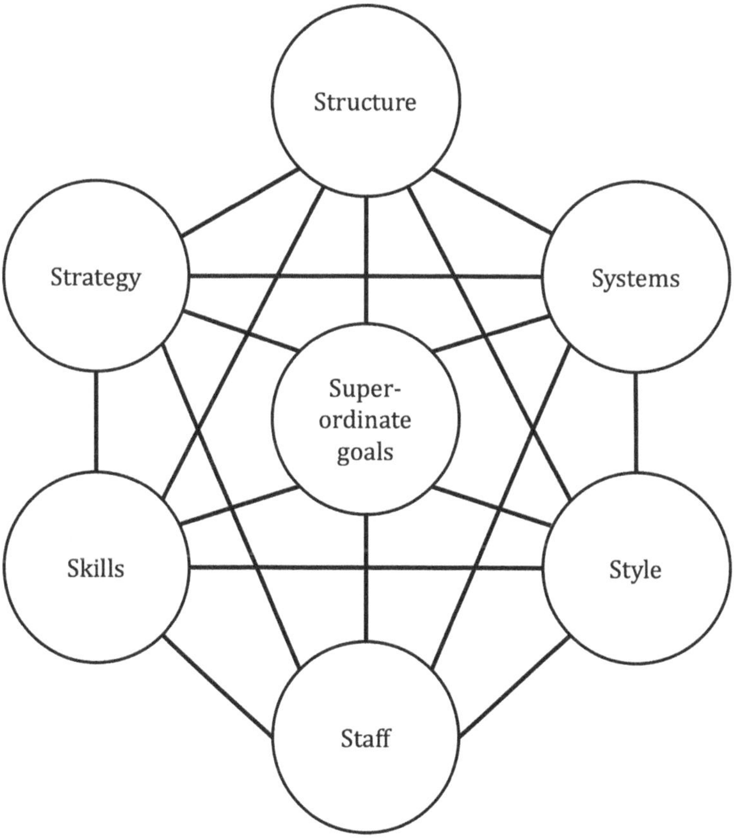

Fig. 2.4 The 7-S framework (Waterman et al., 1980, p. 18)

Many of the messages of the two frameworks are similar, especially when it comes to broadening the thinking beyond structure. The elements of the frameworks also greatly overlap. What sets the 7-S framework somewhat apart is its inclusion of 'softer' elements of organizing, such as 'style' (mostly referring to leadership style) and 'superordinate goals' (which in later incarnations of the framework morphed into 'shared values'). The 7-S framework as originally envisioned by Peters, Waterman, and Phillips did not claim to include only elements of the organization that can be designed—as the Star model does—but, rather, to show all elements of the organization that should be considered when orchestrating organizational change. This distinction is also the reason why organizational culture is not present as an element in the Star model, an absence that is often noted by those getting acquainted with the model for the first time. It is Galbraith's position that culture is not one of the elements of an organization that can be designed. Rather, he sees it as a behavioral element—along with performance—which can be influenced by acting through the other elements, which leaders can directly control. He describes what other design disciplines have called a second-order design problem.[7]

Both the Star and the 7-S framework contributed a great deal to having practitioners and scholars move beyond just structure when thinking about organizing and organization design. However, 40 years later, the term 'restructure' is still a common shorthand for the 'redesign' of an organization, much in the same way structure is for design. Using the former term does not necessarily mean the focus will be purely on structure, but it does invoke an image of boxes being moved around on the organization chart rather than a holistic approach considering elements such as management processes, reward systems, and people development. This may come across as a semantic dispute, but if we want to apply the lessons of the 7-S and Star frameworks, we need to take these labels seriously. For the purposes of this book, we will be strict in seeing structure as just one element of an organization's design. It is an important element, but not one to be looked at in isolation, which brings us to the third core message of the Star model.

Restructure, Reorganization, or Redesign?

When we talk about organization design, you could say that what we actually mean is *organization redesign*. In most cases there will be an existing organization, the design of which we aim to improve. However, as we will see later on in this book, the preferred design approach is one where we start from a blank slate. Rather than move lines and boxes around in an existing organization chart, we take a fresh look at the design that best fits with the organization's goals and context. The end result may be close to or far removed from the current design. So, organization design also encompasses the design of existing organizations.

If the focus of the design effort is purely on the structure—which we will argue against throughout this book—you could speak of a restructuring effort or *restructure*. If the aim of the effort is simply to reduce the headcount, organizations

[7] This is a term from video game design, where game designers use the rules of the game to indirectly design player behavior; see Salen and Zimmerman (2004).

tend to speak of *downsizing* or—to use a euphemistic term—rightsizing. Downsizing efforts rarely look at the organization design, but typically focus purely on reducing team sizes or eliminating roles. The pressure to show quick results to stakeholders usually drives this constricted view, even though looking more fundamentally at the organization design may very well pay off in the long run.

Implementing a new organization design,[8] a restructure or a downsizing, in almost all cases, involves a *reorganization*. By this we mean that any or all of the following occur: management structures and reporting lines change, composition and objectives of team and department change or new teams and departments are created, and role and job change or new roles and jobs are created. A reorganization involves moving people into new teams or into new roles (including new management roles), a process that is circumscribed by labor laws in most countries.

This is not a book about reorganization, downsizing, or restructuring. However, it is important to be aware of the links that exist between organization design and these common organizational change efforts. ◂

The Elements of the Model Should Be Aligned

Besides broadening the thinking beyond structure, another important insight was expressed by the Star model (as well as by the 7-S framework). That is the idea that all these elements of an organization interact. Changing one should not be done without making sure the others are still aligned. Galbraith (2014) stresses the importance of a consistent message for employees that comes with this alignment. This also extends more broadly to the effectiveness of the organization. Training and coaching teams in self-management without making changes to a highly centralized structure does not make sense neither does creating a structure with highly autonomous units without adapting the traditional, yearly planning and budgeting cycle.

Alignment of the elements of the Star can also work on another level, which is to have one element mitigate the negatives of another. More often than not, it is the negatives of the structure chosen that will need to be mitigated. As we will see in subsequent chapters, information and decision processes as well as reward systems can greatly enhance the strength of a structure or compensate for its weaknesses. Interventions in these elements of the Star are often communicating vessels: they are closely connected and will need to be aligned.

2.2.2 Puranam's Fundamental Problems of Organizing

Whereas Jay Galbraith created his Star model in response to his practical experiences of unsuccessfully trying to 'sell' isolated organizational interventions to managers,[9] Phanish Puranam, Oliver Alexy, and Markus Reitzig came at their set of universal

---

[8] More about implementation in Chap. 9.

[9] As related in Galbraith (2014).

problems of organizing in an attempt to frame theorizing about new forms of organizing. Theirs is not necessarily intended as an organization design framework—it is so universal as to also encompass emergent, that is, not deliberately designed, organizations—but it can productively be used as such. The power of the framework lies in its succinct integration of the existing organization theories into these four universal problems, which together form a logical set, solutions to which are claimed by the authors to be "individually necessary and collectively sufficient for an organization to exist" (Puranam et al., 2014, p. 166). Puranam and his colleagues claim that, taken together, scholarly work on organization design has identified two interlinked problems that need to be solved: the division of labor and the integration of effort. The foundation for this way of conceptualizing organization design was laid by James March and Herbert Simon (1958) who spoke of specialization and coordination, respectively. But perhaps the real founding fathers of this way of thinking about the design of organizations were Paul Lawrence and Jay Lorsch (1967), who spoke of the dual challenge of differentiation and integration,[10] when they laid out their contingency theory. The intuitive logic behind this way of framing organization design still prevails: it is about grouping the tasks of the organization in a manner that makes most sense and then tying these groups of tasks all back together.[11]

Puranam and his colleagues refine this framework by decomposing the two problems into two subproblems each.

- Task division: determining the tasks that the organization needs to perform to achieve its goals
- Task allocation: assigning the tasks (identified in the first subproblem) to individuals or groups in the organization
- Provision of rewards: providing rewards to the organization members to motivate them to perform the tasks that have been allocated to them
- Provision of information: making sure the organization members have the information needed to perform their tasks

There is an important extension to this framework, described by Puranam (2018) under the label of authority. Authority in organizations is superimposed on the four-problem framework in two ways. The first way is what Puranam has called the authority to design, determine, and potentially also enforce the solutions to the four problems. The second way is dispute resolution, the authority to manage exceptions when the solutions to the four problems fall short.[12] Theoretically speaking, authority—to design or resolve disputes—is not necessary for an organization to exist. The design could be emergent—that is, arise without authority—and it could be of such high quality that no exceptions occur that cannot be handled by the solutions chosen for the four problems. Particularly the last condition is unlikely in practice, hence the inclusion of exception management in the framework.

[10] As the terms they employ indicate, both March and Simon and Lawrence and Lorsch focused on an activity-based division of labor, which does not cover the entire spectrum of possibilities as we will see in Chap. 7.

[11] Much more about what this entails in Chaps. 7 and 8.

[12] Puranam mentions a third role—the authority to direct subordinates—which we will discuss in Chap. 8.

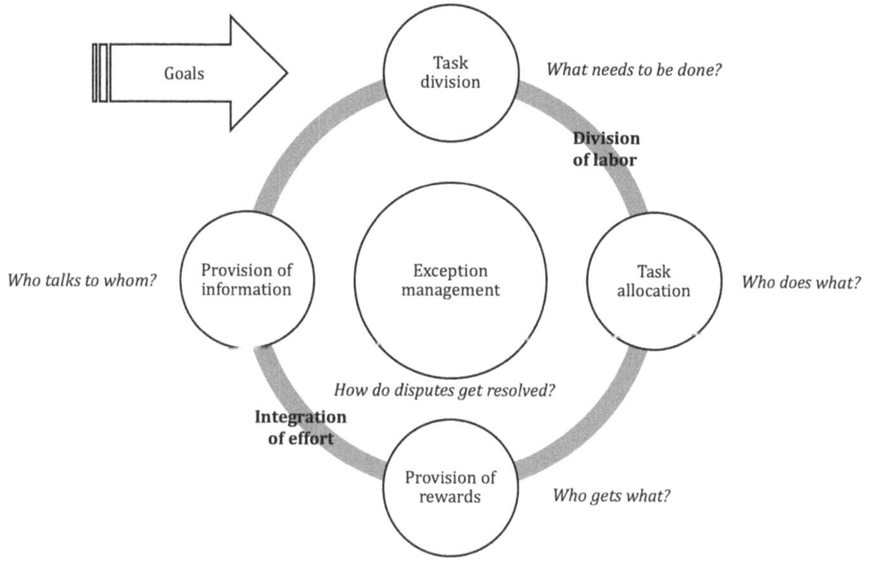

Fig. 2.5 The fundamental problems of organizing (based on Puranam et al., 2014; Puranam, 2018, 2019)

A final point to make about this framework is not so much an extension as it is an explication, regarding the position of strategy. Puranam and his colleagues do not speak of strategy per se, but consider organizations—following March and Simon and others—to be goal-oriented systems. The first of their universal problems takes these system-level goals as a starting point for determining the tasks the organization needs to perform. Combined with setting the goals, this could be considered a strategy process. But to avoid unduly conflating theoretical constructs, let us limit ourselves to goals. The organization's goals are considered an exogenous element in this framework, a starting point which directs the search for solutions to the four universal problems.[13]

Figure 2.5 gives a visual representation of the framework.

A Comparison of the Two Frameworks

Although they come at the topic from different directions and with different purposes, both Galbraith's Star model and Puranam's four fundamental problems offer useful vocabulary for organization designers, specifically when talking about the 'what', the artifacts involved in organization design: the elements that can be designed or the questions that need to be answered. I do not believe a head-to-head comparison of the two frameworks makes much sense—since their stated goals are different—but contrasting the two may help us focus our discussions in the ensuing chapters of this book.

[13] This point is stressed by the authors when they use the framework to compare forms of organizing *between organizations with comparable goals* (Puranam et al., 2014).

First of all, Galbraith's is more explicitly a strategic organization design framework, in the sense that it does not seem to allow for the possibility of an emergent design. The framework assumes leadership of an organization—authority, to use Puranam's term—who actively control the elements of the framework. Related to this, Puranam's framework is more universal in the sense that it uses a very inclusive definition of the organization, which encompasses any size (from two individuals up) and any purpose. Galbraith on the other hand assumes a large, for-profit organization, where concepts such as departmentalization, budgeting processes, and compensation systems have a place.

Looking at the individual elements of the frameworks, there are obvious areas of overlap. Most fundamentally, both frameworks stress the connection of the design to the organization's purpose: it does not make sense to talk about an organization's design without relating it to the organization's goals or strategy. Furthermore, Galbraith's reward systems link closely to Puranam's provision of rewards. Galbraith's elements of task and structure are very similar to Puranam's task division and task allocation. The biggest distinction is Galbraith's inclusion of people processes, albeit while placing it (together with rewards) as ancillary to strategy, structure, and processes. People processes is where Galbraith's Star extends beyond pure organization design into the implementation of the design. It is a useful extension, necessary for an organization to successfully apply a new design. The fact that it is so closely tied to implementation makes it a logical omission from Puranam's framework, which has analysis and comparison as its main goal. Finally, Puranam's provision of information is closely associated with Galbraith's information and decision processes. However, the latter also contains elements of what Puranam would call authority, where it concerns the vertical decision processes.

A final aspect to highlight when contrasting the two frameworks is that of alignment. An important message of the Star model is that the elements need to be aligned (hence the star shape which connects them) to communicate a clear message to the employees. Instead of alignment, Puranam and his colleagues speak of the complementarity of the solutions to the four problems, a slightly different concept. They consider "a pair of solutions to these problems [to] be 'complements' when adopting one increases the value of the other" (Puranam et al., 2014, p. 173). This opens the door to a description of configurations, or sets of solutions that fit together. It is something Galbraith stays away from. Rather, he speaks of 'offsetting' the negatives of a choice in structure by choices made for the other elements. He also suggests that certain information and decision processes better fit certain structural choices, such as when he speaks of the multidimensional firm in later work (Galbraith, 2010). But his framework does not suggest an avenue to configurations. Rather, it suggests a blank slate approach to organization design, merely offering a template. It shows which aspects the leadership of an organization needs to address when changing the design of their organization. The work of Puranam and his colleagues shows a research avenue of empirically identifying (new) forms of organizing as clusters of complementary solutions to the four universal problems, somewhat akin to Mintzberg's earlier work on the typology of five ideal types of organization (Mintzberg, 1980).

Organizations as Open Systems: The Viable System Model

Viewing organizations as open systems means viewing them as "capable of self-maintenance on the basis of throughput of resources from the environment" (Scott & Davis, 2007, p. 95). A well-known open systems model is the viable system model (VSM; Beer, 1979, 1981), developed by Stafford Beer in the 1970s. Beer applied theories about cybernetics, by Ashby (1956) and others, to management systems. At the base of Beer's model lay a belief that organizations and society as a whole need to be more adaptive. The model is recursive in nature in that it acknowledges that a viable system is embedded in a higher-level viable system and may itself contain lower-level viable systems. This means "that a system can be viable whatever level it exists at (individual, group, organisational, or societal)" (Ramage & Shipp, 2020, p. 195). According to Beer's VSM, "there are five necessary and sufficient subsystems interactively involved in any organism or organization that is capable of maintaining its identity independently of other such organisms within a shared environment" (Beer, 1984, p. 14). The first subsystem contains the primary activities (operation, production) and the regulation needed to perform them. Subsystem two deals with coordination between the various primary subsystems. Subsystems three, four, and five set—and (sporadically) monitor—the boundaries for the primary subsystems, gather intelligence about the environment, and develop policies for the system based on these inputs.[14] The VSM model—as well as other applications of general systems theory to organizations—has a distinct design orientation. That is to say, it is not so much intended to describe or understand an organization as it is useful to prescribe what the design of the organization should look like. Systems models are described using rigorous diagrams and mathematical vocabulary, which may scare off some practitioners. However, VSM has recently seen a bit of a resurgence as a framework that is well-suited to the current challenges of organizations and management (Hoverstadt, 2008). Many of the elements (subsystems) of VSM can be recognized in the frameworks we have covered in this chapter, such as the distinction between primary activities (division of labor in Puranam's framework) and the coordination between them (integration of effort). A complementary aspect lies in the sophistication of the VSM model in describing the strategic function (subsystems three, four, and five). The model shows the importance of effective mechanisms and processes for adaptation and change in an organization and gives practical guidelines for how to design this. ◀

[14] This three-sentence summary of the VSM model by no means does justice to its sophistication; please refer to Beer's original work (1979, 1981) for a more in-depth description.

2.3 A Few Words About Practitioner Terms

Now that we have taken an in-depth look at two organization design frameworks, we have some vocabulary at our disposal for talking about organization design. More specifically, we have a vocabulary for talking about the artifacts that an organization design process produces, in other words, the elements of the organization which can be designed. This gives us a more specific understanding of what organization design is. Unfortunately, the world around us—the academic world as well as the business world—is not always so strict. You may hear the term organization design used to designate something different than what we have understood it to mean in this chapter. Or you may hear other terms, which overlap with organization design or are perhaps even considered synonymous. We have already spoken about two of them extensively in this chapter: organization development and organization structure. Let us now turn to three others of these potentially overlapping terms.

2.3.1 Operating Model

One of the terms most closely related to organization design is operating model. It is a term popular with management consultants, who like to speak of a 'target operating model' when referring to the 'to-be' situation that an organizational change project is aiming for. The term operating model is often used rather casually, without a clear definition—and with the apparent assumption that the audience knows what it is—or fluidly, to fit the context of a specific organization. More often than not, you can replace operating model with organization design—in the sense in which we have framed the latter term in this chapter—without changing the message of what is being said.[15] The frameworks that are in use by consulting firms to talk about the operating model often resemble the Star or 7-S model[16]; in other cases, a framework such as Galbraith's Star is implicitly at the base of how the operating model is defined.[17] The implications of the frameworks used also are often similar: there needs to be alignment among the elements of the operating model and between the firm's strategy and its operating model. The extension that is sometimes made in comparison to the frameworks for organization design we spoke about in this chapter is to include aspects of technology in the framework.

There is one notable exception to more or less equating operating model with organization design. That is the framework called operating model canvas, developed by Andrew Campbell et al. (2017). Campbell and his colleagues take a broader perspective on operating models. Besides the usual elements of business processes, organization (i.e., structure), and management systems (encompassing information and decision processes, reward systems, and people processes), they also include locations, information systems, and suppliers in their definition of an operating

[15] See, for example, Atmar et al. (2019).

[16] See, for example, Strategy& (2021) and Blenko et al. (2014).

[17] As in Kesler and Kates (2016).

model. Of course, any framework that takes a broad view of the elements relevant in running an organization has value in preventing isolated interventions. But for the purposes of this book, we will keep our perspective slightly more focused and consider operating model to be synonymous with organization design. And when talking about the latter, we will use the frameworks covered in this chapter: Galbraith's Star and Puranam's four fundamental problems.[18]

2.3.2 Business Model

A popular and concise explanation of the term business model is that it forms a description of how a firm makes money, that is, which activities the firm performs to create and capture value.[19] Although there is debate among scholars about where to position it,[20] using the organization design frameworks employed in this chapter, we would place business models in the strategy domain. In that sense, the design of a business model precedes organization design. The most well-known framework for describing or designing business models is the business model canvas, developed by Alexander Osterwalder and Yves Pigneur (2010). The framework uses nine building blocks to map out the—current or future—business model (Fig. 2.6). These building blocks range from a description of the value proposition itself and its targeted customers to the revenue streams underlying it and the infrastructure needed to deliver it. This final element of infrastructure is where the business model links with the organization design. Especially the key activities needed to execute the organization's value proposition form an important starting point for the organization design, closely associated with 'task' in the original Star model. As such, a completed business model canvas can form an excellent starting point for an organization design effort.

2.3.3 Business Architecture

Business architecture is a term that comes from the information technology field, specifically the field of enterprise architecture.[21] Although definitions tend to vary, in this context business architecture is generally considered to be the necessary link between an organization's goals and its information technology. A business architecture would usually comprise at least the business processes and potentially other elements of what we have called an organization design in this chapter, such as the organization's structure. Besides this more limited scope, a number of things set a business architecture apart from an organization design. First of all, there is a strong

[18] Andrew Campbell enjoys comparing his operating model canvas with other frameworks he comes across in his blog: https://ashridgeonoperatingmodels.com

[19] For an extensive review of definitions, see Massa et al. (2017).

[20] For a review of this debate, see Massa et al. (2017).

[21] For an overview, see Gampfer et al. (2018).

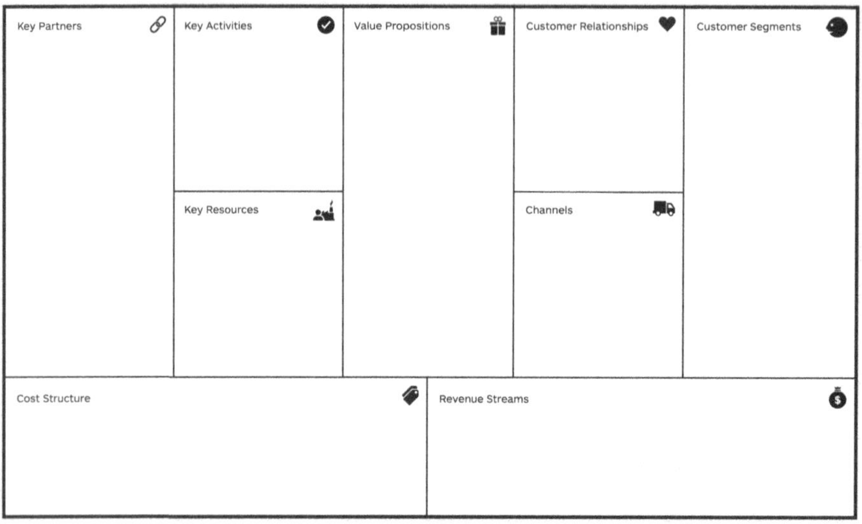

Fig. 2.6 The business model canvas (designed by: Strategyzer AG)

drive toward using modeling and mapping techniques to document the business architecture. Whereas there is no prescribed format for documenting an organization design[22]—other than the lines and boxes of the organigram—the field of business architecture uses highly formalized and standardized modeling techniques.[23] The second thing that sets it apart is that the business architecture is usually considered an intermediate product to get to the main focus of an enterprise architecture endeavor, which is developing the information technology architecture: a description of the data, applications, and technology needed to perform the business strategy. From that perspective, developing an enterprise architecture could be a logical follow-up or extension to developing an organization design. Many foundational elements of the business architecture should be available in the organization design, although possibly not at the required level of granularity or formal comprehensiveness. Because business and enterprise architecture comes from the world of IT and organization design comes from the world of management, the two tend to lead different lives. Academic research is conducted in distinct and insulated traditions, the practitioner communities have their own associations that rarely meet, and the two subjects tend to reside in different domains inside the organization: organization design as a general business issue in the domain of the CEO or COO and enterprise architecture confined to the CIO or CTO's domain.

[22] Although work has been done in capturing organization designs—or theories about organization design—in formal models (Puranam, 2018) and in developing algorithms to support the design effort (Worren et al., 2020), we are far removed from an agreed upon modeling technique for organization design; more about these new data-driven developments in Chap. 6.

[23] See, for instance, the business architecture section of the TOGAF framework for enterprise architecture (The Open Group, 2018).

When Business Architecture Meets Organization Design

An insurance company had started a sizeable project for the modernization of its IT systems. After the first steps had been taken in this IT project, the firm's management realized they needed to modernize their organization design as well. As part of the development effort for the modernization of their IT systems, an enterprise architecture had been developed. This included a business architecture in the form of models of the operational business processes. These process models proved to be an excellent starting point for the organization design effort, since the organization's main activities (its 'task' in the Star model) had already been mapped extensively. However, one problem was that the process models were not recognized by the top management team. Although the enterprise architecture had been validated and approved as part of the systems development effort—with the COO as a member of the steering committee—the top management team apparently did not see it as a topic they needed to be intimately familiar with. The enterprise architecture effort itself was not seen as strategic, whereas the organization design effort was. This meant that the high-level process model—based on the business architecture—had to be validated again as part of the organization design project. ◄

To close this chapter, I offer an overview of the key terms used in this chapter, each accompanied by a definition (Table 2.2). These definitions are by no means claimed to be conceptually solid. They merely serve to distinguish these terms for the purposes of this book.

Table 2.2 Definitions of key terms used in this chapter

Concept	Definition
Organization design	A systematic and holistic approach for aligning and fitting together all parts of an organization to achieve its defined strategic intents[a]
Organization development	The work of facilitating change in organizations through a holistic and humanistic approach that puts people at the heart of the process[b]
Organization structure	One element of the organization design: the basic choices about how activities are allocated to units in the organization (individuals, teams, departments, and divisions)
Organizational model	Also: form of organizing; synonymous with organization design
Operating model	Synonymous with organization design
Business model	The activities a firm performs to create and capture value
Business architecture	A model of an organization's business processes

[a]I borrow the definition used by the European Organisation Design Forum (2020)
[b]I borrow from the descriptions used by the Roffey Park Institute (2021)

Review Questions

1. Do you think it makes sense to distinguish between organization design and organization development? Or do you think it should be seen as one integrated discipline?
2. What are some of the commonalities and differences between organization design and other design disciplines such as architecture or industrial design?
3. Do you think that the elements of Galbraith's Star model cover everything that can be designed about an organization? Are there elements you would add or remove?
4. Comparing the Star model to the 7-S model, which one do you consider most useful for organization design? Why so?
5. Do you agree with Puranam et al. that solutions to the four fundamental problems of organizing are necessary for an organization to exist?
6. Do you think an organization can be designed effectively when there is no clear organizational strategy?
7. Do you think the Star model and Puranam's four fundamental problems are applicable to any type of organization (in terms of size, industry, etc.)? If not, to which types of organizations do they not apply?

References

Ashby, W. R. (1956). *An introduction to cybernetics*. Wiley.

Atmar, H., Becdach, C., Kleinman, S., & Rieckhoff, K. (2019). *Bridging the gap between a company's strategy and operating model*. Retrieved January 29, 2021, from https://www.mckinsey.com/business-functions/organization/our-insights/bridging-the-gap-between-a-companys-strategy-and-operating-model

Beer, S. (1979). *The heart of enterprise*. Wiley.

Beer, S. (1981). *Brain of the firm* (2nd ed.). Wiley.

Beer, S. (1984). The viable system model: Its provenance, development, methodology and pathology. *The Journal of the Operational Research Society, 35*(1), 7–25.

Blenko, M., Garton, E., & Mottura, L. (2014). *Winning operating models that convert strategy to results*. Retrieved January 29, 2021, from https://www.bain.com/insights/winning-operating-models-that-convert-strategy-to-results/

Brown, D. R. (2014). *Experiential approach to organization development* (8th ed.). Pearson Education.

Campbell, A., Gutierrez, M., & Lancelott, M. (2017). *Operating model canvas: Aligning operations and organization with strategy*. Van Haren Publishing.

Chandler, A. D., Jr. (1962). *Strategy and structure: Chapters in the history of the American industrial enterprise*. MIT Press.

Cross, N. (2007). *Designerly ways of knowing*. Birkhäuser.

Cummings, T. G., & Worley, C. G. (2015). *Organization development & change* (10th ed.). Cengage Learning.

European Organisation Design Forum. (2020). Retrieved January 29, 2021, from https://eodf.eu

Galbraith, J. R. (1973). *Designing complex organizations*. Addison-Wesley.

Galbraith, J. R. (1977). *Organization design*. Addison-Wesley.

Galbraith, J. R. (2010). The multi-dimensional and reconfigurable organization. *Organizational Dynamics, 39*(2), 115–125.

Galbraith, J. R. (2014). *Designing organizations: Strategy, structure, and process at the business unit and enterprise levels* (3rd ed.). Jossey-Bass.
Gampfer, F., Jürgens, A., Müller, M., & Buchkremer, R. (2018). Past, current and future trends in enterprise architecture: A view beyond the horizon. *Computers in Industry, 100*, 70–84.
Hoverstadt, P. (2008). *The fractal organization: Creating sustainable organizations with the Viable System Model*. Wiley.
Kesler, G., & Kates, A. (2016). *Bridging organization design and performance: 5 ways to activate a global operating model*. John Wiley & Sons.
Lawrence, P. R., & Lorsch, J. W. (1967). *Organization and environment: Managing differentiation and integration*. Harvard Business School Press.
March, J. G., & Simon, H. A. (1958). *Organizations*. John Wiley.
Massa, L., Tucci, C. L., & Afuah, A. (2017). A critical assessment of business model research. *Academy of Management Annals, 11*(1), 73–104.
Mintzberg, H. (1980). Structure in 5's: A synthesis of the research on organization design. *Management Science, 26*(3), 322–341.
Osterwalder, A., & Pigneur, Y. (2010). *Business model generation*. John Wiley & Sons.
Puranam, P. (2018). *The microstructure of organizations*. Oxford University Press.
Puranam, P. (2019). *AI and organization design*. Presented at the Organization Design Community Annual Conference 2019, Harvard Business School, Boston, August 11.
Puranam, P., Alexy, O., & Reitzig, M. (2014). What's "new" about new forms of organizing? *The Academy of Management Review, 39*(2), 162–180.
Ramage, M., & Shipp, K. (2020). *Systems thinkers* (2nd ed.). Springer.
Roffey Park Institute. (2021). What is organizational development. Retrieved January 29, 2021, from https://www.roffeypark.com/expertise/organisational-development-hr/
Salen, K., & Zimmerman, E. (2004). *Rules of play: Game design fundamentals*. The MIT Press.
Scott, W. R., & Davis, G. F. (2007). *Organizations and organizing: Rational, natural, and open systems perspectives*. Pearson Prentice Hall.
Simon, H. A. (1996). *The sciences of the artificial* (3rd ed.). The MIT Press.
Strategy&. (2021). *Our solutions—Operating model*. Retrieved January 29, 2021, from https://www.strategyand.pwc.com/gx/en/unique-solutions/capabilities-driven-strategy/operating.html
The Open Group. (2018). *TOGAF standard, version 9.2*. Retrieved January 29, 2021, from https://pubs.opengroup.org/architecture/togaf9-doc/arch/index.html
Waterman, R. H., Peters, T. J., & Phillips, J. R. (1980). Structure is not organization. *Business Horizons, 23*(3), 14–26.
Worren, N., Christiansen, T., & Soldal, K. V. (2020). Using an algorithmic approach for grouping roles and sub-units. *Journal of Organization Design, 9*(1), 1–19.

3 What Are the Triggers for Organization Design?

Abstract

Contingency theory offers the rationale for why organizations choose to revise their design: to achieve a fit between the organization design and the context that the organization operates in, which is necessary for the organization to perform well. This implies that a redesign is needed if the internal or external context changes, preferably before dysfunctional behaviors begin to occur that point to a misfit. This contingency rationale can be hindered by inertial forces that lead a top management team away from reviewing and revising their organization design, even though there are clear reasons for doing so. These forces can be internal, such as the dynamics of political coalitions, or external, such as a threat to legitimacy if the organization were to adopt a new design. It is important to acknowledge that these and other forces will sometimes prevent the implementation of the design that has the best fit. At times, organizations arrive at a new organization design without following the contingency logic, but rather through processes of isomorphism that can make organizations in a particular field start to look alike. Isomorphism can stem from pressures from the environment, professionals sharing norms and practices across organizations, and from the tendency of organizations to model themselves after peers they perceive to be successful. These processes come with important caveats from the perspective of organization design.

Keywords

Organization design • Contingency theory • Inertial forces • Isomorphism • Mimetic isomorphism

J. van Bree, *Organization Design*, https://doi.org/10.1007/978-3-030-78679-3_3

Learning Objectives

- Explain the rationale behind contingency theory, and apply it to organization design.
- Identify triggers and symptoms for reviewing the organization design.
- Recognize inertial forces that can hold back a redesign of the organization.
- Critically reflect on isomorphic processes taking place in an organization.

Now that the previous chapter has given us a clearer picture of what organization design is, we can take a look at the reasons for paying attention to it. Why go through the trouble of uprooting the way you are organized, potentially moving people into new teams and new roles, impacting how collaboration takes place and performance is managed, and putting your employees on a—sometimes stressful—learning curve? The rationale for answering this 'why' lies in contingency theory.

3.1 Contingency Theory: Making Sure the Organization Design Fits the Context

In the early days of management theory, one of the driving forces was the search for what you could call the best way to organize or, rather, the *one* best way to organize. Frederick Winslow Taylor is generally viewed as the founding father of an approach that sought to rationalize the production process, including the role of the individual workers in that process. Taylor laid down his ideas in *The Principles of Scientific Management* (1911), which became the label for his approach and that of his followers. The claim of scientific management was that maximum efficiency could be achieved by closely analyzing the tasks performed by workers and then designing that work in the best way, captured in a standardized procedure. Taylor acknowledged that redesigning the work had implications for other aspects of the organization, primarily the way in which work was managed. The role of the manager, in Taylor's philosophy, was to design the optimal work arrangements—based on scientific analysis of the tasks, through time utilization studies—and to make sure workers followed the standards they developed. A fairly paternalistic attitude pervades Taylor's work, in that he viewed workers as limited in their ability to optimize their own tasks. Their bosses, by following the principles of scientific management, would optimize their work for them and tell them how to perform their tasks most efficiently. And why would workers object to this, since this increased efficiency would mean higher wages? As Scott and Davis note in their review of scientific management and related schools, "Taylor's methods were by no means restricted to manufacturing plants but rapidly spread to the organization of schools, fast-food restaurants, and even amusement parks" (Scott & Davis, 2007, p. 43).

A second important figure in the early days of management theory is the French industrialist Henri Fayol. Like Taylor, he derived his ideas from his practical experience—Fayol was the director of a large mining company—but unlike Taylor, his starting point was not the tasks on the shop floor. His administrative theory (he preferred the term administration to management) set out a number of general principles about how an organization should be governed. Many of these principles seem self-evident today, a matter of common sense. That probably shows how foundational Fayol's work was, and the work of those who built on it in the United States after his *L'Administration industrielle et générale* had been translated into English (30 years after its original publication). Fayol's principles cover aspects such as how to allocate authority and responsibility, the importance of unity of command, and the optimal degree of centralization (Fayol, 1949).

Although both Taylor and Fayol prescribed no more than principles, they set in motion a search for the single best way to organize. It was not until the mid-1960s that this paradigm began to be challenged. At that time, a number of scholars published work that, from different perspectives, challenged the validity of the search for this single best way. Woodward (1958), March and Simon (1958), Burns and Stalker (1961), Chandler (1962), and Thompson (1967) all contributed to this paradigm shift, which was most clearly expressed by Paul Lawrence and Jay Lorsch (1967). Their 'contingency organization theory' states that "different organizational forms are required to cope effectively with different task and environmental conditions" (Lawrence & Lorsch, 1967, p. 203). The theory goes on to assert that the performance of an organization—or a part of the organization—is determined by the goodness of fit between the environment and its internal attributes, that is, its organization design.[1] In other words, there is no one best organization design. Rather, an organization design that performs well in one context—because there is a good fit between the organization's environment and its design—may well prove detrimental to performance in another context—because such a fit is lacking.

An important implication of contingency theory is that a redesign of the organization is necessary if the context changes, which is a general answer to the question that underlies this chapter. This idea was further developed by Lex Donaldson (1987) in his SARFIT model: structural adjustment to regain fit (Fig. 3.1). The SARFIT model states that there is an important intermediary stage between a change in the organization's context and a redesign. That intermediate stage is misfit. And misfit manifests itself in dysfunctional behaviors, which in turn lead to low performance. This logic offers some important clues as to when a redesign is necessary. There are two indicators to pay attention to. The first is the occurrence of these dysfunctional behaviors. Donaldson mentions "slow and poor decision-making, miscommunication, demotivation and so on" (Donaldson, 1987, p. 5). From my personal experience as a management consultant, I can add a number of symptoms to that list, such as lack of clarity about responsibilities, lack of collaboration or

[1] Another important contribution that Lawrence and Lorsch make in the same study (1967) is to identify two interrelated challenges in organization design: differentiation and integration.

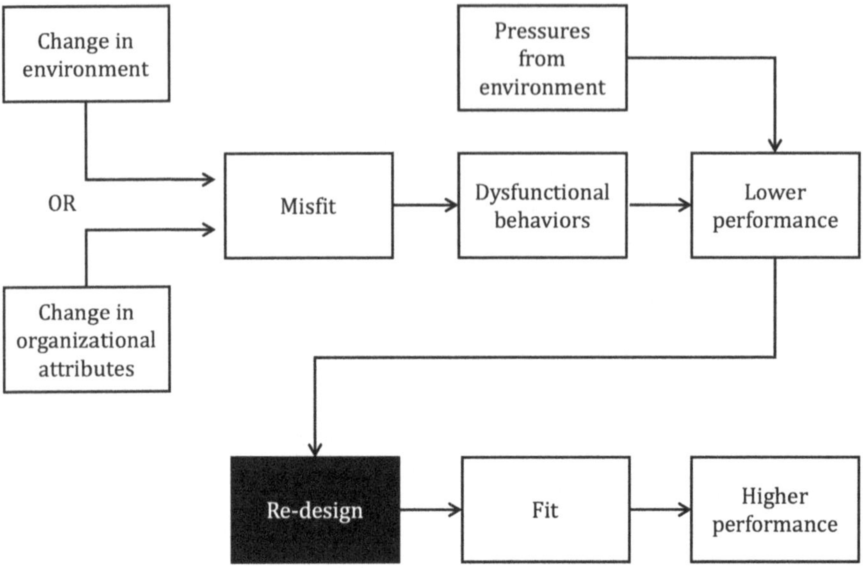

Fig. 3.1 The essential logic behind the SARFIT contingency model (based on Donaldson, 1987)

even conflict between teams or departments, or top management dealing with an overload of operational issues. Nadler and Tushman (1997) also mention underutilized skills and resources, cumbersome work flows, and a proliferation of task forces and committees as examples of dysfunctional behaviors. A change in conditions—causing these dysfunctional behaviors—is not always an autonomous, external event. Conditions may also refer to attributes of the organization itself. Typical examples of changes in attributes include rapid growth of the organization or a shift in competitive strategy. These are typical triggers for reviewing the design of an organization and making the necessary changes, preferably before the dysfunctional behaviors start occurring. Other, more external triggers include a shift in the competitive landscape or regulatory framework and the introduction of new technologies[2] which in turn impact the organization's core work.

Organizational Agility as a Response to an Uncertain Environment

One could easily argue that contemporary organizations deal with more external triggers for redesign than did the firms in the 1960s when Lawrence and Lorsch were putting their contingency theory to paper. In many industries, shifts in the competitive landscape are a common occurrence. Technological developments have enabled new business models which have challenged incumbent firms.

[2] See also Donaldson and Joffe (2014).

Uber and Lyft created the ride-sharing market, Airbnb made short-term rentals a viable alternative to hotels, Booking.com and Expedia replaced travel agencies, Amazon decimated retail stores, Google and Facebook ruined the advertising model of traditional media, and Netflix encroached on the production and distribution model of the movie industry. The list goes on. And it is not only new competitors entering the arena, there are also big global shifts such as the transition to renewable energy and a circular economy and swings in the political balance of power.

This uncertain and unpredictable environment has led organizations to look for organization designs that allow them to continuously adapt to changes. They have been striving for what has become known as organizational agility. One of the few research-based views on this phenomenon comes from Chris Worley and his colleagues (Worley et al., 2014), who attached this label to organizations that were consistently outperforming their industry peers over several decades. When studying these outperformers more closely, they identified a number of routines that made up this agility capability. These routines revolve around sensing the changes in the environment and responding to them. Although this may sound simple enough, the difficulty seems to lie in making sure that what your organization's people see in the environment ends up with the right decision-makers and that potential responses are tested, learned from, and implemented effectively. It is especially this predisposition to action, and to learning through experimentation, that seems to distinguish the agile organizations from the rest.[3] Seeing how widespread the exposure to an uncertain environment is for contemporary organizations—not just for profit-seeking firms but also for not-for-profit and public organizations—achieving organizational agility has become somewhat of a holy grail for many top management teams. This in itself is completely consistent with contingency theory: as the context changes, a misfit occurs, and a new organization design is needed. It starts going wrong when organizations start emulating a practice that seems to deliver agility in other organizations. More about this isomorphic tendency later on in this chapter. ◀

Besides dysfunctional behaviors, the second indicator for a misfit to pay attention to is the performance of the organization, although the relationship between that indicator and the organization design is much less clear. Contingency theory states that it is not a specific way of organizing that leads to performance, but rather the goodness of fit between the way of organizing and the organization's context. Again, an organization design that leads to exceptional performance in one context—say, building your organization around self-managing, Agile teams—could prove disastrous in another. If performance drops, a look at potential misfits is warranted, taking the organization design as an avenue for improvement. There may of course be many other areas besides the organization design to investigate and improve if an organization's performance is lacking. It will be virtually impossible to show that a change in

[3] See also Birkinshaw and Ridderstråle (2015).

an organization's design leads to increased performance, because of all the other factors at play. Chief among those factors is sorting (Puranam, 2018): which individuals are recruited or self-select into which organizations? Take the Dutch bank ING, which decided to adopt a new management model and way of working in 2015, inspired by Spotify, Google, and Netflix. This change significantly improved their performance, with a drop in cost and a boost in both employee engagement and customer satisfaction (Birkinshaw, 2018). But was this due to the new organization design, or was there perhaps a sorting effect? ING used these changes as a prominent tool for employer branding. Their new way of working and their revamped office environment were shown off in numerous articles, YouTube videos, and speaking engagements. It is very likely that this attracted the type of talent ING needed to achieve their goals. Who is to say that it was their organization design rather than this sorting effect which was the explanation for the performance boost they saw?

It is important to note that the dysfunctional behaviors that are associated with a mismatch between an organization's design and its context do not always lead to a drop in performance. Some organizations are able to absorb this dysfunctionality because of the slack resources they have at their disposal. This is a pattern sometimes visible with young organizations scaling up a successful business model. As long as there is a steady income stream and the organization can attract enough talent, there is no urgency to take a fundamental look at the organization's design. There will be a point, however, at which the situation becomes untenable. This point can be reached when employee frustrations mount, because of the aforementioned dysfunctional behaviors, when the organization is no longer able to deliver on its strategy, or because of a change in market conditions which eliminates the slack and dictates efficiency. This effect of the stringency of the environment was identified by Donaldson (1987), who speaks of environmental illiberality. A contemporary example was noted in a case description of GitHub (Burton et al., 2017). In their exploration of the boss-less organizational model of this fast-growing software company, the authors noted that weak selection pressures, that is, an abundance of "paying customers and slack internal personnel resources" (ibid., p. 7), meant most any organization design would work. So environmental illiberality (to use Donaldson's term) is an important catalyst for a misfit to eventually lead to a redesign of the organization. In a very forgiving environment, a misfit and the subsequent dysfunctional behaviors can persist without any pressure on the leadership to change the organization's design.

Scaling Up in a Forgiving Environment

Selling.net is an online retailer.[4] The firm started out in the proverbial garage of two German college students in 1998. It was since acquired by a US-based conglomerate and has grown into an Internet success story, with a current turnover of more than US$10 billion and a workforce of 15,000 employees worldwide. Especially over the past five years, the numbers have been tremendous, with

[4]This is a pseudonym for the actual company that this case description is loosely based on.

double-digit growth in revenue year-over-year and profit margins of 30% and more. New employees flowed in by the thousands each year, especially into their headquarters in Munich, where young professionals of dozens of nationalities were attracted by the perks that came with working at a thriving scale-up: being surrounded by smart people, spending your days in a trendy office with an informal vibe, and enjoying the many parties and getaways organized for the Selling.net staff.

The organization design had not been looked at fundamentally since the days of the company's founding. If an issue arose, the default answer was to 'throw people at it', in other words, to assemble a team—sometimes of new hires—to address this issue. The organization chart grew into an unwieldy web that nobody fully oversaw or really cared about, for that matter. Efficiency was not a consideration, since there was an abundance of resources: money was pouring in, and the Munich tech scene was an excellent talent pool to recruit from. Salaries at Selling.net were highly competitive, and the famed office parties did the rest. This 'throwing people at it' mentality meant that sometimes teams received assignments that they later found out other teams were working on as well. Some of the time, this was intentional, management's way of instilling competition for the best solution. But most of the time, it was by accident. Purely a result of the lack of deliberate thought put into how tasks were divided and allocated in the organization. This lack of deliberate thought also extended to how efforts were linked. The number of meetings needed to tie the operation of Selling.net together was incredible. And since all decision-making was consensus-based, getting real change off the ground took ages. But all this was not seen as a problem. The company was on a growth trajectory and did not need to do much more than execute on its highly successful business model. The forgiving environment allowed the misfit to exist without any negative effects on performance.

This did not mean that the misfit was invisible. The dysfunctional behaviors were all around: employee frustration about the inability to get any real technological innovation off the ground, management frustration about partly implemented strategic shifts, and a general loss of direction and purpose. Things came to a head when Selling.net's Chinese manufacturing partner cut all ties in 2018 in a move presumably instigated by the US-China trade wars. This left a major vulnerability in the company's supply chain completely exposed and sent a shock through its entire system. Revenue dropped by more than 50%, as did its parent company's stock price. All of a sudden, the cost of Selling.net's swollen headcount became a burden and the company embarked on a major downsizing effort to bring costs more in line with their dwindled revenues. It remained to be seen whether a fundamental look at its organization design, in order to regain fit, would be on the agenda of its top management team. Or would the appetite for a redesign disappear once profitability levels were back to what they were before? ◂

Table 3.1 Reasons to review the organization design

Triggers to review the organization design, that is, changes in context	Rapid growth A change in company strategy A changing regulatory framework Introduction of new technologies (which impact the organization's core work) A shift in the competitive landscape A merger, acquisition, or divestiture
Symptoms of the organization design no longer fitting the context	Slow and poor decision-making Lack of clarity about responsibilities Lack of collaboration or even conflict between teams or departments Top management team dealing with an overload of operational issues Underutilized skills and resources Cumbersome work flows A proliferation of task forces and committees

The reader will note that contingency theory does not prescribe which organization design would fit to which environmental conditions, only that there needs to be a fit. It is up to the designer embracing this orientation to decide which design ensures a fit. Research in the contingency theory tradition has only given some very general indications about specific fits. The classic example is Burns and Stalker (1961), who argue that mechanistic (bureaucratic) organizations fit well with conditions of certainty, while organic (flexible) organizations fit with an uncertain environment. Organizations would often require more specific guidance to achieve a fit. Design criteria can be an important tool to assist in this process, as we will see in the next chapter.

To close this section, Table 3.1 summarizes our discussion. It lists triggers to review the fit between your organization design and your context, as well as common symptoms that there may already be a misfit.

PartsPoint Group: A Redesign in Response to Rapid Growth

PartsPoint Group (PPG) is a distributor of vehicle parts in the Benelux with revenues of €250 million and some 1100 employees. PPG is a mid-sized player in a highly competitive market, in which economies of scale and a cost-efficient operation are essential for survival. PPG had been employing a strategy of growth through acquisitions and had gobbled up several smaller players in the Benelux market in recent years. Each of these acquired firms had its own distribution network, sourcing and procurement channels, and marketing apparatus. And each firm's managing director had simply been added as a direct report to PPG's CEO, creating an organization chart which had become unwieldy and an executive team of almost 20 members. The misfit between context and organization design, and the ensuing dysfunctional behaviors, was obvious. The time had come to channel this growth by revising PPG's organization design. The result of the redesign effort was a unified and much more streamlined organization. PPG's supply chain was now managed centrally—which allowed for a much-needed optimization project—and its distribution network was on track to be integrated under one brand, with much clearer commercial direction by a newly instituted Chief Commercial Officer position. The executive team was brought down to a group of five, which made deliberations and decision-making easier. A fit between PPG's context and its organization design had been restored. ◀

3.2 Inertial Forces: Why Not Redesign an Organization?

Now that we have looked at reasons to review or revise your organization design, let us look at the counterargument. What are some of the reasons not to do this? An obvious first possible answer to that question is that none of the triggers or symptoms mentioned in Table 3.1 are present. If an organization is operating in a steady context, is performing well, and is not showing any of the symptoms of dysfunctional behavior, one can safely assume its organization design is not in need of much attention. If there is a loss of performance, the dysfunctional behaviors start occurring frequently, or a shift in the context was perceived, the logic of the previous section would dictate a closer look at the organization design. However, not every organization follows this logic. One reason for this may be a matter of beliefs and convictions. Every top management team has their own beliefs about the levers they can pull to improve their organization's performance, which can be based on previous experience, what they have read, or what their consultant has told them. Levers to pull—other than the ones we have defined as part of organization design in the previous chapter—may include the use of technology, business process improvement, replacing or developing leadership, or an effort to change the company culture. Each of these efforts can have merit, and they may very well impact the performance of an organization positively. However, the specific triggers and symptoms mentioned in Table 3.1 will most directly be remedied by pulling the levers of the organization design. Apart from their personal convictions, why would a top management team not embark on a redesign if the need for it is obvious? The answer lies in the inertial forces at play.

As mentioned at the start of this chapter, embarking on an organization redesign entails upheaval and insecurity. Positions and potentially jobs are at stake, there may be new leadership, and employees move into new teams with a different manager. In general, the organization's members need to let go of what they know or even what they know to work (at least in their corner of the organization). What is wrong with the way we do things? What is the problem we are trying to solve? These are some of the questions that come up when the current organization design is reviewed. This common dynamic stresses the need for a clear rationale when embarking on a redesign, something we will return to in Chap. 7. In many European countries, a change in the organization's structure will need to be discussed with a body representing employees, such as the worker's council or labor unions. Not every management team looks forward to these discussions. All of these considerations can lead a top management team away from reviewing and revising their organization design, even though there are clear reasons for doing so.

A different, more macro perspective at these inertial forces comes from population ecology theory. This research tradition states that forms of organizing replace each other as environmental conditions change. The underlying—rather simplifying—premise is that organizations are subject to such strong inertial forces that they are unable to adapt, or at least, adapt timely and effectively, to environmental changes. As such, it stands diametrically opposed to contingency theory, which works from the rational conviction that organizations *are* able to adapt their design, improve their performance, and survive. Some of the inertial forces mentioned in one of the founding works on population ecology are listed in Table 3.2.

Connected to these inertial forces hampering adaptation is a belief in population ecology theory that there is only a loose coupling between the earnest efforts of many a top management team, devoted "to predicting the future and to developing

Table 3.2 Some common inertial forces to organization redesign (based on Hannan & Freeman, 1984)

Inertial force	Explanation
Sunk costs in plant, equipment, and personnel	Personnel is an especially relevant factor to take into consideration. An organization may not have the people that can navigate any new organizational model. Especially complex or nontraditional models such as a matrix structure or self-managing teams may require specific competencies. Investing the time and resources into developing or acquiring these competencies—either by training current staff or by replacing them with new hires—is sometimes not considered a viable option.
Dynamics of political coalitions	As many readers will recognize, decision-making in organizations is not a neat, linear, and purely rational process. The actual road to a decision involves consensus-building, coalitions, and opportunism.[a] This can serve as a strong inertial force to organizational change, including implementing a redesign.
Tendency for precedents to become normative standards	"This is the way we have always done things around here." In many organizations, it is hard to question—let alone change—structures and processes which have become deeply engrained in the organizational fabric.[b]
Threat to legitimacy	Certain stakeholders—such as regulators, shareholders, or employees—may look at some organization designs unfavorably. A loss of legitimacy—and a subsequent loss of access to markets, capital or labor—will prove detrimental to an organization's performance. This could make the implementation of a rationally speaking ideal organization design into an infeasible option.

[a]Scholars in the Carnegie Mellon School have written extensively about this, prominent examples being Cohen et al.'s (1972) 'garbage can model' and Cyert and March's (1963) 'dominant coalition'
[b]This notion is further explored in theories on imprinting, which we will not cover here; the interested reader is referred to Marquis and Tilcsik (2013) and Alexy et al. (2021)

strategies for coping with expected events" (Hannan & Freeman, 1984, p. 150), and actual organizational outcomes. That is a valid point. As mentioned before in this chapter, connecting a specific organization design to organizational performance is a tenuous endeavor. There are too many variables at play. However, the choice of doing nothing has serious consequences if the triggers and symptoms mentioned in Table 3.1 have come into play. Even though there will almost always be some unexpected consequences of an organization redesign, it is the opinion of this author that a well-managed organization design process is always better than waiting for the evolutionary forces to wipe your organization away. But this perspective does show us that there are forces at play in organization design projects which may prevent us from implementing the design that has the best fit with the context.

AST Logistics: Managers as a Prime Inertial Force

Air & Sea Transport Logistics[5] (AST Logistics) is a medium-sized Belgian company in the logistics industry (350 employees, €170 million in revenues), which wanted to improve its organizational agility. The executive team (CEO, CFO, and COO) had recently been on a study trip to China and had become convinced that their organization needed to adapt more rapidly to the market forces coming their way. AST had been working on innovation projects along several roadmaps, but progress was slow. The pace of change that the executive team had seen in China had scared the living daylights out of them. A considerable number among their employees shared their ambition and welcomed a new organizational model that would entail more autonomy for them and their teams and fewer managers. At least, that is how they saw the change. But a large faction of personnel saw absolutely no need to change the way they were organized. Profit margins were close to 50% in recent years, and their contracts with clients were very long-term. There was not a cloud in the sky, as far as they were concerned.

The executive team initiated an organization design project, engaging a design team of about ten representatives from different parts of the organization. The team contained skeptics as well as enthusiasts about the idea of moving to more organizational agility. The end result after five days of intense design work and debate was that there were two options: a rather radical option, which would mean a big shift away from the current way of organizing, but which met most of the design criteria, and an alternative model, which was much closer to the current situation. Implementing this second option was considered a waste of energy by some in the design team, because it would mean upheaval without really moving the needle on the goals they were trying to achieve. These members of the design team wanted to take the plunge and implement the radical option. The team reached a stalemate when it turned out preferences in the group about the two options were split exactly down the middle. They decided to communicate their considerations to the executive team and hand the decision back to them.

[5] This is a pseudonym for the actual company that this case description is loosely based on.

The executive team struggled as well. The radical option would mean merging some departments, creating a new one, removing some management roles, reshuffling teams, and placing a lot more decision-making power into the hands of autonomous client units. The CEO made the rounds of the managers who would be impacted. Some graciously accepted that this much-needed change might mean their role would change or even disappear. They were able to see the bigger picture. Others were openly resistant to the change, claiming they did not see the need for it. The executive team decided that the radical option was not going to be acceptable to a considerable number of their current managers. They worked with the design team to come up with a lighter, intermediate option, which did not include the reshuffle needed to create the new, autonomous client units.

As the design team went ahead with the operational design of this new, intermediate option, some managers began using their involvement in this process to further remove some of the sharp edges. The merging of departments and creation of a new one disappeared from the design, replaced by management processes to improve collaboration. And even when the operational design of this newly diluted version of the design was ready for sign-off by the managers, there was still resistance to the proposed change. The CEO had to throw in his full weight—implicitly threatening to step down—to force the approval for implementation.

Looking back on the whole process six months later, he said he was happy with the outcome. Even though the design that was implemented was only an incremental change, it had set something in motion. The direction that was signaled by the changes—less influence of management, more autonomy for teams—had released energy. It had also made it clear to a few of the existing managers that this was no longer the organization for them; one had already left for a position elsewhere. The CEO had not completely discarded the radical option. He said, "I will pull it out of my folder again when the time is right." ◀

3.3 Isomorphism: Why Are Organizations So Similar?

In the first part of this chapter, we have looked at reasons for reviewing and revising the organization design. We worked from the rational perspective of the contingency theory, which claims organizations need to achieve a fit between their design and their context in order to achieve satisfactory performance. We also looked at not so rational, but very real, inertial forces that prevent an organization from changing its design. We now need to look at a third category of processes that explain why organizations adopt new designs. These processes cannot really be considered organization design, but often have the same outcome: the implementation of a new organizational model. However, the starting point is not the organization's context—as contingency theory prescribes—but the behavior of its peers.

We work from a rather naïve perspective if we assume that organizations make choices about their design without looking at what their peers are doing. I am reminded of an organization design project we did at a mid-sized insurance company. We had gone through all the necessary steps to reach a comprehensive, solid strategic design that met the design criteria and was supported by the design team and the steering committee, when, in the very last design team meeting, the CFO said: "This design looks good, but why don't we go out and visit some other companies to see how they are doing things." I consider this an example of a fundamental sense of insecurity that arises in many leadership teams when it comes to designing their own organization. They often doubt that their organization has the people and the competencies to come up with a design that fits their context. I can think of some reasons for this doubt. First of all, redesigning your organization is not something you do every day. Furthermore, it has a fundamental and somewhat unpredictable impact on many people. This combination can create doubts: what if we are doing this all wrong and send our organization off the cliff? An understandable emotion. A second reason for doubts is that a leadership team may be aware of their limited view on the matter. Based on their own experience and background, they can only imagine a limited number of options for their future organization design. There may be this nagging feeling that there are options out there that they have not considered yet. Looking at all the options is something that can be addressed in a well-considered design process, as we will see later on in this book. Even the urge to look at peer companies is something that can have a place in the process, to broaden the minds of the design team. Where we depart from the design process as advocated in this book is if an organization starts simply mimicking others.

The market for ideas about new ways of organizing seems to be growing. Many organizations have realized that putting their way of organizing on show can be a great tool for employer branding and generally positive public relations. Stories about organizations that have introduced self-managing teams, lean start-up methods, intrapreneurs, moonshot campaigns, Holacracy, Agile practices, or a Teal organization[6] can be found not just in management journals but just as easily in mainstream media. There are conferences, blogs, webinars, and podcasts for you to learn more from gurus and academics. And there is a whole industry of consultants and trainers out there that can educate and certify you in these practices, as well as help you introduce them in your organization. And that is where companies are in danger of diverging from the tenets of contingency theory because, as Julian Birkinshaw—who has studied this system of management ideas extensively—writes, "all too often, the practices used successfully at one company prove disastrous at another" (Birkinshaw, 2014, p. 53). His advice is to not focus on the surface of these practices but to look for the underlying principles, which may be more valuable and durable than the practices that are currently in fashion. It is very likely that some of the terms I mention in this paragraph—such as Agile—will be looked

[6] If you have no clue about most of these terms, that is perfectly fine; we will return to some of them later on in this book, and for the rest there is always Google (the search engine, not the company and their management model).

at quite differently in 10 or 20 years' time just as we currently look differently at the matrix organization, total quality management, or the balanced scorecard. But it is equally likely that some of the underlying principles and ideas of Agile will endure, such as more autonomy for development teams and an iterative way of working to address search and exploration problems.

The desire to mimic is hard to ignore in many organizations. It is a second force—besides the inertia discussed in the previous section—that makes it hard for a top management team to conduct an organization design project in the way this book proposes. A useful theoretical lens to apply to this force is that of institutional isomorphism. In 1983, Paul DiMaggio and Walter Powell asked: "What makes organizations so similar?" (DiMaggio & Powell, 1983, p. 147). Their unit of analysis is the organizational field, for which we could use the shorthand of industry or sector: hospitals, public schools, health insurance companies, online travel agencies, and so on. The field does not only include organizations producing similar products or services but also their suppliers, consumers, and regulators. DiMaggio and Powell see "an inexorable push towards homogenization" (ibid., p. 148) as an organizational field matures. The tool they offer to explain this process of homogenization is institutional isomorphism. They distinguish between three mechanisms: coercive, normative, and mimetic isomorphism.

Redesigning for the Wrong Reasons

Besides isomorphism, we see many other reasons for an organization redesign that do not conform to contingency theory and as such should be considered 'the wrong reasons'. Many of these have to do with power relations in the organization's leadership. Marking the beginning of a new CEO's tenure ('first 100 days'), concentrating power in a particular part of the organization, or simply getting rid of certain managers can be among these reasons. Other starting points for a redesign that lack an adequate rationale can be to reduce the number of layers or the number of managers. Although this sounds like a noble pursuit—and some of the principles we will be covering in the next chapter will steer an organization in that direction—in and of itself this is a wrong reason for embarking on a redesign of the organization. There need to be clear symptoms that lie at the base of this decision, such as slow and poor decision-making, lack of clarity about responsibilities, or any of the other symptoms listed in Table 3.1. Simply using the elimination of management layers as a starting point creates the risk of taking the wrong design decisions and creating uncertainty in the organization about the need for change. ◀

3.3.1 Coercive Isomorphism

Almost all organizations experience pressure from their environment to conform their organization design to certain standards. These pressures can be formal, as is common in sectors such as the financial services industry. Regulators have launched many demands over recent years, such as requiring each firm to have a Chief Risk

Officer and forcing the implementation of Know Your Customer (KYC) processes to prevent money laundering. Both examples have had a fundamental impact on the organization design of financial services firms. Pressures can also be more informal, expressing a conformance to cultural norms. Examples include efforts to increase diversity and inclusion in the workforce, conduct business in a socially responsible way, or reduce the carbon footprint of companies. This is not to say that there cannot be an intrinsic motivation on the part of an organization's leadership and employees to make these changes. The point is that these societal influences can ultimately have an impact on the design of the organization. And even if installing a Corporate Social Responsibility department is considered purely ceremonial by an organization's leadership, the staff of this department will take their task seriously and will attempt to exert their influence where they can. Subtler still are the examples of influence cited by DiMaggio and Powell (1983): neighborhood organizations and schools organized using participatory and collectivist principles felt the need to develop formal hierarchies and roles to be able to interact with their donors and outside agencies. I am reminded of a start-up company I worked with that had done away with the role of managing director to become a purely self-managing team, but still needed someone with that title on their business card from time to time, to interact with their clients and investors.

3.3.2 Normative Isomorphism

Two software developers from different organizations may very well be more similar than a software developer and a business controller from the same organization. Education and professional networks are what drive normative isomorphism. Take software development as an example. Professionals in this field are in extremely high demand. They can and do move from company to company in search of the best work environment, the most challenging and prestigious projects, or simply the highest pay. They meet in online forums, in training courses, and on conferences. New practices propagate rapidly in this community, permeating organizational boundaries. As a result, technology groups in organizations will start looking alike in terms of their structures and processes. That is not to say that they are identical. Developers that come from Google have a different philosophy than those from Amazon and different still from coders who worked at Facebook. But many of the practices under the Agile umbrella—such as Scrum—have become de facto standards in a lot of IT groups. It is possible to extend this example to many professional fields, such as marketing, finance, and human resources.

3.3.3 Mimetic isomorphism

For the purposes of the discussion in this book, the most interesting form of institutional isomorphism is that of mimetic isomorphism. Many organizations have the tendency to model themselves after organizations they perceive to be successful.

DiMaggio and Powell (1983) hypothesize two important predictors for this behavior. The first is the extent of uncertainty an organization has to deal with. Put simply, if there is no easy answer for how to design your organization in response to the unpredictability of the environment, it becomes tempting to copy the form of organizing of a peer who seems to be successful. And since DiMaggio and Powell conceptualized this 40 years ago, the environment for organizations has only become more uncertain and the market of ideas about new ways of organizing more vibrant. But as DiMaggio and Powell and Birkinshaw (2014) note, the focus is often on structures and practices that are easy to observe and thus seem easy to import. This carries with it a definite risk. The organizational model of Chinese appliance maker Haier is a case in point. Their way of organizing is currently the subject of many a glowing review,[7] and it is not difficult to put the observable features of their model to paper, as many have done: entrepreneurial teams that form an internal market, using a number of standardized processes to collaborate. That does not mean it is easy to mimic the performance this company is achieving, using this organization design. For Haier, it has been a journey of decades to get to this point. The observable parts of the end result tell only a small part of this success story.

There is an aspect of legitimacy at play here as well. If a large and visible firm adopts a certain way of organizing, that will make it more acceptable or even desirable for others. It will legitimate the solution (Mol et al., 2019). It may even increase the legitimacy of those who adopt that solution.

> It is important to note that each of the institutional isomorphic processes can be expected to proceed in absence of evidence that they increase internal organizational efficiency. To the extent that organizational effectiveness is enhanced, the reason will often be that organizations are rewarded for being similar to other organizations in their fields. (DiMaggio & Powell, 1983, p. 153)

A final aspect to note about mimetic isomorphism is the internal political process that may play a role in the organization that does the mimicking. As we mentioned when discussing inertial forces in the previous section, politics will often play a role in organization design processes. A process of mimetic isomorphism may serve political purposes in several ways. It may serve the agenda of a senior executive who has just taken office and has taken the model with him from a previous position. Or, in a rather painful hypothesis that DiMaggio and Powell (1983) introduce, it may just be easier for a top management team to adopt a 'tried and true' model than to go through the disruptive discussions needed to review where they stand as an organization, where they need to go, and which organization design is the best fit for that context. In other words, it is easier than the hard work that this book prescribes.

[7] We will cover Haier in more depth in Chap. 5.

Mimetic Isomorphism: The Case of 'the Spotify Model'

In 2012, Henrik Kniberg, a Swedish Agile consultant who was working with Spotify at the time, put to paper his interpretation of Spotify's way of working, together with one of their own Agile coaches, Anders Ivarsson. Their whitepaper called "Scaling Agile @ Spotify with Tribes, Squads, Chapters and Guilds" and the accompanying videos Henrik made about Spotify's engineering culture became immensely popular,[8] especially after the apparently successful implementation in 2015 by Dutch bank ING of an organizational model that was heavily inspired by Spotify and used the same terminology (tribes, squads, etc.). Even though Kniberg and others have warned against taking his whitepaper as a model, it became the latest and greatest management hype after ING and the consulting firms involved started publicizing their success.[9] Everyone wanted to know about it, and many organizations—especially in the European financial services industry—went on to implement it in some form or other. The rise of the Spotify model coincided with the growth in Agile practices, which were going beyond isolated pockets in the IT department and were taking over other parts of the organization (Rigby et al., 2016). Since there was no established solution for working with Agile teams on a large scale, this was fertile ground for mimetic isomorphism. Spotify and ING supplied the legitimate models that many organizations were in search of. In research conducted between 2016 and 2018, Daniel Gerster and his colleagues listed 12 large, multinational firms in a variety of industries that had implemented the Spotify model, or some variation of it, in parts of their organization (Gerster et al., 2020). And that was the tip of the iceberg. In those years, you could not do an organization design project without at some point being asked about the Spotify model and whether it was applicable. Some organizations simply came right out and asked consultants to implement it. And most consultants were happy to oblige. At some point I was even asked by a director at a museum whether it would be a fit for their organization.

Even though many in the Agile community have been railing against it and Spotify employees themselves have stated this is not how they are organized (Lee, 2020), the Spotify model is still a popular template for implementing a way of organizing composed mainly of relatively autonomous, cross-functional teams, with members that have a home base in their functional departments. In Chap. 5, we will take a closer look at ING's implementation of the model and compare it to older, but similar organizational, set-ups. ◄

[8] Both the whitepaper and the videos can be found on the website of Kniberg's consulting firm Crisp (Kniberg, 2014).

[9] See, for example, Jacobs et al. (2017).

Discussion Questions

1. Which relationship do you see between an organization's design and its performance?
2. Do you think there is one best way to organize in today's turbulent and uncertain environment? If so, describe that way of organizing.
3. If the diagnosis is 'lack of collaboration between departments', which elements of Galbraith's Star model would you focus on in an organization redesign?
4. Do you think it is a good idea to implement a design which has been watered down because of top management politics? Or should only a design that achieves the optimal fit be implemented?
5. Is it a good thing or a bad thing that organizations in a particular field look so much alike? Why so?
6. What could the value be of mimicking a peer organization that seems to be successful? ◀

References

Alexy, O., Poetz, K., Puranam, P., & Reitzig, M. (2021). Adaptation or persistence? Emergence and revision of organization designs in new ventures. *Organization Science*. https://doi.org/10.1287/orsc.2021.1431.

Birkinshaw, J. (2014). Beware the next big thing: Before you adopt a new management idea, figure out if it's right for you. *Harvard Business Review, 92*(5), 50–57.

Birkinshaw, J. (2018). What to expect from agile. *MIT Sloan Management Review, 59*(2), 39–42.

Birkinshaw, J., & Ridderstråle, J. (2015). *Adhocracy for an agile age*. Retrieved January 29, 2021, from https://www.mckinsey.com/business-functions/organization/our-insights/adhocracy-for-an-agile-age

Burns, T., & Stalker, G. M. (1961). *The management of innovation*. Tavistock.

Burton, R. M., Håkonsson, D. D., Nickerson, J., Puranam, P., Workiewicz, M., & Zenger, T. (2017). GitHub: Exploring the space between boss-less and hierarchical forms of organizing. *Journal of Organization Design, 6*(10), 1–19.

Chandler, A. D., Jr. (1962). *Strategy and structure: Chapters in the history of the American industrial enterprise*. MIT Press.

Cohen, M. D., March, J. G., & Olsen, J. P. (1972). A garbage can model of organizational choice. *Administrative Science Quarterly, 17*(1), 1–25.

Cyert, R. M., & March, J. G. (1963). *A behavioral theory of the firm*. Prentice Hall.

DiMaggio, P. J., & Powell, W. W. (1983). The iron cage revisited: Institutional isomorphism and collective rationality in organizational fields. *American Sociological Review, 48*(2), 147–160.

Donaldson, L. (1987). Strategy and structural adjustment to regain fit and performance: In defence of contingency theory. *Journal of Management Studies, 24*(1), 1–24.

Donaldson, L., & Joffe, G. (2014). Fit—The key to organizational design. *Journal of Organization Design, 3*(3), 38–45.

Fayol, H. (1949). *General and industrial management*. Pitman.

Gerster, D., Brenner, W., & Dremel, C. (2020). How enterprises adopt agile forms of organizational design: A multiple-case study. *The Data Base for Advances in Information Systems, 51*(1), 84–103.

Hannan, M. T., & Freeman, J. (1984). Structural inertia and organizational change. *American Sociological Review, 49*(2), 149–164.

Jacobs, P., Schlatmann, B., & Mahadevan, D. (2017). *ING's agile transformation*. Retrieved January 29, 2021, from https://www.mckinsey.com/industries/financial-services/our-insights/ings-agile-transformation

Kniberg, H. (2014). Scaling agile @ Spotify with squads, chapters & guilds. Retrieved January 29, 2021, from https://blog.crisp.se/2012/11/14/henrikkniberg/scaling-agile-at-spotify

Lawrence, P. R., & Lorsch, J. W. (1967). *Organization and environment: Managing differentiation and integration*. Harvard Business School Press.

Lee, J. (2020). *Failed #SquadGoals: Spotify doesn't use "the Spotify model" and neither should you*. Retrieved January 29, 2021, from https://www.jeremiahlee.com/posts/failed-squad-goals/

March, J. G., & Simon, H. A. (1958). *Organizations*. John Wiley.

Marquis, C., & Tilcsik, A. (2013). Imprinting: Toward a multilevel theory. *The Academy of Management Annals, 7*(1), 195–245.

Mol, M., Birkinshaw, J., & Foss, N. J. (2019). The system of management ideas: Origins, micro-foundations, and dynamics. In A. Sturdy, S. Heusinkveld, T. Reay, & D. Strang (Eds.), *The Oxford handbook of management ideas* (pp. 25–41). Oxford University Press.

Nadler, D. A., & Tushman, M. L. (1997). *Competing by design: The power of organizational architecture*. Oxford University Press.

Puranam, P. (2018). *The microstructure of organizations*. Oxford University Press.

Rigby, D. K., Sutherland, J., & Takeuchi, H. (2016). Embracing agile: How to master the process that's transforming management. *Harvard Business Review, 94*(5), 40–50.

Scott, W. R., & Davis, G. F. (2007). *Organizations and organizing: Rational, natural, and open systems perspectives*. Pearson Prentice Hall.

Taylor, F. W. (1911). *The principles of scientific management*. Harper.

Thompson, J. D. (1967). *Organizations in action: Social science bases of administrative theory*. McGraw-Hill.

Woodward, J. (1958). *Management and technology*. H.M.S.O.

Worley, C. G., Williams, T., & Lawler, E. E., III. (2014). *The agility factor: Building adaptable organizations for superior performance*. Jossey-Bass.

4 What Makes for a Well-Designed Organization?

Abstract

Based on contingency thinking, specific guidelines for the design of an organization should come from its internal and external context. Design criteria are a way to express these guidelines, specific to the organization in question. More generally, there are a number of design principles that can guide organization design efforts, based on the work of various scholars and practitioners. The first principle prescribes that tasks that have a high level of interdependence should be combined into one organizational cluster. In this way, the clusters created have optimal autonomy, thus preventing coordination cost, collaboration problems, and conflict. The second principle is to allocate these autonomous clusters of tasks to teams that are self-sufficient. Self-sufficiency means that teams have the resources, skills, and information at their disposal to perform the tasks assigned to them. Acknowledging and managing the tensions between organizational units is the third principle. Principle four is preventing redundant management layers. The fifth principle is to create enough flexibility in the design to fit the context. And the final guideline is to not overdesign.

Keywords

Organization design • Design criteria • Design principles · Interdependence • Coordination • Autonomous task clusters • Self-sufficient teams • Management layers

J. van Bree, *Organization Design*, https://doi.org/10.1007/978-3-030-78679-3_4

geographies. He uses the divisional structures described by Chandler a decade earlier as an example (Galbraith, 1977). Galbraith also notes the downsides of this design strategy: foregoing economies of scale (because some resources need to be duplicated for each self-contained group) and reducing the benefits of grouping positions according to skill (such as building a critical mass of expertise). In his later work, he describes how organizations can combine both orientations in multidimensional structures (Galbraith, 2010).

The logic of self-contained groups also underlies much of the work in the Lowlands SocioTechnical Systems Design (L-STSD) tradition. Interdependencies between groups create coordination work. And coordination work is not only costly in itself—we will cover the range of coordinating mechanisms available to organizations in Chap. 8—but is also prone to cause errors, confusion, or even conflict. So, it needs to be avoided by dividing the labor in such a way that semiautonomous groups are created, with as few interfaces as possible between them (De Sitter et al., 1997; Kuipers et al., 2020). L-STSD speaks of semiautonomous groups as Thompson does of conditionally autonomous groups—and Simon (1996) of nearly decomposable systems—because "we must recognize that autonomy is modified; the fully autonomous unit would not be or remain a part of the organization" (Thompson, 1967, p. 58). The design logic that Thompson follows, based on this principle, is a different one than that of L-STSD.[1] Thompson describes a logic that is bottom-up: an organization first tries to contain the interdependencies in the smallest possible unit (what he calls the first-order grouping). If it is not possible to contain all interdependencies in that unit, an overarching unit is created to contain the remaining interdependencies and so on. In this way, a hierarchy is formed, in the sense of an inclusive clustering (not in the sense of power differences or formal reporting relations). The L-STSD approach on the other hand follows a top-down logic. It starts with the complete value chain of the organization that is in scope and then clusters and sub-clusters those tasks down to the level of teams. This book follows the latter design logic, which we will cover extensively in Chap. 7.

It is important to make a distinction here between agent interdependence and task interdependence. As Puranam et al. (2012) have shown, this distinction has not always been maintained in conceptualizations of interdependence. When we speak of interdependence in the context of this design principle, we are referring to task interdependence: the situation where the performance of one task in an organization is affected by the performance of other tasks (McCann & Ferry, 1979; Kumar et al., 2009; Puranam et al., 2012). In the design logic of this book, we are not speaking of agent interdependence—or position interdependence, as Thompson calls it—quite simply because tasks have not yet been allocated to agents at the point where we apply this design principle.[2]

Important related work to this logic of creating autonomous clusters has been done by Carliss Baldwin and her collaborators on what they have labeled the "mirroring hypothesis", which contends "that there exists a correspondence (…) between

[1] Which is not surprising, since Thompson does not study organization design, but rather the behavior of organizations, from a social science perspective.

[2] We will cover the different types of interdependence in greater detail in Chap. 8.

the network of technical dependencies between tasks and the network of organizational ties between the people performing the tasks" (Colfer & Baldwin, 2016, p. 715). Baldwin points to Thompson as the originator of this hypothesis when it comes to the organization mirroring the technical system. There is an extensive body of literature that deals with the mirroring hypothesis based on Baldwin and Clark's seminal work from 2000, and we lack the room in this book to do justice to the nuances involved. For the purposes of our discussion of this first design principle, the mirroring hypothesis shows us that there are situations in which we can base the creation of autonomous clusters of tasks on the dependencies that exist in the underlying technology. An example of this is Spotify, where a specific module of their software (such as the payment solution) can be assigned to an autonomous team (called squad, in their language).[3] The important nuance here is that the organization designers need to understand the technical interdependencies involved in order to create the corresponding organizational modules (i.e., autonomous clusters).[4] Generalizing this approach from technical systems to systems of activities, Srikanth and Puranam (2011) speak of the modularity strategy:

> decompose a system of activities into subsystems (also known as modules or components), such that activities within a module are highly interdependent with one another, but there are few dependencies between activities that are part of different modules. (Srikanth & Puranam, 2011, p. 853)

Although the principle in itself is quite intuitive, putting it into practice is far from a trivial matter.[5] It requires what Puranam and his colleagues call architectural knowledge: "the designer's knowledge of how to divide and allocate tasks" (Puranam et al., 2012, p. 430). We will return to the approach for this design activity—what we will later refer to as 'grouping'—in Chap. 7.

Other authors have added complementary perspectives to this logic. Lawrence and Lorsch (1967) described the differences that arise between differentiated organizational units in terms of their work styles, attitudes, and the objectives they pursue. This makes collaboration between units more difficult to manage than collaboration within units. This point is echoed by Goold and Campbell, who advise managers to be wary of "any source of advantage that requires cross-border links" (Goold & Campbell, 2002, p. 118). Albert Cherns, working from the sociotechnical perspective, encourages the 'principle of boundary location', which states that "boundaries should not be drawn so as to impede the sharing of information,

[3] As described by Kniberg (2014); although, to be fair, a payment solution might be so technically complex that it requires several teams collaborating on it.

[4] An important other nuance lies in the fact that mirroring does not always lead to higher performance, most notably because firms may get stuck in the 'mirroring trap', where they fail to see technical innovations because they fall outside the framework of their strictly mirrored organization design (Colfer & Baldwin, 2016).

[5] In fact, it may have become more difficult since originally proposed in the 1960s; the complexity of organizations—in terms of the different inputs and outputs that must be dealt with simultaneously—has increased vastly since then and with it the number of interdependencies (a point made by Joseph et al., 2019).

knowledge, and learning" (Cherns, 1987, p. 156). This principle has been practically translated as 'keep work whole': "identify whole units of work and strive to keep them as whole as possible when defining organizational boundaries" (Schmitz, 2019, section 5. Keep Work Whole). Lastly, Von Hippel (1990) offers the extension of looking at problem-solving when identifying task interdependence; in his view, it is cross-boundary *problem-solving* that needs to be avoided. When allocating tasks, the organization designer must "first, (…) predict which tasks are likely to be the source of important new information: second, (…) predict which other tasks in the network are likely to be affected by that new information" (Von Hippel, 1990, p. 411). Clustering the interdependent tasks identified in this way reduces the problem of cross-boundary problem-solving.

In sum, this first principle prescribes that tasks that have a high level of interdependence should be combined into one organizational cluster. In this way, the clusters created have optimal autonomy, thus preventing coordination cost, collaboration problems, and conflict. We will show the practical application of this principle in Chap. 7.

Semiautonomous Clusters in Action: The Cell Division Philosophy

Eckart Wintzen (1939–2008) was a Dutch entrepreneur who founded a software company called BSO (later BSO/Origin) in 1977 and built it into a multinational firm with 6000 employees in 21 countries when he left in 1996, after a merger of BSO/Origin with a Philips subsidiary. The management philosophy for which he became famous—at least in Dutch business circles—was that of cell division.[6] Wintzen never let a unit of his firm grow over 65 people. As soon as a cell had more than 50 employees, it started preparations to split into two. The result was a collection of autonomous units, with their own market segment, HR services, offices, and support staff. The managing director of a cell had full profit and loss responsibility. Boundaries of cells were set according to the geographic region they served, the specific services they provided, or a combination of both. Wintzen was very careful not to create any centralized support staff (HR, legal, procurement, and the likes) even though he was often advised to do so to avoid duplication of effort. He stuck to his conviction that centralized support staff would eventually become more expensive than some duplication of effort by the cells. The only two things that had a centralized component at BSO/Origin were finance and corporate communication: finance in the sense that every cell had to use the financial software mandated by headquarters, in order to make consolidation of the accounts easier, and corporate communication in that Wintzen was very strict when it came to corporate identity and brand. If he happened to see even just the wrong color desk in an office, he would intervene and have it removed. In spite of the independence of the cells, he felt it was crucial that BSO/Origin presented itself as one unified company to the outside world, with one brand image. Without any formal training in sociotechnical principles or organizational modularity, Wintzen was able to create a company that adhered perfectly to this first design principle. ◀

[6] He described his philosophy extensively in Wintzen (2007), which unfortunately is only available in Dutch.

4.2.2 Principle 2: Create Self-Sufficient Teams

If the first principle is followed down to the lowest organizational level, the result is a collection of semiautonomous clusters of tasks, ordered in a hierarchy. The lowest-level clusters in this hierarchy can then be allocated to teams. That is where the second principle comes into play. Let us assume for now that the tasks in this semi-autonomous cluster need to be executed by a team of humans.[7] As this allocation of tasks to a team takes place in the design process, it is quite common that interdependencies are created between this team and others—interdependencies that do not arise from the tasks themselves, but nevertheless impact the semiautonomous nature of the cluster that was so carefully designed using the first principle. To give an obvious example, if this team does not have the resources (funds, equipment, manpower) needed to perform the tasks allocated to them, they will need help from others inside or outside of the organization. This creates what we could label resource interdependence,[8] as opposed to the task interdependence we discussed with respect to the first principle. To reap the benefits of the first principle, we will need to adhere to this second principle of creating self-sufficient teams.

First off, let me make clear that a self-sufficient team is not the same as a self-managing team. The team being self-sufficient does not say anything about whether or not it has a manager. Having said that, making a self-sufficient team self-managing is easier than going through the same process with a team that is not self-sufficient. I would go as far as saying that self-sufficiency and having a semiautonomous cluster of tasks allocated to it—that is, adhering to the first two design principles—are prerequisites for a team to become self-managing. These design aspects of introducing self-managing teams are often disregarded when an implementation is limited to removing a layer of managers and adding a cadre of team coaches.

So, what does self-sufficiency entail? Albert Cherns introduced a number of principles from a sociotechnical design perspective that are useful starting points. The first one is his 'principle of power and authority'.

> Those who need equipment, materials, or other resources to carry out their responsibilities should have access to them and authority to command them. In return, they accept responsibility for them and for their prudent and economical use. (Cherns, 1987, p. 157)

In other words, give the team the authority and responsibility to use the resources they need to perform the tasks allocated to them. Although this may sound self-evident, implementing this principle is where a lot of organizations run into problems. Giving each team the authority to command the resources they need will either lead to duplication of these resources—if teams are given exclusive access to them—or to the need for a process or authority that prioritizes the access to the resources that are shared. This issue is exacerbated if the resources in question are scarce, such as manufacturing equipment, specific expertise, or access to funds. This is one of the main points where firms encounter difficult trade-offs in their

[7] Although the same reasoning, mutatis mutandis could be followed for nonhuman actors.

[8] Which we will discuss in more detail in Chap. 8.

organization design. Economies of scale will go at the expense of the self-sufficiency of teams and vice versa. Matrix structures and shared service centers are examples of mechanisms that organizations have employed to solve this dilemma, to varying degrees of success. But the general tendency of many organizations is to let the scale tip toward economies of scale. Duplication of resources is considered so counterintuitive to many managers that it is often not seriously considered. One of the reasons may be that economies of scale are quite easy to quantify, whereas the gains of a self-sufficient team are much more difficult to calculate. It is important to be aware of this trade-off and to make deliberate design decisions to tackle it. We will return to this topic in subsequent chapters on grouping and linking (Chaps. 7 and 8).

Another set of Cherns' principles that are relevant for self-sufficiency of teams deal with variance control and information flow. The first is that variances (by which Cherns refers to exceptions or errors) should not be exported across unit borders, that is, they should be dealt with as close to their points of origin as possible. This is a principle similar to some of the principles behind Lean and the Toyota Production System (Liker & Morgan, 2006), which promote the shop floor (or *gemba*) as the place to diagnose and solve problems. A related principle by Cherns prescribes that information should be provided to those who require it when they require it. Cherns is talking primarily about information about the team's performance. He states an organization cannot hold a team responsible for the performance of a certain task or set of tasks, if it is "doling out information about its performance in arrear and through a higher authority" (Cherns, 1987, p. 157). Combined, these two principles mean that in order to be self-sufficient, a team needs to have both the information and the authority to solve problems and improve performance.

This leads to another aspect of self-sufficiency, which is whether the team has the skills and expertise among its members to perform the tasks required and solve the problems that impact its performance. In many cases, this requirement calls for a number of different skills to be combined in the team. This can be achieved by combining several team members, each with their deep expertise, in a cross-functional team. It can also be achieved by promoting a certain fluidity in roles of the team members. Both have been shown to have a positive influence on the performance of self-sufficient teams (Magpili & Pazos, 2018). The cross-functional team composition is an important building block of the Agile practices which have found their way to an increasing number of organizations in the past years (Rigby et al., 2016). Agile practices also promote a certain level of role fluidity, so that team members can (temporarily) step into roles of other team members, who may be overburdened or unavailable. However, Agile teams seem to favor members with deep expertise over members with more broad skills. In the sociotechnical tradition, this focus on broad skills is much more prominent. Cherns expounds this as the 'multifunctional principle', which promotes enlarging "the response repertoires of individuals and teams" (Cherns, 1987, p. 158) instead of hiring another expert. A certain level of task overlap is seen as improving the flexibility of the team and thereby its self-sufficiency. Cherns' comments should of course be seen in the context of his time. When we are talking about highly specialized skills such as user interface design, front-end development, or machine learning, it is only to a limited extent that task overlap can be designed into teams.

> The more complex the knowledge and skills required for the total group task, the more frugal one should be with regard to job redundancy. (Kuipers et al., 2020, p. 284)

It is important to note here that this design principle (self-sufficiency), as well as the previous one (autonomous clusters of tasks), has important positive effects on team members' motivation. Designing team tasks according to these two principles will result in a higher motivational potential according to Hackman and Oldham's Job Characteristics Theory (Hackman & Oldham, 1976; Hackman & Wageman, 2005; Oldham & Hackman, 2010). The first factor contributing to this is the team task as a self-contained—and as such hopefully meaningful—piece of work. The second is the fact that the team members have autonomy, in the sense of having the skills and resources at their disposal to perform the team tasks. And finally, the fact that teams are provided with feedback about their performance will positively impact team members' motivation.

The Four Most Important Aspects That Make a Team Self-Sufficient

- The team is assigned a semiautonomous cluster of tasks (a prerequisite stemming from the first design principle).
- The team has the authority and responsibility to use the resources they need to perform the tasks allocated to them.
- The team needs to have both the information and the authority to solve problems and improve performance.
- The team has the skills and expertise among its members to perform the tasks required and solve the problems that impact its performance.

4.2.3 Principle 3: Manage the Tensions Between Organizational Units

The first two design principles have focused on what we might call the micro level of the organization: teams and their tasks. If we zoom out and consider these teams—or let us use the more neutral term units—in relation to each other, the third principle comes into play. It is rare that we find an organization that has an entirely singular focus. By this I do not mean its high-level strategic goals, because those *should* of course be aligned across the organization. But I am referring to sources of tension that can be found one level deeper, between the organizational units. It is what Nicolay Worren describes as "coupling between functional requirements" (Worren, 2018, p. 60). The third design principle states that these tensions need to be identified, acknowledged, and managed.

Let me give two examples from my own professional experience. One is a company in the public transportation sector. The majority of its resources—people and equipment—are dedicated to its operational goals of letting trains and buses run according to the timetable, with a comfortable experience for travelers, and against acceptable costs. This means that the organizational unit responsible for that goal tends to favor qualities such as efficiency and predictability and the indicators used for its performance are around these aspects of operational excellence. Senior management of this unit will do their best to direct this part of the organization toward these goals. However, there is also another part of the organization, which is responsible for the commercial aspects. It collects customer insights, develops new products and services, and generally has goals around increasing market share and turnover. The commercial unit needs the operations unit to make good on its sales promises, but the operations unit is primarily interested in running a reliable transportation network. If the commercial unit decides that a smartphone app will replace paper tickets—because that is what they hear the modern traveler wants—that is not necessarily something the operations unit is eager to integrate into its processes. The same may be true for adding extra stops or increasing the number of trains on a line. In the past, there had been instances where the commercial unit promised more than the operations unit could deliver. In this specific example, this tension is managed by instituting an internal customer-supplier relationship, in which the operations unit supplies a catalogue of what they can offer and the commercial unit negotiates with them to achieve what they consider the best deal for their customers. This is then settled with a formal 'handshake' in the top management team of the company, between the Chief Commercial Officer and the Chief Operations Officer.

An example from a completely different sector shows a similar dynamic. This is a museum, which obviously has as one of its main tasks to preserve priceless art treasures for posterity. And that is how its Head of Conservation sees his mission and that of his department. This means managing optimal conditions inside the museum's buildings, making sure objects are not unnecessarily moved or loaned out, and undertaking conservation projects where needed. The museum also has a department called Development, which concerns itself with securing funds from sponsors, estates, and grants. One of the perks offered to tier 1 sponsors is that they are allowed to dine in one of the galleries of the museum once or twice a year, with a group of their employees or business relations. The Development department tries to maximize the availability of the Gallery of Honor for this, because their mission is to pamper their sponsors and thus secure the maximum amount of funds. The Conservation department mainly sees the risks of objects being exposed to groups of people eating and drinking and of not being able to use the gallery at night for conservation work. Both departments have objectives which are important for the museum's survival, so there is a need to actively manage this tension and strike the right balance.

The organizations you are familiar with will likely have similar tensions that play out. And there is nothing wrong with that. The healthy dynamic that can arise from this is one where the units challenge each other and keep each other in check. If the museum would only focus on conservation, it may not secure enough funds to expand its collection, whereas if it would only cater to its sponsors, the long-term conservation of its art treasures may be at risk. The unhealthy version of this dynamic occurs if the tension is not explicitly managed or if the balance of power tips too far to one side. That is why these tensions need explicit attention in the design of an organization. And that is where this third design principle comes in.

Probably the most universal tension of all—and the one most extensively explored in scholarly work—is that between exploration and exploitation. This tension was first identified by James March (1991) in the context of organizational learning. Exploitation in his framework referred to applying existing organizational knowledge (skills, capabilities) and exploration to developing new knowledge. In a review of the literature on exploration and exploitation, Dovev Lavie and his colleagues describe the opposite ends of this continuum.

> Whereas exploration engages individuals and organizations in search, experimentation, and variation, exploitation enhances productivity and efficiency through choice, execution, and variance reduction. (Lavie et al., 2010, p. 110)

These activities are contradictory, yet equally necessary for organizational survival. Every organization will encounter this tension in some form or other. Another label used for what is essentially the same dynamic is 'running the business' (exploitation) versus 'changing the business' (exploration) (Nieto-Rodriguez, 2014). Because it is so universal, several strategies have emerged to manage the necessary balance. These strategies are predicated on the notion that it is exploration in particular that needs attention. This is the activity which will only yield returns in the longer run and with less certainty. The typical example is research and development work. In most organizations, if no specific management attention is directed at these exploration activities, they will be crushed by the 'exploitation machine', which runs the day-to-day business. That short-term focus on selling products, serving clients, and running projects will always take precedence if left unchecked. As a consequence, exploration tasks need to be protected from or even freed from the rest of the organization. In a similar vein, Goold and Campbell (2002) speak of "specialist cultures" that need to be sufficiently "insulated" from the rest of the organization. The most common way to achieve this protection of the exploration tasks is by assigning them to a separate unit. This is what Lavie et al. (2010) label "organizational separation", which yields what has been described in the literature as a structurally ambidextrous organization (Tushman & O'Reilly, 1996). In this mode of balancing exploration with exploitation, the exploratory units are often small teams, given a large degree of autonomy, and with cultures and processes geared toward innovation and creativity. Although this type of organization design addresses the problem of exploitative activities encroaching on the exploration, it comes with its own challenges. Prime among them is creating the right interface between exploration and exploitation to make sure the results of exploration can be exploited to yield returns. Because the distinction between these units is structurally accentuated in this mode, crossing the divide becomes a less than trivial matter. The organization runs the danger of letting the exploration units drift away, without the innovations they produce ever being effectively absorbed in the exploitation units. An example I came across is from one of the largest Dutch banks, which ran an 'intrapreneurship' program for a number of years. In this program, internal start-up teams—made up of bank employees—were facilitated to develop new banking services. If their idea was deemed viable, they were freed up to work on this full-time. Some of these teams were even physically placed outside the headquarters building, to stress their unique status. This helped tremendously in instilling an entrepreneurial, exploration-oriented drive in these teams. The downside was that some of them did not want to return to the bank anymore. After one team had developed a potentially successful new app that was ready to go to market, their team lead said: "I don't care whether you or some venture capital firm is going to finance us going forward, but I'm not going back to my old job at the bank."

The example of exploration and exploitation shows three important steps that need to be taken when it comes to the tensions that arise between organizational units, stemming from their distinct goals:

- Identify and acknowledge the tension.
- Direct management attention to the tension.
- If needed, adapt the design of the organization to remove or manage the tension.

It is important to note that these types of tensions will be relatively limited if the first two design principles of this chapter are followed, resulting in self-sufficient teams. However, as the examples of the public transportation company and the museum show, shared resources (a rail network or an art collection) may get in the way of following those principles all the way through and eliminating all interdependencies and ensuing tensions. We will cover these trade-offs in the design process in Chap. 7 on grouping.

As we saw in this section so far, the most common way to manage these tensions is to place the conflicting units under separate leadership and to let the tension play out at the senior management level of the organization. This can be supported by management processes such as the internal customer-supplier process in the public transportation company example.[9] We will cover interdependencies, of which these tensions are a subset, and linking mechanisms, of which management processes are a subset, more extensively in Chap. 8.

The tensions can also be managed without resorting to separate organizational units. An attempt can be made to reconcile conflicting goals inside one unit or even assigned to one role. When applied to the exploration-exploitation tension, this is known as contextual ambidexterity (Gibson & Birkinshaw, 2004): contextual in the sense that the right context needs to be created for individual employees to be able to divide their time between exploitation and exploration activities. That context can be an incentive system that rewards both types of activities or a culture in which it is accepted or even respected that employees sometimes retreat from their day-to-day work to explore new business opportunities. Many mid-sized consulting firms—including all those I have been employed by—work according to these principles of contextual ambidexterity. Consultants are expected to meet their targets by acquiring and running client projects, but they are also rewarded for assimilating new

[9] Another excellent example of an internal customer-supplier process is described as part of the FMC Technologies case study in Worren (2017).

knowledge, developing new services, or entering new markets. Contextual ambidexterity avoids many of the coordination problems that arise with organizational separation. However, creating the right context—specifically, creating enough room for exploration—puts high demands on managers as well as employees.

4.2.4 Principle 4: Prevent Redundant Management Layers

After organizations grow beyond a certain size—let us take Eckart Wintzen's threshold of 65 employees—introducing some form of structure beyond just a single unit becomes inevitable. In the case of Wintzen's BSO, this took the form of a large number of comparable cells, all reporting into the same corporate parent. However, a structure this flat is atypical. Most organizations of that size—over 5000 employees—will have several management layers between the lowest-level units and the top management team. Each layer brings additional cost and creates a further separation between the teams that do the core work and the part of the organization where strategic decision-making takes place. In the public transportation company mentioned in the previous section, there are four management layers between the men and women running the train service and the senior executives running the company. It is inevitable that this divide is felt and has distinct effects on how the organization functions—which is not the same as saying that this is the wrong organization design. Considering the context of this organization (e.g., the size of the operational workforce and the geographic scope of their train network), this number of layers may very well be the best fit. This fourth design principle simply aims to prevent organizations from adding layer after layer without taking their added value into consideration.

So, when is an additional management layer necessary? Let us take an organization that consists of 20 teams. According to the first two design principles, these teams have been made as self-sufficient as possible. If this was done successfully, there is no need for management layers beyond the corporate parent that all units report into. This was the situation at BSO/Origin and is the situation at Buurtzorg, a Dutch neighborhood nursing organization.[10] However, as we will see in the second part of this book, creating semiautonomous clusters of tasks and self-sufficient teams is highly challenging in most organizations. BSO and Buurtzorg happen to have short value chains. Teams can cover the value chain in its entirety for a specific neighborhood (Buurtzorg) or customer segment (BSO), thus creating autonomy. Unfortunately, short value chains are the exception. Most organizations will need more than one team to cover their end-to-end value chain. If this is the case, some type of coordination will be needed between these teams, to make sure the right products or services are delivered to clients. Bringing the teams that need to be coordinated together under one manager is a default way to manage this interdependence. As we will see in Chap. 8, it is only one of many linking mechanisms available to organizations and one of the most expensive ones, at that. But if this formal and strong form of linking is necessary, that is certainly a valid reason to add a layer of management.

[10] See Laloux (2014, pp. 62–73), for an extensive description of this case.

A second valid reason for adding a management layer is if that layer can add value to the units reporting into it. In the context of corporate headquarters, Goold and Campbell (2002) refer to this as 'parenting propositions'. In the case of BSO/ Origin, there was the added value of being able to use a closely guarded, strong brand across all the individual cells. This is an example of what Goold and Campbell call the 'leverage proposition'. The example above of using a management layer for coordination purposes across a value chain would fall into the category of 'link propositions'. The other three parenting propositions that Goold and Campbell identify are 'select' (acquiring or disposing of units), 'build' (helping expand the size and scope of units), and 'stretch' (setting ambitious targets for units). Following Goold and Campbell's logic, management layers that do not have clear and distinct parenting propositions should be considered redundant.

However, many organizations would fail this test for at least some of their management layers. Can there be another rationale at work? Why yes, there is the matter of span of control. Many management layers exist simply because they make the span of control of the layer above tenable. These managers are quite unceremoniously referred to as span breakers (Kesler & Kates, 2016). Span breakers are a dangerous phenomenon, because they have the potential to create costly management layers without much added value. In most cases, the need for span breakers arises from not following—or not being able to follow—the first two design principles. If these principles are followed—and self-sufficient teams are the result—span of control is not really an issue, because the control aspect is very light or not present at all. There may very well be a need for coordination—a valid reason for an additional management layer, as we have seen—but hardly ever for control. We will see some examples of how this plays out in different organizations in the next chapter. If the control part is absent, the span that a senior management team can handle can be quite large. The example of Buurtzorg shows there is no need for a management layer between its 900 teams of neighborhood nurses and the CEO Jos de Blok. The same was true for BSO/Origin. But again, these organizations are the exceptions, where creating self-sufficient teams is relatively easy because of the nature of their business. We will look at how difficult this puzzle is in most organizations in Chap. 7. There are certainly instances where introducing span breakers is warranted, and there is some value that this layer can add.

> The span-breaker role—often called a group executive—can add value by overseeing business unit strategies, by reviewing the performance of businesses on a regular basis, and by coaching and developing general managers. (Kesler & Kates, 2016, p. 52)

The message here is that it needs to be considered a last resort, not a default option, and that the layer should be kept lean (i.e., without a lot of support functions such as HR or finance).

Stratified Systems Theory: A Different Way to Look at Management Layers

A very particular way of looking at the management layers in an organization is by using the framework of Stratified Systems Theory. This theory was developed by Elliott Jaques[11] and is based on the idea that the different hierarchical levels in an organization—what Jaques calls strata—differ in their time span: the time it takes for the longest task to be completed. "At the lower levels, the longest task will be completed in a year or even in a day; at the higher, 'strategic' levels the longest tasks may not be completed for twenty years or more" (Jaques & Stamp, 1995, p. 1). Jaques and his collaborators identified eight strata, with only the very largest of corporations needing senior management at stratum VIII and seven strata of management below. A smaller firm or department may only need three levels. In Stratified Systems Theory, the capability of managers needs to be matched to the stratum at which they operate: not everyone can be expected to deal with decisions that have a time span of five years. This is the part of the theory that is controversial, to the extent that Jaques and his collaborators were largely shunned from the academic community. Viewed through an unfavorable lens, his theory puts employees into categories that they cannot escape from. Jaques himself has claimed an analysis of the suitable stratum for an employee can be made by observing them for 15 minutes and that you can only progress one stratum every 15 years (Kleiner, 2001). The ultimate consequence would of course be that investing in the lower stratum managers is a waste of time and money, because they will never progress up the hierarchy. Leaving aside the controversial aspects of the theory—the focus on employee cognitive capacity—looking at an organizational hierarchy using the stratified systems framework unquestionably has merit. The notion that each management layer needs to have a distinct time span can highlight flaws in an organization's design, especially if two management layers are dealing with similar time spans. "A manager at the same stratum as you makes you feel like they are breathing down your neck. One who is two or more strata above you feels too distant" (Dutrisac et al., 2008, p. 42). When adding management layers in an organization design, this is a valuable test to use: does this layer deal with the same time span as the layer below or above? If so, do we really need it? ◀

This fourth design principle states that we need to prevent redundant management layers. Another way to phrase this is to say that we need to minimize the number of management layers. The starting point is that as much autonomy and self-sufficiency as possible needs to be moved to the unit and team level of the organization—following the first two design principles—and that there are only a few valid reasons for adding additional management layers:

- The management layer is needed as a strong linking mechanism for the units below.

[11] For an accessible summary of his theory, see Jaques (1990).

- The management layer has one or more clear and distinct parenting propositions.
- The management layer is needed as a span breaker for the layer above.

4.2.5 Principle 5: Create Enough Flexibility in the Design to Fit the Context

If we follow the principles of contingency theory (as put forward in Chap. 3), the organization design needs to fit the context of the organization. Further, a change in context will need to lead to a redesign of the organization, to prevent a drop in performance. If we look at the current context that organizations are dealing with, not only is it characterized by rapid changes, but the direction of change is also highly unpredictable. The COVID-19 pandemic is only the latest and most extreme example of this unpredictable change. But organizations were already dealing with climate change, trade wars, and rapid technological change such as machine learning. If an organization is to maintain a fit between its rapidly changing context and its design, it either needs to be in an almost constant state of redesign or needs a certain amount of flexibility built into the design of the organization.

The good news is that most of the design principles covered so far will greatly increase this flexibility. Semiautonomous clusters of tasks allocated to self-sufficient teams reduce the interdependencies that exist in an organization. The same goes for minimizing the number of management layers. This means that grouping teams in a different way or adding new teams can be done without the need for an overhaul of the organization's structure. However, the principles still assume that a stable cluster of tasks is allocated to a unit or team with a permanent nature. If we were to let go of this stability, an even greater amount of flexibility would be the result. If teams can be assembled, extended, and disbanded when needed, and if the tasks allocated to a team can be altered quickly and effectively, a perfectly flexible organization would be the result. This is what Mintzberg (1980) has described as the adhocracy, of which we will see some contemporary examples in the next chapter. For our discussion in this chapter, it is important to highlight two important pre-conditions for this flexible way of organizing:

- Regardless of the fluidity of the team set-up, employees will always need a stable 'home base' in the organization, to develop in their professional field or simply "for housekeeping purposes" as Mintzberg (1980, p. 337) calls it.
- There need to be clear management processes in place for assembling and disbanding teams and for setting and adapting their assignment (i.e., the tasks allocated to them).

This extreme form of flexibility is not required for every organization or for every part of an organization. As with all aspects of an organization design, there needs to be a fit with the context. Although the uncertainty of the environment has certainly increased over the last decades, there are still many organizations that do not need to be 'reconfigurable' in the manner described above.

In sum, the fifth design principle states that the requisite amount of flexibility needs to be built into the design. In some cases, following the earlier design principles suffices to achieve this. Contingent on context, additional measures are needed.

4.2.6 Principle 6: Do Not Overdesign

The final design principle is the easiest to state, but perhaps the most difficult one to follow. As Albert Cherns phrased it: "it is a mistake to specify more than is needed because by doing so, one closes options that could be kept open" (Cherns, 1987, p. 155). While we may readily agree with his statement—seeing as it will also increase the flexibility mentioned in the previous design principle—the question is of course how we can tell when we are specifying 'more than is needed'. Cherns offers some further guidance by stating that "[w]hile it may be necessary to be precise about what has to be done, it is rarely necessary to be precise about how it is done" (ibid., p. 155).

Let us take Puranam's four fundamental problems framework (covered in Chap. 2) to investigate what the 'minimal critical specification' of an organization design is. Puranam and his collaborators (2014) state that an organization cannot exist without solutions to the four problems; that is, there needs to be a way to identify and allocate the tasks an organization needs to perform, and the efforts of organizational actors or units need to be integrated by means of information exchange and provision of rewards. So, if we return to Cherns, this means being specific about *what* needs to be done and *who* needs to do it (division of labor) but also about *who talks to whom* and *who gets what* (integration of effort). So indeed, it is not necessary to be specific about how tasks are performed—the standardized procedures of scientific management—but it may very well be necessary to be specific about how these efforts are integrated: the information and decision processes of Galbraith's Star model (which we will cover as part of the linking mechanisms in Chap. 8). Marianne Livijn's case study of the redesign of a large food production company (2019) shows what can happen when only a new structure is introduced and the accompanying management processes have not been specified: middle managers start filling in the gaps. There is nothing wrong with that—and in the case that Livijn describes the middle managers' interventions stayed within the overall intent of the design—but regardless of who specifies these management processes, these efforts need to be acknowledged as part of the design process. In Livijn's case, the organization could not function adequately before solutions had been found for the (fundamental) problems that arose after implementation of the macro-level design developed by the top management team.

Perhaps a better way to look at overdesign is to return to our first two design principles. Organizational theorist Karl Weick, when he spoke of the danger of overdesign,[12] identified the demands for coordination as the primary problem. The

[12] This was at a workshop convened at Case Western University, at the occasion of the opening of the Peter B. Lewis Building, designed by renowned architect Frank Gehry; Gehry was in attendance and contributed to the workshop proceedings.

aim of the designer, in Weick's view, should be to "moderate the demands for coordination" (Weick, 2004, p. 43) by fostering "loosely coupled systems" (ibid., p. 43), in other words, to create semiautonomous clusters of tasks and assign them to self-sufficient teams. The root of the problem in many organizations is not so much that management processes—to achieve coordination—are specified, because if they are not the organization will have trouble functioning. Rather, the root of the problem lies one step before: the structure which has been designed requires too much coordination, because it does not sufficiently adhere to the first two design principles of this chapter.

So with this, we come full circle to the decentralized, modular ideal type of organization design prescribed by the first two design principles. The theoretical advantages of this ideal type should now be apparent. The practical feasibility of this design is a matter we will explore in the remaining chapters of this book. First, in the next chapter, we will look at some practical examples of organizations that seem to have come a long way in achieving the ideal (either by design or by accident). Then, in the second part of this book, we will go on to cover the practical design steps that are needed to put the principles into practice.

Review Questions

1. Do you think that organization designs that look alike will always be based on similar design criteria? Why or why not?
2. Which factors determine whether it is easy to decompose an organization's system of activities into semiautonomous clusters of tasks?
3. Do you agree that coordination efforts between organizational units should be kept to a minimum? Why or why not?
4. Does a team need to be self-sufficient before it can become self-managing? Why or why not?
5. How broad or specialized do you think team members' skills should be in a self-sufficient team?
6. Can you think of organizations that do not have to deal with the exploration-exploitation tension?
7. List some of the possible symptoms of a management layer being redundant.
8. Imagine an organization where employees do not have a home base, but are completely flexible to join and leave teams. What would the conditions be for this model to work?

References

Baldwin, C. Y., & Clark, K. B. (2000). *Design rules, volume 1: The power of modularity*. The MIT Press.

Cherns, A. (1987). Principles of sociotechnical design revisited. *Human Relations, 40*(3), 153–162.

Colfer, L. J., & Baldwin, C. Y. (2016). The mirroring hypothesis: Theory, evidence, and exceptions. *Industrial and Corporate Change, 25*(5), 709–738.

De Sitter, L. U., Den Hertog, F., & Dankbaar, B. (1997). From complex organizations with simple jobs to simple organizations with complex jobs. *Human Relations, 50*(5), 497–534.
Dutrisac, M., Koplowitz, H., & Shepard, K. (2008). An executive's guide to RO-based organization design. In J. L. Gray, J. G. Hunt, & S. McArthur (Eds.), *Organization design, levels of work & human capability*. The Global Organization Design Society.
Galbraith, J. R. (1977). *Organization design*. Addison-Wesley.
Galbraith, J. R. (2010). The multi-dimensional and reconfigurable organization. *Organizational Dynamics, 39*(2), 115–125.
Gibson, C. B., & Birkinshaw, J. (2004). The antecedents, consequences, and mediating role of organizational ambidexterity. *Academy of Management Journal, 47*(2), 209–226.
Goold, M., & Campbell, A. (2002). Do you have a well-designed organization? *Harvard Business Review, 80*(3), 117–124.
Hackman, J. R., & Oldham, G. R. (1976). Motivation through the design of work: Test of a theory. *Organizational Behavior and Human Performance, 16*(2), 250–279.
Hackman, J. R., & Wageman, R. (2005). When and how team leaders matter. *Research in Organizational Behavior, 26*, 37–74.
Jaques, E. (1990). In praise of hierarchy. *Harvard Business Review, 68*(1), 127–133.
Jaques, E., & Stamp, G. (1995). *Level and type of capability in relation to executive organization*. U.S. Army Research Institute for the Behavioral and Social Sciences. Public domain. Retrieved January 29, 2021, from https://archive.org/details/DTIC_ADA298621
Joseph, J., Baumann, O., Burton, R., & Srikanth, K. (2019). Reviewing, revisiting, and renewing the foundations of organization design. *Advances in Strategic Management, 40*, 1–23.
Kesler, G., & Kates, A. (2016). *Bridging organization design and performance: 5 ways to activate a global operating model*. John Wiley & Sons.
Kleiner, A. (2001). *Elliott Jaques levels with you*. Retrieved January 29, 2021, from https://www.strategy-business.com/article/10938
Kniberg, H. (2014). Scaling agile @ Spotify with squads, chapters & guilds. Retrieved January 29, 2021, from https://blog.crisp.se/2012/11/14/henrikkniberg/scaling-agile-at-spotify
Kuipers, H., Van Amelsvoort, P., & Kramer, E. (2020). *New ways of organizing: Alternatives to bureaucracy*. Acco Nederland.
Kumar, K., Van Fenema, P. C., & Von Glinow, M. A. (2009). Offshoring and the global distribution of work: Implications for task interdependence theory and practice. *Journal of International Business Studies, 40*(4), 642–667.
Laloux, F. (2014). *Reinventing organizations: A guide to creating organizations inspired by the next stage of human consciousness*. Nelson Parker.
Lavie, D., Stettner, U., & Tushman, M. L. (2010). Exploration and exploitation within and across organizations. *The Academy of Management Annals, 4*(1), 109–155.
Lawrence, P. R., & Lorsch, J. W. (1967). *Organization and environment: Managing differentiation and integration*. Harvard Business School Press.
Liker, J. K., & Morgan, J. M. (2006). The Toyota way in services: The case of lean product development. *Academy of Management Perspectives, 20*(2), 5–20.
Livijn, M. (2019). Navigating in a hierarchy: how middle managers adapt macro design. *Journal of Organization Design, 8*(1), 1–27.
Magpili, N. C., & Pazos, P. (2018). Self-managing team performance: A systematic review of multilevel input factors. *Small Group Research, 49*(1), 3–33.
March, J. G. (1991). Exploration and exploitation in organizational learning. *Organization Science, 2*(1), 71–87.
McCann, J. E., & Ferry, D. L. (1979). An approach for assessing and managing inter-unit interdependence. *The Academy of Management Review, 4*(1), 113–119.
Mintzberg, H. (1980). Structure in 5's: A synthesis of the research on organization design. *Management Science, 26*(3), 322–341.
Nadler, D. A., & Tushman, M. L. (1997). *Competing by design: The power of organizational architecture*. Oxford University Press.
Nieto-Rodriguez, A. (2014). Ambidexterity Inc. *Business Strategy Review, 25*(3), 34–39.

Oldham, G. R., & Hackman, J. R. (2010). Not what it was and not what it will be: The future of job design research. *Journal of Organizational Behavior, 31*(2/3), 463–479.
Puranam, P., Alexy, O., & Reitzig, M. (2014). What's "new" about new forms of organizing? *The Academy of Management Review, 39*(2), 162–180.
Puranam, P., Raveendran, M., & Knudsen, T. (2012). Organization design: The epistemic interdependence perspective. *Academy of Management Review, 37*(3), 419–440.
Rigby, D. K., Sutherland, J., & Takeuchi, H. (2016). Embracing agile: how to master the process that's transforming management. *Harvard Business Review, 94*(5), 40–50.
Schmitz, D. (2019). 9 principles for success. Retrieved January 29, 2021, from https://blog.on-the-mark.com/blog/organization-design-principles
Simon, H. A. (1996). *The sciences of the artificial* (3rd ed.). The MIT Press.
Srikanth, K., & Puranam, P. (2011). Integrating distributed work: Comparing task design, communication, and tacit coordination mechanisms. *Strategic Management Journal, 32*(8), 849–875.
Stanford, N. (2018). *Organization design: The practitioner's guide* (3rd ed.). Routledge.
Thompson, J. D. (1967). *Organizations in action: Social science bases of administrative theory*. McGraw-Hill.
Tushman, M. L., & O'Reilly, C. A., III. (1996). Ambidextrous organizations: Managing evolutionary and revolutionary change. *California Management Review, 38*(4), 8–30.
Von Hippel, E. (1990). Task partitioning: An innovation process variable. *Research Policy, 19*(5), 407–418.
Weick, K. E. (2004). Rethinking organizational design. In R. J. Boland & F. Collopy (Eds.), *Managing as designing*. Stanford University Press.
Wintzen, E. (2007). *Eckart's notes*. Lemniscaat.
Worren, N. (2017). The matrix as a transitory form: The evolution of FMC technologies 2001–2016. *Journal of Organization Design, 6*(1), 1–14.
Worren, N. (2018). *Organization design: Simplifying complex systems* (2nd ed.). Routledge.

What Do New Ways of Organizing Look Like?

5

Abstract

The design of a number of contemporary organizations is reviewed: Vinci, a French builder and operator of infrastructure; ING, a Dutch bank; Zappos, an American online retailer; Haier, a Chinese appliance maker; and Hyperloop Transportation Technologies, a firm bringing the hyperloop transportation system to market. Several common design elements are found in their way of organizing. The most striking commonality is that they all have a modular organization structure, with relatively small teams as the main building blocks. A second important common feature is that these teams are to a large extent self-governing. The third way in which their organization designs are alike is the presence and importance of common management processes, needed to hold the structure together in the absence of a traditional hierarchy. These processes have two important aims: to achieve coordinated action between the teams and to set organization-wide strategic goals. A final point of similarity is that all the organizations reviewed here accept a certain level of duplication of effort. Some of them have even actively resisted the tendency to pool resources, believing it will diminish the autonomy of their teams.

Keywords

Organization design • Vinci • ING • Zappos • Haier • Hyperloop Transportation Technologies • Modular structure • Self-organization • Management processes

J. van Bree, *Organization Design*, https://doi.org/10.1007/978-3-030-78679-3_5

Learning Objectives

- Describe examples of organizations that reflect contemporary developments in organization design.
- Understand the common design elements that run through these examples.
- Connect general principles of organization design to specific examples.
- Discuss advantages and downsides of the choices made by these example organizations.

Now that we have covered the most important frameworks and principles connected to organization design, it is time to take an in-depth look at what this looks like in the field. In this final chapter of the first part of the book, we will look at some current organizational trailblazers to discover how their organization designs relate to the frameworks and principles we have covered so far. We will first introduce the six organizations we will be looking at in this chapter. We will then go over some common threads in their organization designs and relate those back to the design principles of the previous chapter. Let me stress that by trailblazer, I am not referring to the performance of these companies. Even though most of them are doing quite well, if the history of management literature has taught us anything, it is that today's heroes may disappear from the business landscape before the ink on this book is dry. Without any claim to show the recipe for success, I am simply calling attention to the atypical organization designs that these firms employ. In that sense, they are worthy of our attention.

5.1 Introducing Our Trailblazers

The organizations we will be discussing in this chapter hail from Europe, the United States, and China, with one organization not readily pinned down to a geographical region, as we will see. Most of the organizations selected for this chapter are relatively large. That is intentional, because the real complexity of organization design usually does not come to the fore until an organization grows to a size larger than a few hundred people. We can find many examples of innovative and unique organization designs in small organizations. But the value of those organizations as an example of how to organize is usually limited for the larger firms. All the organizations in this chapter are profit-seeking firms, in a variety of industries, ranging from financial services to construction, manufacturing, and retail. The decision to look at relatively traditional industries and to not include internet scale-ups or established Silicon Valley firms is intentional, because it is difficult for companies in the more traditional industries to draw the right lessons from technology-based firms. This is not to say that it is not interesting to study how they are organized. It is just more difficult to see the principles behind their way of organizing that are generally applicable, because technology is such a dominant factor in their organization design. On that note, let us look at the first organization we will be discussing in this chapter.

5.1.1 Vinci

Vinci Group is a Paris-based investor, builder, and operator of buildings and infrastructure in more than 100 countries. The group counts some 220,000 employees (end of 2019) and a total annual revenue of 48 billion Euros.[1] These are impressive numbers, but a much more interesting statistic is that the company is divided into 3200 business units. That means there are on average only 70 employees per business unit. In addition, only around 250 of their 220,000 employees work in the head office in Paris (Huillard, 2017). The organization is characterized by a highly decentralized structure, with these 3200 business units designed to work autonomously, like small enterprises. Xavier Huillard, Vinci's CEO, sees this autonomy and accountability of employees in the field as an important guiding principle of his management philosophy. Much like Eckart Wintzen did at BSO/Origin (covered in Chap. 4), Huillard feels he needs to contain the tendency toward centralization.

> Not surprisingly, consultants regularly advise us to pool our support functions between business units. This is an unproved means of optimisation and rationalisation. I am convinced that the savings made to do this would be negligible compared to the value created if each business unit manager acts as if he were an entrepreneur. (Huillard, 2017, p. 2)

One of the entities of Vinci Group is Vinci Energies, which we will use as the example in this chapter. Vinci Energies is a contractor for energy infrastructure projects. Its 2019 revenue was around 14 billion Euros, and it employed some 82,500 people in that year.[2] Like the rest of Vinci, it is organized as a large number of small business units (about 1800 of them). Micro-segmentation guarantees that no business unit infringes on the territory of another.

> This segmentation is so precise that, for example, one of our companies in Nantes specialises in industrial information technology aimed at manufacturers of pet food. (Huillard, 2017, p. 3)

Each business unit develops its strategic plan in collaboration with the director they report to (who is also overseeing some 12 other business units). The director is also authorized to restructure business units if they are constantly losing money. Once a business unit becomes too big, it is divided in two (again, much like BSO/Origin).

5.1.2 ING

ING is a European bank headquartered in Amsterdam. It employs some 53,000 people (as of 2020) and is active in 40 countries.[3] ING considers itself to be a 'data-driven digital bank', a strategic shift in how they saw themselves which took place around 2014. After having visited technology companies such as Spotify, Google,

---

[1] Data supplied by Vinci (2020).

[2] Data supplied by Vinci Energies (2021).

[3] Data supplied by ING (2020).

and Netflix, they decided to overhaul the organization structure, way of working, and people processes for their entire 3500 staff member group headquarters. The model they chose was largely inspired by Spotify's way of organizing and uses the same terminology. A team is referred to as a squad, a collection of teams forms a tribe, and the functional home base of employees is called a chapter. The main change compared to their old model was that employees would now be working on client-related objectives in semipermanent cross-functional teams (the squads), according to Agile principles.[4] Employees do most of their work in the squad, but their home base is formed by the chapter, led by a chapter lead. Chapters cover a discipline such as user experience design, software development, or marketing. The chapters are what used to be the departments in the traditional hierarchical structure. The model is represented in broad strokes in Fig. 5.1.

The implementation of this new model in 2015 meant a considerable overhaul of ING's management structure. All senior managers had to reapply for the newly defined positions, and when all was said and done, about one-third of them had left

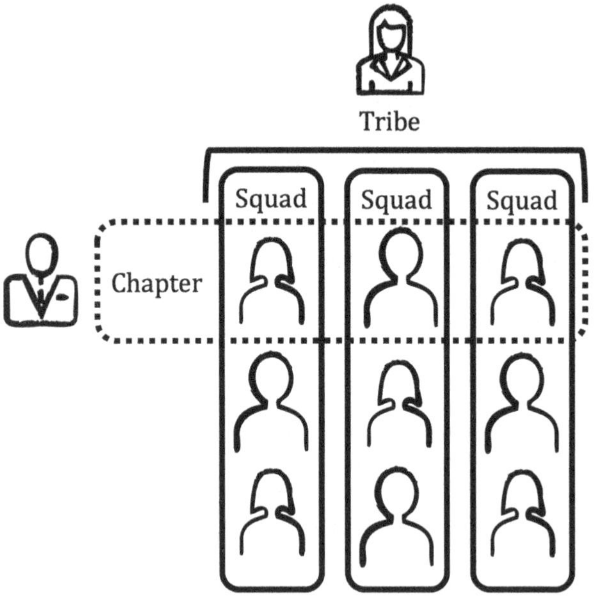

Fig. 5.1 A visual representation of ING's organization model (icons by Ralf Schmitzer from the Noun Project)

[4] We will not cover Agile principles in depth in this text, but the reader is referred to Rigby et al. (2016) for a good, business-oriented introduction.

the company (Birkinshaw, 2018). Since then, ING has continued to roll out this new model across their organization. Published reports show it seems to be paying off, in terms of its improved cost-to-income ratio—mostly because of declining staff numbers—but also in terms of growing customer satisfaction with the digitally enabled services the bank provides (Birkinshaw, 2018).

5.1.3 Zappos

Zappos is an online fashion retailer, based in Las Vegas. Zappos was acquired by Amazon in 2009 but remains an independent entity. It employs around 1500 people and has an annual revenue of some $2 billion.[5] Zappos became a well-known name in business circles, because of its implementation of an organization model called Holacracy. They were not the first organization to implement it, but seemed to be the biggest one at the time. And their CEO, Tony Hsieh,[6] did not shy away from media attention. Like ING, his way of implementing the new organization model was fairly ruthless. In early 2015, he offered severance packages to all employees who felt the model was not a good fit for them. Around 18% of them left, although only the minority cited Holacracy as the reason (Bernstein et al., 2016).

The Holacracy framework was developed by Brian Robertson, a software engineer and entrepreneur. It takes most of its inspiration from a management system developed in the 1970s called Sociocracy,[7] which is predicated on a distributed form of leadership which resides in interlinked, self-managed teams, or 'circles' (see Fig. 5.2). The idea is that this makes a more circular form of management possible, where power and information do not just flow down the hierarchy but there is also a link back up, in the form of elected delegates that represent their circle one level higher in the hierarchy (Romme & Endenburg, 2006; Romme, 2016). It also uses a structured way of group decision-making in these circles, based on the so-called consent principle. This allows a group to come to a decision without the time-consuming search for full consensus or the authority-based final call by a leader.[8] Robertson took these sociocratic principles, further evolved them at his own software firm Ternary, and then repackaged and successfully marketed this 'organizational operating system' as Holacracy.[9]

As Zappos' implementation of Holacracy in 2015 drew quite a bit of media attention, some more negative experiences also started coming out. Especially the number of meetings that the Holacracy model seemed to mandate was quoted as a

[5] Zappos does not report its earnings, so these figures are estimates from the company's Wikipedia (2021) page.

[6] Tony Hsieh tragically passed away in November of 2020 at the age of 46, shortly after stepping down as Zappos CEO.

[7] More information about present-day uses of Sociocracy can be found on the website of The Sociocracy Group: https://thesociocracygroup.com

[8] For a brief explanation of this principle, the reader is referred to The Sociocracy Group (2021).

[9] See Robertson's HolacracyOne website for more information: https://www.holacracy.org

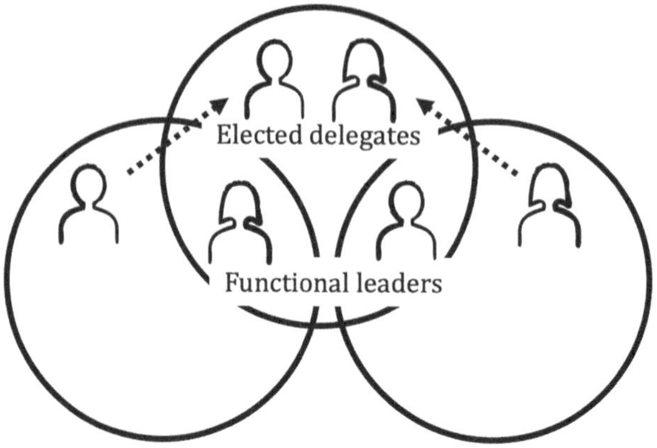

Fig. 5.2 Double linking between circles in the sociocratic management model (icons by Ralf Schmitzer from the Noun Project)

drain on productivity, with some employees reportedly spending five hours a day in conference rooms (Gelles, 2015). The main reason for all this meeting time seems to be that employees can have several roles (seven roles on average in the Zappos implementation) and can be part of more than one circle.

> If every circle has a monthly governance meeting, as is common in holacracies, and if employees are in 4.1 circles, on average, the meeting time adds up. (Bernstein et al., 2016, p. 46)

Recently, Zappos seems to have moved away from the very strict implementation of Holacracy to mitigate some of these disadvantages (Groth, 2020). For our discussion in this chapter, we will take Zappos' initial implementation of Holacracy in 2015 as a starting point.

A Different Incarnation of Holacracy: Spark

Around the same time that Zappos implemented Holacracy, there was another similarly sized online retailer that was doing the same, with much less media attention. Dutch bol.com—part of Ahold Delhaize, one of the world's largest food retail groups—implemented what they called Spark, a simplified version of Holacracy. They decided not to adopt all the rules and processes—and subsequent meetings—that come with the full implementation prescribed by the 'Holacracy constitution'. Bol.com also opted to make adopting Spark voluntary. There was no top-down mandate as there was at Zappos. The implementation did not originate with senior management, but rather bottom up, with two teams at the logistics department. It grew from there to 1300 people—out of a total staff of 2200—who are working according to the Spark principles as of 2020 (Minnaar, 2020). ◄

5.1.4 Haier

Chinese appliance maker Haier has in recent years become the darling of the business press, because of their heavily decentralized management model. We have seen decentralized models before, but not often in such a large, multinational firm operating in a relatively traditional industry. Haier Smart Home—the group's home appliance business—reported a total annual revenue of 200 billion RMB (around 25 billion Euros) in 2019[10] and employs almost 100,000 people across China, Southeast Asia, the United States, Africa, and Europe (Fig. 5.3).[11] It is not the type of firm you would expect to have a radical organization design.

One of the secrets of the apparent success of Haier's model is probably that this is not something that was implemented overnight, not even after a few months of pilots (as in the case of ING and Zappos). Rather, it was a journey of many decades under the leadership of the group's CEO and founder Zhang Ruimin.[12] He grew Haier from a decrepit refrigerator factory in Qingdao to a global appliance brand. Meanwhile, their organization design evolved from a traditional functional hierarchy, to decentralized business units, to further decentralization with self-managing teams. But what Haier has become most famous for is its *rendanheyi* model, which entailed the transformation of all departments into so-called microenterprises in 2014, letting 10,000 middle managers go in the process (Luo et al., 2018; Ruimin, 2018).

Fig. 5.3 Haier Industrial Park in Qingdao, China (Photo: Matthias Holthus)

[10] According to their 2019 annual report (Haier Smart Home, 2021).

[11] It is important to note here that Haier has not fully implemented the organization model they use in China overseas; some nuances of how the model is implemented in the United States—where Haier acquired GE Appliances—are discussed in Van der Lecq (2021).

[12] The interested reader can find an account of that journey in Minnaar (2018).

Haier now consists of more than 4000 microenterprises (or MEs), most of which have 10–15 employees. MEs are expected to be completely self-managing in hiring, setting compensation, and choosing their leader. Targets for MEs are ambitious, and they can and do go out of business if they underperform. The microenterprises can be either front-end units (handling sales and marketing for a specific segment), back-end units (taking care of R&D, manufacturing, or logistics), or functional units (providing support services such as finance and HR). They meet in an internal marketplace of sorts, where they can buy services, or not, from other MEs. Collaboration and knowledge exchange is facilitated by bringing MEs together in platforms, for instance, around a product category. But Haier claims the platform should not be seen as a management layer; that is, MEs do not report to the platform owner. Even more so than similarly sized Vinci Energies, Haier is intended to be an extremely flat organization (Luo et al., 2018; Hamel & Zanini, 2018).

5.1.5 Hyperloop Transportation Technologies

The final organization that is covered in this chapter is a bit of an outlier. It is non-traditional in many ways and probably the least well-known organization on the list. Hyperloop Transportation Technologies (HyperloopTT) was founded in 2013, as one of a handful of firms trying to bring the hyperloop technology to market: a high-speed mode of transport using vacuum tubes and magnetic levitation (Fig. 5.4). This was following an early system design by entrepreneur Elon Musk,[13] which showed the hyperloop to be a profitable and sustainable transportation system.

HyperloopTT has been able to mobilize more than 800 contributors to their mission, across the world. Many of them are not employed by the company, but contribute their time (one or a few days per week) in exchange for stock options. There is a larger community beyond that, who can decide to get involved on specific projects (typically without compensation) and may opt for a more permanent commitment by moving to the group of core contributors. There is also a small group of permanent employees who head one of the domains such as operations or marketing. And at the core of HyperloopTT is a seven-person leadership team, including the CEO and COO.[14]

What characterizes HyperloopTT's organization design is the freedom that teams have to start tasks that they think will benefit the organization in moving forward on its mission. There is no attempt to divide and allocate tasks in a centralized manner,

[13] Musk's original 'Hyperloop Alpha' system design can be found on the Tesla website: https://www.tesla.com/blog/hyperloop

[14] Core team members can be found on the HyperloopTT website: https://www.hyperlooptt.com/about/

Fig. 5.4 The HyperloopTT test facility in Toulouse, France (Photo: Hyperloop Transportation Technologies)

partly because the path to an operational hyperloop is still highly uncertain. HyperloopTT lets the teams explore different avenues, as the opportunities arise. The risk that efforts may be duplicated is par for the course. The large number of people who are willing to contribute their time to this mission—which many consider to be an inspiring one—makes the cost of duplicated efforts negligible (Majchrzak et al., 2018).

5.2 Common Design Elements

After this short introduction of the organizations, let us delve a bit deeper into the common threads in their way of organizing. We discuss four elements of the organization design that stand out in some or all of these organizations.

5.2.1 Modular Structure

The most striking commonality between the design of all these organizations is the fact that it has a modular structure, with relatively small teams as the main building blocks. Whether they are called circles at Zappos, squads at ING, microenterprises at Haier, or business units at Vinci, they share two important common features.

Autonomous assignment. The most important feature is the fact that these teams have been assigned a semiautonomous cluster of tasks (in the terms we used for the first design principle in the previous chapter). In other words, they have an 'end-to-end responsibility', as it is called at ING (Jacobs et al., 2017), that they can perform relatively autonomously from the rest of the organization. This autonomy means less coordination effort and more focus on the team's performance. At ING as well as at Vinci, the modular structure is deliberately designed. As we have seen in the previous chapter, designing a modular structure requires 'architectural knowledge' (Puranam et al., 2012). Vinci uses micro-segmentation to make sure each business unit can autonomously serve a very specific, small market segment. ING uses an overarching structure of 'tribes' to group the teams according to product lines: for example, mortgage services, securities, and private banking (Barton et al., 2018). Zappos and Haier have a more emergent structure, where teams form based on market opportunities or internal needs. At the very end of the spectrum is HyperloopTT, where task division and allocation are completely emergent. The underlying philosophy there is that the extreme uncertainty of their environment "[renders] a priori task division moot or even counterproductive" (Majchrzak et al., 2018, p. 476).

Fluid status. The second common feature between the teams in these organizations is that they do not have a permanent status. In other words, without restructuring or redesigning the organization, teams can be formed, disbanded, or given a new assignment. The permanence of the teams differs from one organization to the next. At Vinci, the business units are fairly stable, with a redesign only taking place if the unit has grown too big or is losing too much money. The same is true for Haier, where microenterprises are formed easily and can go out of business quickly if they underperform, but have a relatively permanent nature otherwise. At ING, the assignment that a squad has can be a short-term one. But it is more common for a squad to work on a specific assignment on a semipermanent basis. And even if an assignment is short-term, the team is usually kept together for the next assignment. However, the structure at ING makes it easy to shuffle teams around. Employees do not report into a squad leader—there is none, for that matter—but into a chapter lead, who represents their craft. So, moving to a new squad does not mean you report to a different manager. Your 'home base' stays the same. At Zappos and HyperloopTT, teams are even more fluid. At Zappos, it is common to be part of several circles, which may lead to a very different dynamic than the focus and commitment that being part of—only one—squad or microenterprise would instill. And at HyperloopTT, only the overarching domains themselves are stable (such as operations and marketing), but teams are formed on a completely ad hoc basis, around a task the community has identified as important.

Mintzberg's Adhocracy and Galbraith's Reconfigurable Organization

When discussing the organization models of the 'trailblazers', it is important to be aware that much of what we are seeing is not entirely new. In 1980, Henry Mintzberg described five simplified 'configurations' in which a number of design parameters—such as coordinating mechanism and type of decentralization—come together to form an archetypical organization design, suitable for a specific type of contingency factors. One of these configurations was the adhocracy,[15] which Mintzberg had observed at consulting firms, advertising agencies, NASA, and Boeing (in the 1960s and 1970s). The workforce of the adhocracy is dominated by highly trained professional specialists, who are grouped in functional departments with others of their craft. However, they do most of their work in project teams that have a high level of autonomy (or decentralization, to use Mintzberg's terminology). Mintzberg distinguishes between the operating adhocracy, in which the project teams carry out work on behalf of the client—a consulting firm being a typical example—and the administrative adhocracy, in which the project teams serve the organization itself. ING's organization model is a good example of a contemporary administrative adhocracy.

Thirty years after Mintzberg, Jay Galbraith (2010) was noticing a design similar to the adhocracy at a number of large, multinational firms (IBM among them). He used the term reconfigurable organization to describe a model characterized by the ability to assemble (and disband) teams to address opportunities, such as customer opportunities or product development opportunities. As in the adhocracy, groups of experts are gathered into functional units (Galbraith uses the term 'pools') from which they can be deployed to these teams.

It seems the principles behind this model have stood the test of time and are now reemerging in the context of Agile ways of working. This quote from Henry Mintzberg is as valid today as it was some 40 years ago: "[F]ashion seems to be an important factor, because every characteristic of Adhocracy is very much in vogue today (…) Adhocracy seems clearly to be the structure of our age" (Mintzberg, 1980, p. 338). ◄

5.2.2 Self-Governance

A second important common feature between the designs of these organizations is that the teams that make up the structure are to a large extent self-governing. That is to say, a lot of decision-making resides with the teams themselves. At Haier, the level of self-governance is probably the most extreme of the examples in this chapter. Among other things, Haier's microenterprises can determine their own strategic priorities, hire new colleagues, and set pay rates (Hamel & Zanini, 2020). The circles at Zappos are also largely self-organizing, although the way in which they govern themselves is prescribed in the Holacracy constitution.

[15] Mintzberg is not the only author to use the term adhocracy; it was also employed by Robert Waterman (1990) to describe a similar organizational setup and was recently dusted off by Birkinshaw and Ridderstråle (2015) to be placed in the context of organizational agility.

> The constitution doesn't say how people should do their tasks. It explains in a broad-brush way how circles should form and operate: how they should identify and assign roles, what boundaries the roles should have, and how the circles should interact. (Bernstein et al., 2016, p. 43)

So, the circles are allowed to govern themselves, as long as they stay within the guardrails set by the Holacracy framework. HyperloopTT is once again at the other end of this spectrum, where standardized practices are seen as useless, "because the process for achieving [HyperloopTT's] mission is too unpredictable" (Majchrzak et al., 2018, p. 489). At ING, the teams work according to Agile principles,[16] which include self-organization as an important starting point. Self-organization in this context means setting priorities, dividing tasks, and managing the flow of work without a formal team lead. It does not extend to aspects such as shifting the assignment of the team, hiring people, or determining compensation. There is still a management layer of chapter leads and tribe leads in place at ING for those types of decisions.

Whether or not the team has a leader differs from one organization to the next. At Haier, the microenterprises have leaders who are chosen by the ME team and can also be removed by them. "If the ME is (…) failing to reach its (…) targets, a two-thirds vote of ME members can oust the existing leader" (Hamel & Zanini, 2020, p. 100). At Zappos, the circles do not have formal leaders and are considered to be self-managing. There are so-called lead links, who are elected by the team to represent them to other circles. But these lead links do not have the formal authority that a team leader would have. Since employees can be part of multiple circles, Zappos went from 150 team leaders to 300 lead links after adopting Holacracy (Bernstein et al., 2016). At ING, there is also not a formal team lead position. The squad's priorities are set by a 'product owner' (a role defined as part of the Agile framework), who represents the customer perspective and determines what the team needs to build. There is also typically an Agile coach, who helps in facilitating the team process and in following the practices associated with the Agile way of working. Reallocating these responsibilities has been one of the more difficult aspects of the transformation for ING.

> [I]n ING's old way of working, a manager was responsible for everything: the product, the process, and the people. With agile, each element is the responsibility of a different person. It's been an adjustment for chapter leads, product owners, and agile coaches to grow comfortable with all of their new responsibilities. (Birkinshaw, 2018, p. 42)

Vinci has a relatively traditional leadership structure, with its units being led by a business unit manager. This is combined with stressing the need to constantly develop the autonomy and accountability of employees, instilling an entrepreneurial spirit. This is one of the main aims of Haier's model as well. Facilitating this entrepreneurship—instilling it in their employees as well as their ME leaders—was shown to be one of the biggest challenges that Haier experienced in their transition to the *rendanheyi* model (Luo et al., 2018).

---

[16] See Agile Alliance (2021) for the 12 Agile principles.

5.2.3 Common Management Processes

As we have seen so far, the organization designs we are discussing in this chapter are characterized by a highly decentralized structure, made up of small units that are to a large extent autonomous. What also becomes apparent when studying these organizations is that—in the absence of a traditional hierarchy—they require new types of glue to be held together. That is where common management processes come in. Even though each of these organizations offers a lot of freedom to its teams to conduct their business in the way they see fit, there are strict rules and protocols when it comes to the interaction with other teams and with the organization at large. These common management processes have two important aims: achieving coordinated action and setting strategic goals.

Achieving coordinated action. First of all, there is a need for common protocols when these decentralized units start interacting. If we look at the 4000 microenterprises of Haier that interact in an internal marketplace, chaos would ensue if these interactions were not bound by rules or procedures. That is why the process of internal contracting is facilitated by so-called presets: "predefined rules about minimum performance standards and margin splits that reduce friction during negotiations" (Hamel & Zanini, 2020, p. 89). Another important integrating mechanism at Haier is the platform. This is not a management layer, but instead a subset of microenterprises—usually around 50 of them—that have interdependencies between them. These interdependencies can, for instance, exist because the MEs operate in similar product categories. The platform owner is charged with identifying the areas where coordination is needed or resources can be shared. In addition, there are some standards set by shared platforms that focus on manufacturing and marketing. Although some of these ways of coordinating sound fairly traditional, what sets them apart is the absence of reporting relationships. And what is almost entirely absent as well is the default coordinating mechanism that a lot of organizations resort to: the meeting. Reports about Zappos' implementation of Holacracy pointed to the downsides of using meetings as a primary coordinating mechanism (Gelles, 2015; Bernstein et al., 2016). No matter how efficiently these meetings are run—and they are when using the Holacracy protocols—an excessive amount of them can wear an organization down. This meeting fatigue need not necessarily be a consequence of using Holacracy, but may rather be a result of how the circles are structured. If they are not—or cannot be—structured according to the first design principle of the previous chapter (semiautonomous clusters of tasks), then too many links between circles will exist. And more links mean more meetings in Holacracy. To counteract that problem, recent reports indicate that Zappos has evolved their organization design to something a bit more like Haier's, with entrepreneurial units in a market-based structure (Bell, 2019; Groth, 2020).

In most of the organizations we are discussing in this chapter, hierarchy plays a role in achieving coordinated action. What is meant here is a hierarchy in the sense of an inclusive clustering—"the boxes-within-boxes structure that characterizes most organizations" (March & Simon, 1993, p. 3)—not in the sense of levels of graded authority. At Haier, microenterprises are clustered into platforms. At ING, squads are clustered into tribes. At Zappos, circles are clustered into super-circles.

Even though the traditional authority relations associated with the hierarchical levels are absent, there seems to be a natural tendency to cluster units together. This is easily explained by the interdependencies that exist between these units, which give rise to a need for coordination.[17] The only exception is Vinci, which through its strategy of micro-segmentation is able to adhere to the first design principle. This means there is much less of a need to cluster business units together for coordination purposes. There are levels of graded authority, however, with around 12 business unit managers reporting to one director.

Setting strategic goals. Apart from achieving coordinated action, the biggest challenge that the decentralized organization designs in this chapter bring is how to keep this fleet of little ships sailing in the same direction. Bernstein and his colleagues state—in their discussion of the Zappos case—that the way in which strategic direction is established in Holacracy is not viable for organizations that need "a clear, stable, consistent overarching strategy" (Bernstein et al., 2016, p. 48). Strategy has an emergent nature at Zappos, as well as at HyperloopTT, and to a lesser extent at Haier. Despite its increased agility, ING is still one of those organizations that needs a consistent, overarching strategy. One of the management processes they use for this is the quarterly business review (or QBR for short), something they picked up from Google and Netflix (Jacobs et al., 2017). The QBR is a large-scale meeting in which the tribes come together to exchange experiences from the last quarter, challenge each other, and set goals for the next quarter. Despite the decentralization that characterizes ING's new structure, senior executives realized that they still need to supply a framework for goals and reporting and to keep the level of ambition high (Birkinshaw, 2018). That same need for setting stretch goals is acknowledged at Haier. Ambitious, leading targets are set for each microenterprise, based on market research. The entrepreneurial autonomy of the ME comes with an expectation that they will outperform the market.

5.2.4 Accepting Duplication of Effort

Probably the most fundamental and at the same time most difficult shift that many of the organizations in this chapter make is to accept a certain level of duplication of effort. The highly decentralized nature of the organization designs in this chapter has many advantages, as we have seen. But there are also disadvantages associated with these models. Some of these can be remedied by the right structural design—ensuring self-sufficient teams are working on semiautonomous clusters of tasks—or by adding the right management processes (as we saw in the previous section). But there is one disadvantage which more or less comes with the territory: it is difficult to achieve economies of scale in a highly decentralized model. Pooling resources is the default mechanism for achieving the advantages of scale. By consolidating functions such as manufacturing and supply chain, and sometimes product development

[17] We will have much more to say about interdependencies and coordination in Chap. 8.

and product marketing as well, a globally operating firm can achieve economies of scale—that is, the percent increase in output will exceed the percent increase in cost. This cost advantage can be based quite simply on not having to duplicate equipment or infrastructure. Lower costs can also be based on learning curves, where more experience allows a firm to repeat a production or delivery activity more efficiently. Regardless of its exact source, the lure of economies of scale drives many organizations toward consolidation efforts, not just for activities in the primary value chain but also for support functions such as HR and finance. In some industries, pooling these support resources in shared service centers that serve several business units—and subsequently offshoring them, in some cases—has become standard practice.

As we saw earlier on in this chapter, large decentralized firms such as Haier and Vinci—and BSO/Origin before them, see Chap. 4—have actively resisted this tendency. This seems to be based not so much on a cost analysis, but on a belief. That belief is three-fold: first, the belief that consolidating functions will diminish the entrepreneurial spirit in the business units, because they no longer have full control over their resources; second, that placing functions at a distance from the business unit will lead to additional coordination cost; and third, that the centralized functions tend to expand and start defending their own position in the organization, rather than facilitating the customer-facing units. All three aspects combined will likely nullify the potential cost savings. I call this a belief because it is very difficult to back this rationale up with a financial analysis. The reduction of entrepreneurial energy and the increase of coordination efforts are hard to quantify—even though they may be quite visible—whereas it is much easier to put a Euro amount on the cost reduction of pooling resources.

The guidance here can come from the design principles covered in the previous chapter. The search for semiautonomous clusters of tasks and maximum self-sufficiency of units should be leading. The organization should then decide how much duplication of effort they are comfortable with to adhere to these principles.[18] If we look at HyperloopTT, we see an extreme tolerance for duplication. This organization needs to cast its nets as wide as possible, to make sure they engage in every opportunity that arises to bring their new technology a step closer to commercial exploitation. Trying to pool these efforts would cause delays and would disturb the explorative energy. However, as we have seen, HyperloopTT operates in a very atypical context. Most organizations will want to move a bit more toward the benefits of scale on this continuum. That does not mean that resources need to be fully consolidated. There are other ways to reap the benefits of knowledge accumulation and specialization. And attention to these aspects is important, since reduced knowledge accumulation has been documented as a potential downside of using a decentralized organization model, such as one consisting of self-directed Agile teams (Annosi et al., 2020). Even at a radically decentralized company such as Haier,

[18] Chapter 7 on 'grouping' contains practical guidelines on how to make this trade-off.

platforms are in place as a way to share specialized capabilities and knowledge between microenterprises. As we saw in relation to setting strategic goals in the previous section, an organization design based on autonomous units requires an overarching level where more strategic trade-offs are made. The strength of the autonomous team lies in their focus on achieving their own objectives. This singular focus cannot logically be combined with efforts to share resources or knowledge. That is something that needs to be facilitated—or enforced, depending on the management style—by another layer in the organization: the platform in the case of Haier or the tribe in the case of ING.

A Different Label for a Similar Phenomenon: The Actor-Oriented Scheme

A number of years ago, Øystein Fjeldstad, Charles Snow, and their colleagues identified a new type of organization design which they labeled the actor-oriented scheme (Fjeldstad et al., 2012; Snow et al., 2017). Driven by the need for rapid adaptation to their competitive environment, this type of organization shares many of its characteristics with the examples we covered in this chapter. The actor-oriented scheme is characterized by a high level of decentralization, with self-organizing actors—either individuals or teams—as the building blocks. Two important elements of the organizational architecture that are needed to make this actor-oriented scheme work are *commons* and *protocols*. Commons refers to resources—in the broadest sense of the word—that are collectively owned by and available to the actors. What is meant here is primarily knowledge and information-based resources, some of which we have been discussing in this section. Protocols can be equated with the management processes we discussed in the previous section: 'codes of conduct' that ensure collaboration between the actors runs smoothly. Fjeldstad and his colleagues show how the actor-oriented scheme can be applied to organizations in a number of industries, including management consulting and open-source software development. ◂

The examples in this chapter have shown how the design principles of the previous chapter can be applied in practice. Table 5.1 shows how the common design elements of the organizations discussed in this chapter relate to these design principles.

Their manifestation in the field shows the endurance of these principles or perhaps even their renewed importance. We have seen it is possible to apply the principles in today's business environment, even though the circumstances are quite different from the time when the underlying theories originated. But we have also seen that these organization designs come with, at times very difficult, trade-offs. That is why a deliberate design process is needed to generate the right solutions and make the right choices for a specific organizational context. The second part of this book is about that design process.

Table 5.1 The link between the common design elements found in the organizations of this chapter and the design principles from the previous chapter

Common design element	Organizations	Design principle (Chap. 4)
Modular structure	Vinci ING Haier	(1) Create autonomous clusters of tasks (5) Create enough flexibility in the design to fit the context (6) Do not overdesign
Self-governance	ING Zappos Haier	(2) Create self-sufficient teams (4) Prevent redundant management layers (6) Do not overdesign
Common management processes	ING Haier	(3) Manage the tensions between organizational units
Accepting duplication of effort	Vinci Haier HyperloopTT	(2) Create self-sufficient teams

Review Questions

1. How would you describe the role of the CEO in the organizations reviewed in this chapter?
2. Do you see any common threads in the attributes of these organizations (size, geographic base, products or services offered, market segments served, etc.)?
3. Review the organizations in this chapter: to what extent do you think there was a deliberate design effort behind the organization as we see it now?
4. Which of these organization designs do you think is most sustainable? And which one do you think will quickly be replaced by another design?
5. Do you see a relationship between the design of these organizations and their performance? If so, explain that relationship.
6. Do you see any differences between the models stemming from national cultures (French, Dutch, American, Chinese)?
7. Why is it, do you think, that we are seeing structures that resemble those described by Galbraith more than 10 years ago and by Mintzberg more than 40 years ago? What does this say about the field of organization design?
8. As a general rule, do you think the teams in these types of organizations should be self-managing (i.e., not have a formal team lead)? Why or why not?
9. What do you think would happen to the teams in these organizations if there was no overarching mechanism in place to set strategic goals?
10. Do you think that profit-seeking organizations should always strive for economies of scale? Why or why not?

References

Agile Alliance. (2021). 12 Principles behind the Agile Manifesto. Retrieved April 27, 2021, from https://www.agilealliance.org/agile101/12-principles-behind-the-agile-manifesto/

Annosi, M. C., Foss, N., & Martini, A. (2020). When agile harms learning and innovation (and what can be done about it). *California Management Review, 63*(1), 61–80.

Barton, D., Carey, D., & Charan, R. (2018). One bank's agile team experiment: How ING revamped its retail operation. *Harvard Business Review, 96*(2), 59–61.

Bell, J. (2019). Exclusive: Zappos is looking beyond e-commerce to ensure it lasts for 1000 years. Retrieved January 31, 2021, from https://footwearnews.com/2019/business/retail/zappos-culture-retail-future-strategy-interview-1202777453/

Bernstein, E., Bunch, J., Canner, N., & Lee, M. (2016). Beyond the Holacracy hype: the overwrought claims—And actual promise—Of the next generation of self-managed teams. *Harvard Business Review, 94*(7/8), 38–49.

Birkinshaw, J. (2018). What to expect from agile. *MIT Sloan Management Review, 59*(2), 39–42.

Birkinshaw, J., & Ridderstråle, J. (2015). *Adhocracy for an agile age*. Retrieved January 29, 2021, from https://www.mckinsey.com/business-functions/organization/our-insights/adhocracy-for-an-agile-age

Fjeldstad, Ø. D., Snow, C. C., Miles, R. E., & Lettl, C. (2012). The architecture of collaboration. *Strategic Management Journal, 33*(6), 734–750.

Galbraith, J. R. (2010). The multi-dimensional and reconfigurable organization. *Organizational Dynamics, 39*(2), 115–125.

Gelles, D. (2015, July 19). Pushing shoes and a vision. *The New York Times*, p. 1 (section BU).

Groth, A. (2020). *Zappos has quietly backed away from holacracy*. Retrieved January 31, 2021, from https://qz.com/work/1776841/zappos-has-quietly-backed-away-from-holacracy/

Haier Smart Home. (2021). *Haier Smart Home*. Retrieved January 31, 2021, from https://smart--home.haier.com/en/

Hamel, G., & Zanini, M. (2018). The end of bureaucracy: How a Chinese appliance maker is reinventing management for the digital age. *Harvard Business Review, 96*(6), 50–59.

Hamel, G., & Zanini, M. (2020). *Humanocracy: Creating organizations as amazing as the people inside them*. Harvard Business Review Press.

Huillard, X. (2017). Expanding without getting fat: Managing the Vinci Group. *Le journal de l'école de Paris du management, 125*(3), 8–14.

ING. (2020). *ING at a glance*. Retrieved January 31, 2021, from https://www.ing.com/About-us/Profile/ING-at-a-glance.htm

Jacobs, P., Schlatmann, B., & Mahadevan, D. (2017). *ING's agile transformation*. Retrieved January 29, 2021, from https://www.mckinsey.com/industries/financial-services/our-insights/ings-agile-transformation

Luo, J., Van de Ven, A. H., Jing, R., & Jiang, Y. (2018). Transitioning from a hierarchical product organization to an open platform organization: A Chinese case study. *Journal of Organization Design, 7*(1), 1–14.

Majchrzak, A., Griffith, T. L., Reetz, D. K., & Alexy, O. (2018). Catalyst organizations as a new organization design for innovation: The case of hyperloop transportation technologies. *Academy of Management Discoveries, 4*(4), 472–496.

March, J. G., & Simon, H. A. (1993). *Organizations* (2nd ed.). John Wiley.

Minnaar, J. (2018). *The world's most pioneering company of our times*. Retrieved January 31, 2021, from https://corporate-rebels.com/haier

Minnaar, J. (2020). *Two large-scale Holacracy experiments: Zappos.com vs. bol.com*. Retrieved January 31, 2021, from https://corporate-rebels.com/zappos-versus-bol/

Mintzberg, H. (1980). Structure in 5's: A synthesis of the research on organization design. *Management Science, 26*(3), 322–341.

Puranam, P., Raveendran, M., & Knudsen, T. (2012). Organization design: The epistemic interdependence perspective. *Academy of Management Review, 37*(3), 419–440.

Rigby, D. K., Sutherland, J., & Takeuchi, H. (2016). Embracing agile: How to master the process that's transforming management. *Harvard Business Review, 94*(5), 40–50.

Romme, A. G. L., & Endenburg, G. (2006). Construction principles and design rules in the case of circular design. *Organization Science, 17*(2), 287–297.

Romme, G. (2016). *The quest for professionalism: The case of management and entrepreneurship*. Oxford University Press.

Ruimin, Z. (2018). *Rendanheyi: Maximizing everyone's value*. Presented at the Global Peter Drucker Forum 2018, Imperial Palace, Vienna, November 30.

Snow, C. C., Fjeldstad, Ø. D., & Langer, A. M. (2017). Designing the digital organization. *Journal of Organization Design, 6*(1), 1–13.

The Sociocracy Group. (2021). *4 principles*. Retrieved January 31, 2021, from https://thesociocracygroup.com/4-principles/

Van der Lecq, B. (2021). *An American icon being acquired by a Chinese giant: The story of GEA*. Retrieved January 31, 2021, from https://corporate-rebels.com/an-american-icon-being-acquired-by-a-chinese-giant-the-story-of-gea/

Vinci. (2020). *2020 essentials*. Retrieved January 31, 2021, from https://www.vinci.com/essentiel/en/

Vinci Energies. (2021). *Our key figures*. Retrieved January 31, 2021, from https://www.vinci-energies.com/en/group/key-figures/

Waterman, R. H. (1990). *Adhocracy: The power to change*. W.W. Norton & Company.

Wikipedia. (2021). *Zappos*. Retrieved January 31, 2021, from https://en.wikipedia.org/wiki/Zappos

How to Approach an Organization Design

6

Abstract

The organization designer has two important dimensions to consider when approaching an organization design project. One is the mode of intervention, which can range from providing expert knowledge to the client to engaging in a collaborative process. The second dimension is the number of people involved in the design process, which can range from just a few members of the leadership team to groups of up to thousands (in so-called large group interventions). The approach described here uses a collaborative approach that engages a design team of a manageable size. The design team represents the organization and is mandated by the leadership team to perform the design work. Elements of approaches from other design disciplines can offer useful inspiration for the organization design approach, such as the importance of prototyping and testing. Still, a lot of challenging aspects of the design process remain, especially having to do with the inevitable political aspects at play. Data-driven tools that support the organization design process are increasingly on offer. They may offer support in analyzing the current situation, in prototyping design options, and even in generating new designs.

Keywords

Organization design • Design process • Management consultant • Leadership team • Process consultation • Prototyping • Data-driven design

J. van Bree, *Organization Design*, https://doi.org/10.1007/978-3-030-78679-3_6

Learning Objectives

- Compare and contrast organization design to other design disciplines.
- Critically reflect on the choices an organization designer makes when it comes to the approach of a project.
- Understand the rationale behind a collaborative and co-creative approach for designing an organization.
- Understand the role of three important groups in the organization design process: the steering committee, the design team, and the consultant team.
- Recognize some of the practical challenges associated with organization design projects.
- Identify when data-driven tools and approaches have added value to an organization design process.

In this second part of the book, we turn to the 'how' of organization design. What is needed to put into practice the frameworks and principles covered in the preceding chapters? What are the steps that need to be taken in a design project, and what are some of the tools and guidelines available to the organization designer? Before we go into the actual approach, perhaps it is a good idea to start by identifying who the organization designer is.

6.1 Who Is the Organization Designer?

In many design disciplines, we can identify a designer: the individual whose name will be attached to the designed—and produced—product, for example, Yves Saint Laurent in fashion, Frank Gehry in architecture, and Jonathan Ive in product design. Often, these individuals will be gracious and humble enough to acknowledge that it was a team effort, but it is still their face on the cover of magazines and their name that is attached to the trapeze dress, the Guggenheim Museum, or the iMac. Even though—as we shall see later in this chapter—there are useful parallels to be drawn between organization design and other design disciplines, the role of the designer is not one of them. It is rare to find a specific name attached to an organization design. The exceptions are the CEOs who take their organization in a very specific direction: Zhang Ruimin at Haier (see Chap. 5), Dee Hock at Visa,[1] and Eckart Wintzen at BSO/Origin (see Chap. 4). But I doubt that they would consider themselves to be organization designers. What they seem to be doing is channeling and reifying ideas that were already present and showing courage to deviate from the norm. The other instances in which we may be able to identify the organization designer are when a consultant or consulting firm plays an important role in the process. Let us look a bit closer at whether it is the organization design consultant then who shapes the organization.

[1] Recounted by the man himself (Hock, 1999, 2005).

6.1.1 The Stance of the Consultant as Organization Designer

A redesign is not something an organization goes through very often, which makes it a typical topic for which consulting support is engaged. The expectation of the client about the type of intervention that the consultant will provide will fall somewhere on the spectrum from an expert mode to a mode which Schein (1990) has described as process consultation. In the expert mode, the imprint of the consultant as organization designer will be most clearly visible. The client transfers the responsibility for the design to the consultant. There is an assumption of a knowledge asymmetry between consultants and clients (Nikolova & Devinney, 2012). The knowledge that the consultant brings to bear is often in the form of standardized solutions. These solutions can be benchmark data, such as the average ratio of managers to staff (span of control) or the average number of support staff in a certain industry. Standardized solutions can also take the form of an entire organization model such as Holacracy (see previous chapter) or the 'Spotify model' (discussed in Chap. 3). The assumption underlying the expert mode is that this knowledge about organization design can be transferred to and implemented in a different context, with a slight customization. As we have seen in Chap. 3—where we covered contingency theory and isomorphism—this assumption is highly problematic. Still—as theories about isomorphism show—it is a seductive and understandable position for an organization's leadership to take, especially if the uncertainty is high about which model to adopt for addressing new challenges.

On the other side of the spectrum is process consultation or the social learning mode. In this mode, organization design is a collaborative process, in which the consultant takes the role of guide or facilitator. Rather than rely on standardized solutions, "consulting knowledge is 'constructed' through individual actions embedded in the client-specific context rather than existent prior to action" (Nikolova and Devinney, p. 396). What is required of the consultant is not the knowledge of specific models or benchmark data, but knowledge about which questions need to be answered in which order. In addition, the consultant needs to have the skills to manage this specific process of interaction with their client, which is characterized by openness—sometimes even vulnerability—on both sides. It is my experience that this is often more demanding of the client than it is of the consultant. In a collaborative organization design process, the question that is inevitably posed to the consultant at some point is: "What do *you* think we should do? Which design do *you* think is best? How do other organizations do this?" As Edgar Schein (1990) has pointed out, the consultant should of course not withhold their expertise if the client really needs it. The key is to be able to move out of the expert role again, once the consultant's expertise has been inserted into the process. In the case of organization design, that expertise is about showing available options, clarifying advantages and disadvantages, and pointing out trade-offs. It is not about recommending a specific option.

The approach to organization design that this book offers is founded on principles of co-creation. The idea underlying this approach is that the organization design consultant needs to be the expert in the relevant frameworks, principles, and approaches—the topics of this book—not in solutions. This is not to say that specific solutions—such as the examples of organizations discussed in the previous chapter—cannot have a role in an organization design process. They can offer inspiration and can be used to illustrate certain principles, but it is essential that they come with a disclaimer: these are not 'best practice' that can be copied.

Edgar Schein's Process Consultation

Social and clinical psychologist Edgar Schein has made many important contributions to the field of organization development, notably with his work on organizational culture (Schein, 2017). The work that extends most in relevance to the field of organization design is that on process consultation (Schein, 1990, 1999). With process consultation, Schein describes a set of guidelines and principles for what he calls a helping relationship. This relationship can be between a counselor and patient, between a parent and child, but also between a consultant and client. Besides his background in psychology, Schein draws on decades of his own consulting work as well as many other helping situations. The essential dynamic that Schein tries to ward off is that of the helper adopting the position of expert, when being asked for help. In a consulting setting: the client asks a question; the consultant supplies the answer. This seems simple enough, but Schein points to several assumptions underlying this dynamic. Chief among them are the assumptions that the client knows what the real problem is and that they have communicated it truthfully. "Sometimes the helper (…) must think about these assumptions and assess the consequences of providing expert information. And sometimes, based on this assessment, the helper must choose not to operate in that model even if requested to do so" (Schein, 1990, p. 59). Even a more interactive model of 'playing doctor'—clients invite consultants to investigate, make a diagnosis, and suggest a cure—comes with serious limitations according to Schein: for example, has the client correctly identified the sick area? Will the client accept the diagnosis and the prescription? Based on the issues with these modes of helping, Schein proposes the mode of process consultation. It assumes that clients seeking help often do not know exactly what their problems are and would benefit from participation in the diagnosing process. Process consultation also works from the assumption that it is the client who knows best which remedy will work in their organization and that they will benefit from being involved in the development of solutions. Many of the principles of process consultation underlie the approach for organization design described in this book. Perhaps the most important one is that "[i]n process consultation, it is essential to create a situation in which clients continue to own their own problems" (Schein, 1990, p. 61). ◀

There is no consensus in the professional field of organization design that a collaborative approach is best. Especially some of the larger consulting firms—who take care of a sizeable part of the organization design work, particularly for large multinationals—tend to work more from the expert mode. And there are definite advantages to that way of working. For one, having a solution that is validated by an expert—especially if it is a big-name consulting firm—can increase the legitimacy of that solution in the eyes of external stakeholders such as (supervisory) boards, shareholders, or regulators. In addition, the expert mode makes it easier to conduct a confidential organization design process. In some cases—such as a merger or downsizing—that may be an important consideration. A third advantage of the expert approach that is often mentioned is that it is less time-consuming than the collaborative approach. This may be true if measured by the time from trigger of redesign to finished design. However, if the time is measured from trigger to a fully implemented design, it may be a different story. The expert mode—due to its limited involvement of the organization—will likely take more effort to implement. I have seen many examples of organizations trying to make sense of a 200-page slide deck, which was the deliverable of a consulting firm working in the expert mode. In a collaborative design approach, the change and transition process starts in parallel with the design work, because the organization will be owner of the problems as well as the solutions.

There is an important second dimension that determines what an organization design project looks like, besides the choice between a collaborative and expert way of working. That is the question of who to involve in the design process. Albert Cherns (1987) made a strong case for involving those who will be occupying the new design: the employees and managers of the organization. His argument is that first of all, the data that are needed in designing the organization—such as the strengths and weaknesses of the current organization design or the tasks and their interdependencies—may be unreliable or incomplete if only a small group, say, the top management team, is involved. And second, perhaps even more importantly, "conclusions from those data in the form of design or redesign will otherwise be only weakly accepted" (Cherns, 1987, p. 154). On a related note, Cherns puts forward the 'compatibility principle': the way in which design is done should be compatible with the design's objective. In other words, if the objective is to move to a more decentralized structure consisting of autonomous teams, the design process should not be a top-down affair. Cherns would not have agreed with the way Tony Hsieh implemented Holacracy at Zappos, by basically issuing an 'accept or leave' directive (see previous chapter).

Cherns' principle does not tell us how many in the organization need to be involved in the design process. As a rule of thumb, the group that is involved in the design process should have first-hand access to the data that is needed. In other words, the design team should be a representative cross-section of the organization—or part of the organization—that is in scope of the design effort. That means that not just all (functional) domains are represented but also all relevant management layers. So, the scope needs to be covered both horizontally and vertically. The design team should contain what Paul Tolchinsky—eminent practitioner and co-creator of the Whole-Scale Change methodology[2]—calls a 'microcosm' of the organization. This requirement should be balanced by the need to keep the core design team of a manageable size. There are methods to perform design work with large groups—using so-called large group interventions—but these place such high demands on facilitators that we will not consider them as a standard part of the organization designer's toolkit. For the purposes of the approach as described in this book, we will assume there is a design team consisting of 6–12 representatives of the organization (with 20 as the upper limit). More about the role and mandate of this design team later on in this chapter.

Large Group Interventions: Design Work on a Larger Scale

A large group intervention (LGI) is "a planned meeting or conference of organization members and other stakeholders to address organizational problems and opportunities" (Worley et al., 2011, p. 405). There are many examples of methodologies in use for these types of meetings, such as Future Search, Open Space, World Café, Decision Accelerator, and Whole-Scale Change.[3] LGI meetings can vary in terms of the number of people involved—starts around 50 and can go up to thousands—as well as the length, although they usually extend beyond one day. Participation in an LGI is always broad, sometimes including external stakeholders. The meeting agenda is typically very deliberately designed—plenary sessions alternating with breakout groups—and there tends to be a lot of preparatory work performed by a core team. Despite the fact that LGIs address some crucial issues that organizational researchers might be interested in, there is very little connection between this practice and organizational theory (Bartunek et al., 2011). Empirical evidence of the outcomes of LGIs is mostly qualitative and case-based. What the available case descriptions suggest, however, is "that LGIs can shorten decision-making cycle times, generate creative responses and strategies, and increase commitment to action" (Worley et al., 2011, p. 406). Two important principles of the LGI are 'getting the whole system in the room'—bringing together all internal and external stakeholders—and searching for 'common ground' (Bunker & Alban, 2006; Weisbord & Janoff, 2010). An empirical investigation of the LGI called decision accelerator by Chris Worley, Sue Mohrman, and Jennifer Nevitt showed that "getting the whole system in the room is more than simple representation; it must be balanced representation" (Worley et al., p. 420). In addition to achieving this balanced representation, a large responsibility lies with the facilitators of the LGI in making sure that the right interactions take place during the meeting and that participants feel free to share their perspectives, even when more high-powered stakeholders are involved in the discussions. Using an LGI as part of an organization design process can be a very powerful intervention, but it may also steer a project off a cliff if used without thoughtful and skilled preparation and facilitation. ◀

[2] See Dannemiller Tyson Associates (2000).

[3] For an overview, see Holman et al. (2007).

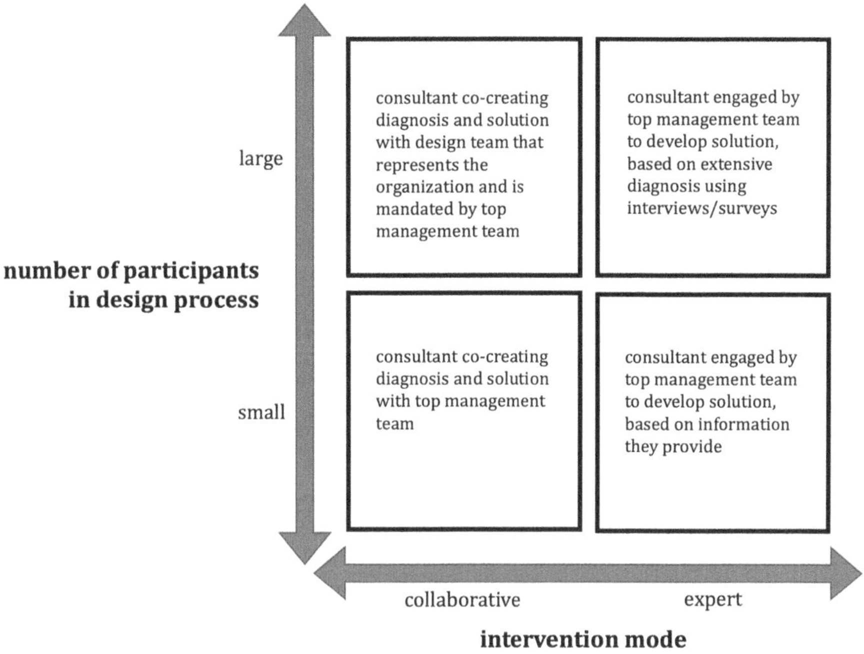

Fig. 6.1 Two dimensions to consider in the approach of an organization design project and typical settings that they produce

To close off this section, Fig. 6.1 summarizes the dimensions that the organization designer can consider when deciding how to approach a design project. It also shows examples of typical settings that the combination of dimensions can produce.

6.2 A Generic Approach for Organization Design

Relatively little attention has been paid in the academic literature to the process that practitioners use in (re)designing organizations. There are a few exceptions of studies that investigate the development or evolution of a specific instance of an organization (re)design (Engler et al., 2013; Worren, 2017; Meyer et al., 2017; Livijn, 2019), but the focus of these studies is almost entirely limited to the content, rather than the process of the designs. In addition, some monographs suggest approaches to organization design (Nadler & Tushman, 1997; Galbraith et al., 2002; Kesler & Kates, 2011; Stanford, 2018; Worren, 2018)—which were used as a basis for the approach presented in this chapter—but the authors do not investigate the practice of applying these approaches. Although the approaches advocated offer a useful framework—and, in my experience as an organization design consultant, are widely used—these works do not offer empirical evidence of outcomes or challenges,

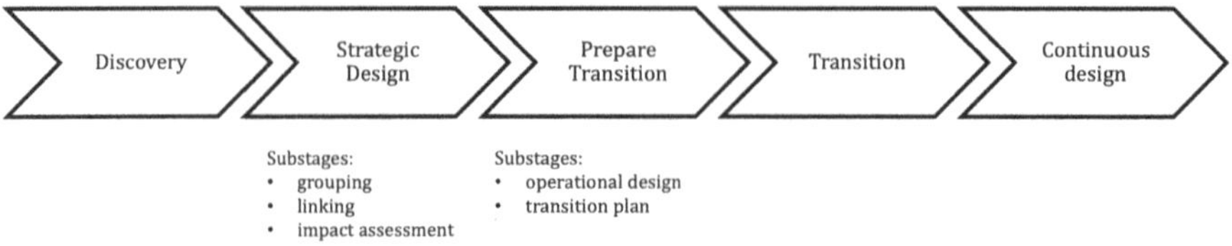

Fig. 6.2 A generic organization design approach (based on Nadler & Tushman, 1997; Galbraith et al., 2002; Kesler & Kates, 2011; Stanford, 2018; Worren, 2018)

specifically related to the process of organization design.[4] Having said that, the approach presented in this chapter aims to represent the current consensus among practitioners in organization design. I call it a generic approach to stress that individual organizations or consultants may use a different flavor, using different terms or placing some activities in a different stage. But three important principles remain in place in the approach:

- A design project starts with a diagnosis or discovery stage to clearly identify the need for change and the desired outcomes.
- The results of the discovery stage need to be translated into useful guardrails for the design project, usually referred to as design criteria.
- The design effort works from the overall, macro level (usually referred to as strategic design) down to the detailed, micro level (operational design).

Figure 6.2 gives a visual representation of the stages in the generic approach. Even though the chart implies a linear process, there are many iterative aspects to it, as we will see in the course of this and the next few chapters. We will cover all the stages of the approach in the subsequent chapters of this book, but our main focus will be on the strategic design stage, more specifically, on the grouping and linking substages (in Chaps. 7 and 8, respectively).

Even though this approach can be applied in a collaborative as well as an expert mode of intervention, in this book the assumption will be that a collaborative mode has been chosen. A key role in this collaborative way of working lies with the design team. The design team consists of a representative cross-section—or 'diagonal slice'[5]—of the organization, who:

- Collectively have all the information—or have access to the information—about the different domains and elements of the organization impacted by the organization design
- Can engage in abstract, conceptual thinking, as well as more operational discussions
- Have a constructive and future-oriented mindset
- Can place the interests of the organization above their own
- Have credibility and respect in the organization

[4] Exceptions notwithstanding, such as Chasserio and Botte (2020).

[5] A term used by Paul Tolchinsky (personal communication, March 2021).

This is quite a list of requirements. It is rare to have a design team that meets all of them. To complicate matters further, a balance needs to be maintained in the team. There usually is a mix of managers and employees, of operations and support staff, of creative and practical thinkers, and of dreamers and critical naysayers. All have their place in the design process, and it is up to the facilitator to manage the balance. That facilitator is typically an organization design consultant, someone who brings expert knowledge about the frameworks, principles, and approaches of organization design and combines that knowledge with the skill to manage group processes.

Essential in working with a design team is the mandate or charter that this team is given. This is especially relevant in situations where the organization's leadership is not part of the design team. The leadership team needs to then give the design team clear guardrails for their design work. One of those guardrails is the set of design criteria, something we introduced in Chap. 4 and will return to in the next chapter. However, it is rare that a leadership team feels comfortable enough to accept any solution that the design team comes back with, as long as it meets the design criteria. The solution space that is circumscribed by a set of design criteria can be quite large. It may be hard to imagine beforehand the types of solutions that may be generated. One way to achieve more control over the design process is by adding negotiables and nonnegotiables, or boundary conditions, as they are referred to in Whole-Scale Change (Dannemiller Tyson Associates, 2000). These may be statements around the leeway for headcount or cost increases (or a target for cost cuts), the room for eliminating or creating management layers, employment guarantees, or even suggestions of design directions that management would like the design team to explore.

What needs to be crystal clear in the charter for the design team is who designs and who decides. I am reminded of a project in a large public transportation company where that was not sufficiently clear. The design team in this project had set to work enthusiastically, mandated by the leadership team. Drivers, conductors, office staff, and managers were working in unison to do discovery work and generate a number of exciting new design options. Energy was flowing, and there was a real sense of accomplishment after the second design workshop. But when the leadership team—who acted as the steering committee in this project—were informed of the three intermediate options that the design team had generated, they intervened. One of the options was considered infeasible and was vetoed. This decision was not based on any boundary conditions that had been communicated to the design team nor had the possibility of the steering committee being allowed to veto options even been explicitly discussed. When the steering committee decision was reported back to the design team at their next design workshop, this was met by disbelief and disappointment. The incident put a real dent in the team's confidence, and it took time to get the energy levels back to what they were in previous workshops. What this example points to is the importance of a charter, set up in the early stages of the project, which clearly states who decides, who designs, and which conditions and requirements need to be met. We will have more to say about this in the next chapter.

Who Designs and Who Decides?

A medium-sized company in the logistics industry had embarked on a redesign of the organization. The top management team would act as the steering committee and had mandated a 10-person design team to conduct the actual design work. The guardrails set were fairly broad, clarifying the strategic ambition that lay at the foundation of the project. The design workshops were productive and generated a number of design directions. After a few iterations, the design team converged on two, quite distinct design options. This was an unforeseen development, since the aim had been to converge on one design. It was now unclear how to proceed. Should the design team choose between the two options, or should they leave this choice to the steering committee? The design team decided to vote. Votes were split exactly down the middle. The team decided to see if there were members who had a paramount objection to one of the options. There were objectors to both. The design team then tried to move the decision to the steering committee, because they felt that was where the final responsibility lay. The steering committee pushed back, saying they expected the design team to reach a consensus. Slotting in an extra design workshop did not bring the design team closer to a solution; they tried to reach consensus on an intermediate option, but failed. The team reached the conclusion that they had gone as far as they could. They decided to report both design options back to the steering committee, accompanied by an extensive report on the pros and cons of both options, as members of the design team saw them. The steering committee ended up accepting that, in this case, it was their responsibility to decide which option would be implemented. But a clearer charter on who designs and who decides could have prevented the misunderstanding. ◂

For the approach used in this book, we will assume there is a steering committee which signs off on the charter for the design team and on the design criteria and which will take a decision whether or not to proceed at two additional stage gates: after completion of the strategic design and after completion of the prepare transition stage. The three go/no-go moments are shown in Fig. 6.3.

The design team, besides being charged with doing the design work, has another important responsibility. It forms the interface to the broader organization. Design team members need to act as ambassadors for the design process, informing their

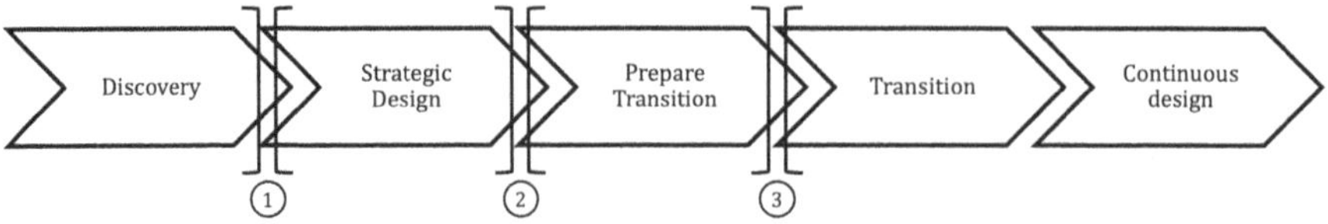

Fig. 6.3 Three stage gates for a steering committee decision in the generic organization design approach

colleagues about what goes on in the design workshops. They need to engage the wider organization and move it forward, as the design work moves forward. The members of the design team also need to be conduits of information, making sure they consult others outside the design team when they realize they do not have the full picture. The facilitators of the design process can choose to give specific assignments for information gathering to members of the design team. In Whole-Scale Change—a large group intervention method—there can even be dedicated research teams tasked by the design team to collect insights that help the process along (Dannemiller Tyson Associates, 2000).

A final point to make about the work of the design team is that it requires a cadence. Organization design work is complex, touches on many aspects, and contains many considerations. If a design team meets irregularly, or with large intervals, a lot of time will need to be dedicated in each workshop to get up to speed again. Careful documentation by the consultant team can be helpful, but cannot fully replace the need to meet in a regular rhythm to sustain momentum. Meeting regularly also helps the design team become a real team, one that can take joint ownership of the design process and its outcomes. Time is needed between design workshops, as a way to let implications sink in and to gather additional information. Depending on the workload the design team has, a two-week interval has been shown to be a good rhythm, in my professional experience.

Implicit in this description of the design team, their role, and their rhythm is that there is an entity that facilitates all this. We will call this the consultant team, which consists of one or more—internal or external—organization design consultants, and, depending on the size of the project, support consultants. The consultant team is responsible for designing and managing the overall design process and for preparing and facilitating the workshops with the design team and the steering committee. Support consultants take a role in documenting results and take care of planning, communication, and logistics. Table 6.1 summarizes the responsibilities of the three teams involved in an organization design project.

Table 6.1 The responsibilities of the three teams involved in the organization design process

Steering committee	Design team	Consultant team
Develops the design criteria Signs off on the guardrails (charter) for the design team Supplies the design team with the resources it needs to do the design work Communicates about the design process with stakeholders that are not represented in the design team Signs off on the design decisions of the design team Takes the deliverables of the design team forward toward implementation	Represents a cross-section of the organization that is in scope of the design process Collects the information necessary for the design work Participates in the design workshops Involves additional colleagues or external parties to broaden the perspective, where necessary Takes responsibility for the design decisions made by the team Acts as ambassadors and key conduits for the design process to the rest of the organization	Designs the overall design process Prepares and facilitates the design workshops Documents the considerations and output of the design work Plans meetings and takes care of logistics and communication

This section only scratches the surface of the group and organizational processes involved in an organization design project. This text is not meant to be a guide for group facilitation or managing group dynamics. There are many other excellent resources available for those topics.[6] The aim of the description of a generic organization design approach in this chapter and the next is to show the order and manner in which steps need to be taken and questions need to be answered, the technical aspects of the design process, if you will. The assumption is that readers have other resources at their disposal to develop their skills in group facilitation.

6.2.1 Design Ability[7]

We have previously touched upon the design aspect of organization design. Earlier in this chapter, we looked at who the organization designer is. In Chap. 2, we briefly framed organization design as a 'science of design', concerned with the knowledge about certain artifacts—such as structures and processes—and about the process for designing them. Let us pick up on that point, specifically when it comes to the approach for organization design.

When trying to understand how designers in 'traditional' design disciplines—such as product design—approach problems, the work of design researcher Nigel Cross is very helpful. He spent several decades teasing out what exactly are 'designerly ways of knowing', based both on laboratory work and theoretical reflections. Cross identified four elements of design ability (Cross, 2007):

- *Resolving ill-defined problems.* Because design problems are inherently ill-defined and complicated, the scientist's approach to first fully understand them is ineffective for reaching an appropriate solution in time.
- *Adopting solution-focusing strategies.* Instead of spending a lot of time with the problem by analyzing it or trying to fit it into a model, designers spend most of their time on generating and testing potential solutions.
- *Employing abductive or productive reasoning.* By working on potential solutions, designers focus on what may be, not on what must be (deduction) or what actually is (induction). This abductive or conjectural logic is essential in the work and mindset of a designer.
- *Using nonverbal modeling media.* Drawings, scale models, and prototypes characterize the way designers communicate about their process.

So, how would these aspects of design ability translate to organization design? One thing that stands out is the importance of testing. Designers quickly move to the generation of design proposals. By testing and evaluating these proposals, those design alternatives that do not meet the requirements are rejected or modified, and a final proposal can emerge. Testing can be based on formal requirements, such as dimensions or physical qualities. It can also be more informal, when something does or does not look right in the designer's eye. This generating and testing

[6] See Forsyth (2019) for a general introduction in group dynamics and Bunker and Alban (2006) and Holman et al. (2007) for methodologies in large group interventions.

[7] This section draws on Chap. 6 of Van Bree (2014).

solutions is essential in surfacing requirements that are hard to make explicit at the start of the design process.

> Often, the problem as set by the client's brief will be vague, and it is only by the designer suggesting possible solutions that the client's requirements and criteria become clear. (Cross, 2007, p. 34)

A similar phenomenon can be seen in an organization design project. It is often hard for a leadership team to fully think through what they are saying yes to when they approve a set of design criteria. It is only through seeing design alternatives that meet or do not meet these criteria that the requirements for the new organization come into sharper focus or additional criteria surface. That is why it is essential to spend enough time on formulating and thinking through the design criteria early on in the process, as we will see in the next chapter.

Another aspect of this central activity of testing is the use of prototypes by designers. What could a prototype of an organization design look like? The central part of an organization design is the way in which the tasks of the organization are grouped; these decisions form the core of the organization's structure. If we start on a relatively high level of abstraction, it does not take a design team long to start generating and visualizing alternative ways of clustering tasks. I have seen that it is also fairly easy for a team to get this concept across to others, to start discussing advantages and disadvantages of their 'prototype', and to generate a revised version of it. As we will see when we cover 'grouping' in the next chapter, there are structured ways of going through this process. Testing prototypes in this way—by discussing them and looking at them from different perspectives—is an essential part of the organization design process (Fig. 6.4). As part of the impact assessment, a more extensive 'stress test' of the organization design can also play a role (see Chap. 9).

Fig. 6.4 Design team members working on an organization design prototype

Game Design as an Inspiration for Organization Design

The game designer is the person who envisions the gameplay or the experience of the player that they would like to see and then designs the high-level framework within which that gameplay will take place. That framework is the rule set. It is not possible to fully anticipate what will happen once the rules are set in motion. Game designers will develop an intuition about the gameplay that certain rules will give rise to, but a test will always be necessary. Game designers are tackling what Katie Salen and Eric Zimmerman call a second-order design problem (Salen & Zimmerman, 2004). They realize that they cannot directly design player behavior, so they do it indirectly through the design of the rules of the game. This also implies an iterative approach, in which rules are designed, set in motion, the resulting gameplay is observed, the rules are adjusted to prevent undesirable behavior, and the rules are set in motion again. Game designers typically use a prototyping process involving the players to constantly evaluate the design goals. They build paper prototypes of their games and invite users to play the prototype in so-called playtesting sessions. The results of these sessions are used to further refine the rule set (Fullerton, 2019). This focus on involving users and having them test intermediate results can serve as an inspiration for organization designers. The co-creative design approach described in this book incorporates some of these elements. ◄

The element of Cross' design ability that is hardest to translate to an organization design setting is the abductive reasoning: focusing on what may be, not on what currently is. As we have seen in the previous section, the team that does the core design work is made up of representatives of the organization in question. Inevitably, they bring their current work context with them. There is a tendency to stay close to what is familiar. It takes real effort—and is not always possible—to put them into an abductive way of thinking. One of the important roles of the organization design consultant is to push the thinking of the design team if they are in danger of getting stuck in the present. There is an upside to this tendency of a design team to stay close to the current work context. It increases the likelihood of an organization design that can be implemented successfully, because the design team is very much aware of the current context and the potential gap that needs to be bridged. The best advice for the design team comes from eminent organization design practitioner Paul Tolchinsky: "Design for tomorrow, or as far as you can see or imagine."[8]

6.3 Practical Challenges in Organization Design Projects

As already noted, little scholarly attention has been given to the organization design process. Academic work has been done in evaluating organizational change more generally, which can be informative in the transition stage (see Chap. 9). But the

[8] Personal communication (March 2021).

practice of the actual design work—the stages before transition—has not been thoroughly investigated. That is why Nicolay Worren, Bill Zybach, and I conducted a study among organization design practitioners to better understand the challenges they face during the design process (Worren et al., 2019).

The first challenge that came out of the study lies in the early 'contracting phase' of an organization design project: creating realistic estimates regarding the time and resources required to complete the project. It is not a challenge because organization design consultants are unable to make the estimate. It is the fact that the project sponsor is likely to underestimate the effort needed. This is caused, in part, by a lack of understanding about what organization design entails. Unfortunately, many managers still think of it as rearranging some lines and boxes on the organization chart. How hard can it be? As the reader of this book will have realized, it is so much more than that. Apart from a lack of understanding, a lack of experience may also be at play. A redesign is not an everyday occurrence for a manager, so they may struggle with attaching a realistic estimate to the time and resources required. Especially a co-creative—and as such, time-intensive—approach may come as a surprise. It is up to the organization design consultant to explain why this effort will pay off in the end.

In the core work of developing the new design, three challenging aspects came out of the study:

- Help participants see the larger picture, as opposed to protecting their own turf
- Make sure that alternative options are explored, before a preferred model is chosen
- Ensure that managers and employees understand the rationale behind the design

We touched on some of these aspects when discussing the generic design approach earlier in this chapter. The first one mentioned is one of the biggest challenges in working with a design team. Members need to work in the organization's interest, not that of their own department or position, in order for a design team to be effective. This is challenging, because organization design by definition concerns the content and context of my work, the team I will be working with, who will report to me, and who I will be reporting to. Again, it comes down to the skill of the organization design consultant to facilitate honest and open discussions with members of the design team about where interests lie. Clear job assurances in the early stages of the design project can help. But there will almost always be a political aspect to an organization design effort, including stakeholders who keep their cards close to their chest.

The second and third elements mentioned above should both be adequately addressed if the design approach proposed in this book is followed. Exploring alternative options is an integral part of the design approach, as we will see in the next chapter. Furthermore, working from a contingency mindset and using design criteria to make the connection between the requirements of the context and the requirements for the organization design explicit should support the communication of a clear rationale.

The study was a clear reminder of the high level of skill that organization design practitioners need.

> They need to be able to build trust with the client and other stakeholders, but also challenge their thinking and help them imagine alternative realities. They need to master analytical tools and use a fact-based approach, but also understand and manage the emotional reactions to change. They need to be strategic while at the same time consider how concepts and ideas are going to be operationalized and implemented. (Worren et al., 2019, pp. 14–15)

6.4 Data-Driven Approaches to Organization Design

Implicit in the description of the organization design approach in this chapter is the assumption that the activities are performed by humans. We have spoken of a steering committee, a design team, and a consultant team, all with their specific role in the design process. The co-creative approach proposed in this book works on the basis of a belief that members of the organization are best able to uncover the problems that are holding the organization back, to formulate a compelling vision for the future, and to design the organization that best fits their context. But seeing how complex organizations and their environments have become, and considering the advances in data science and machine learning, is it not rather naïve to keep relying on purely human computing power in the design process?

Part of the answer to that question lies in the choice of what to use the machine for. Design researcher Nigel Cross, through experiments on computer-aided design back in the 1960s, surmised that

> AI-in-design research can be aimed either at *supporting* design (through interactive systems that aid the designer's creativity) or at *emulating* design (that is, through developing computational machines that design). (Cross, 2007, p. 60)

This first role of computers in design seems to be the least controversial one. It seems obvious that value is added to the design process if those tasks that are routine or that go beyond a human designer's computational powers are taken over by a machine. This is as true for organization design as it is for the more traditional design disciplines, such as product design and architecture. So, what are some of those tasks in the context of organization design? The first thing that comes to mind is the 'prepare transition' stage[9] of the approach presented in this chapter. In that stage of the design process, the detailed, operational design is produced and the transition plan is drawn up. One of the aspects that requires attention in this stage is detailed team compositions, headcount numbers, and a role-by-role comparison of the as-is and to-be situations. In large organization design projects, these databases need to be managed carefully, and most importantly: changes in the design need to be easily reflected in the numbers, without labor-intensive checks and changes by

[9] We will cover this stage in more depth in Chap. 9.

hand. The default option is to use an advanced spreadsheet for this. However, there are dedicated tools in use as well. Some are proprietary, used by consulting firms, and others are commercially available (such as Orgvue[10]). In my personal experience, tools like these can certainly be helpful. However, like any data-driven solution, they are dependent on the quality of the data that goes in. In this case, we are talking about the quality and reliability of the HR data that the organization in question has at their disposal. More often than not, cleaning up this dataset can still take a lot of time and human effort.

These types of 'data-crunching' tools can also be useful in earlier stages of the design process. Depending on what the design criteria and boundary conditions are, it may be necessary to compare several design options quantitatively or to show that a preferred option stays within certain boundaries (e.g., when it comes to headcount). In this case, the tool—be it a spreadsheet or more specialized application—is used for decision support. It shows the quantitative consequences of certain design options. Again, the quality of the support is determined by the quality of the data that is fed into the tool. In addition, these types of calculations will usually require quite a few assumptions, which may diminish their value in supporting decisions. But for some leadership teams, this type of reassurance in the form of 'hard data' is needed to come to decision about taking a certain organization design forward.

So far, we have looked at tools that fall into Cross' first category: supporting design. What about tools that fall into the second category: emulating organization design work? Can the core design work in an organization design project—the 'strategic design' stage in the approach presented in this chapter—be done by a machine? One of the essential tasks in the strategic design stage is 'grouping', which we will discuss in more detail in the next chapter. Grouping entails creating semiautonomous clusters of tasks in such a way that interdependencies *between* the clusters are kept to a minimum.[11] But how do we know which design option, of those generated by the design team, contains the minimum number of interdependencies? Nicolay Worren and his collaborators have developed a tool that aims to use a data-driven approach to improve these design decisions (Worren et al., 2020). The tool—called Reconfig—uses a survey to take stock of interdependencies between roles in the as-is situation, that is, before the design effort. It then uses an algorithm to cluster the roles in such a way that there is the least amount of interdependencies between the role clusters. Worren and his colleagues acknowledge that the tool has limitations[12] and that it should be seen merely as support for the design process, not a full automation. Nevertheless, further development of this and similar tools may offer more data-driven methods to generate design options for the overall structure of the organization. This may even make the role of the organization

[10] See https://www.orgvue.com

[11] See Chap. 4 for more on this important design principle.

[12] Some striking limitations are its focus on agent interdependence rather than task interdependence, its use of the predesign situation as the measure of interdependence, and its bottom-up approach of clustering roles (rather than a top-down approach of clustering tasks, as put forward in this book).

design consultant or the design team less critical, as a leadership team may use a tool to generate design options that would otherwise have been the result of the work of a design team.

As with the other tools mentioned in this section, the added value partly depends on the style of decision-making of the leadership team in question. Using a data-driven tool may give some teams more confidence in the design results. On the other hand, relying more on a design team will usually generate support for the design options more broadly in the organization. In addition, with tools such as Reconfig, faith needs to be put into the algorithm that generates these options. It is unavoidably based on assumptions that the organization in question needs to subscribe to, such as those around how interdependencies can be measured, and the role they need to play in design decisions.

Where Worren sees potential in using data-driven tools for the core of the organization design work—generating design options—other researchers will not go that far. Phanish Puranam and Julien Clement see most potential in data-driven analysis of the current or future internal context of the organization (problematic patterns, potential bottlenecks, etc.)—what they call perception and prediction—and in using algorithms and computer-based simulations to prototype design options (Puranam & Clement, 2020). There is no question that the availability of data can help in surfacing root causes in the discovery stage of an organization design project. As these tools become more accessible and data collection becomes less time-consuming, we will likely see a further proliferation of their use. But again, their adoption will depend on the style of decision-making of the leadership team. Will they be comfortable choosing between two design options based on the results of a computer simulation?

Given the current state of affairs, the ambition of the approach proposed in this book is not to offer a data-driven way of designing an organization, but rather to offer an evidence-based way. Data can be one source of evidence, but there can be many others. In-depth deliberations in a design team may also offer important evidence for the feasibility or infeasibility of a design option. A 'stress test' with a large group of stakeholders—something we will discuss in Chap. 9—can offer evidence of the support a design has and of deficiencies that still need to be addressed. The philosophy underlying this book is that it is this type of rich, qualitative, sometimes even implicit evidence that should play a role in organization design projects. It does justice to the social psychological and political nature of the process. A purely data-driven approach may make us lose sight of that.

Review Questions

1. Do you think organization designers should have their name attached to their designs, in the same way that architects do? Why or why not?
2. What are some of the situations in which a collaborative approach to organization design will not work?
3. What are some of the situations in which involving a design team that represents the organization will not work?

4. Do you think a case could be made for working bottom-up in an organization design approach, instead of from macro to micro?
5. What are some of the ways to avoid personal interests and politics gaining the upper hand in the design team?
6. What are some of the ways to stimulate abductive reasoning in the design team?
7. What would help in making realistic time and resource estimates at the start of an organization design project?
8. Which do you see more potential for: data-driven tools to support design or data-driven tools to emulate design? Why so?
9. Do you think the emergence of data-driven organization design tools will mean less work for organization design consultants? Why or why not?

References

Bartunek, J. M., Balogun, J., & Do, B. (2011). Considering planned change anew: Stretching large group interventions strategically, emotionally, and meaningfully. *The Academy of Management Annals, 5*(1), 1–52.

Bunker, B. B., & Alban, B. T. (2006). *The handbook of large group methods: Creating systemic change in organizations and communities*. Jossey-Bass.

Chasserio, S., & Botte, S. (2020). Transforming corporate headquarters: A case study of a collaborative journey. *Journal of Organization Design, 9*(1), 1–17.

Cherns, A. (1987). Principles of sociotechnical design revisited. *Human Relations, 40*(3), 153–162.

Cross, N. (2007). *Designerly ways of knowing*. Birkhäuser.

Dannemiller Tyson Associates. (2000). *Whole-Scale Change: Unleashing the magic in organizations*. Berrett-Koehler Publishers.

Engler, E., Jones, S., & Van de Ven, A. (2013). Organizing healthcare for changing markets: The case of Ascension Health. *Journal of Organization Design, 2*(3), 3–15.

Forsyth, D. R. (2019). *Group dynamics* (7th ed.). Cengage.

Fullerton, T. (2019). *Game design workshop: A playcentric approach to creating innovative games* (4th ed.). Taylor & Francis Group.

Galbraith, J. R., Downey, D., & Kates, A. (2002). *Designing dynamic organizations: A hands-on guide for leaders at all levels*. AMACOM.

Hock, D. (1999). *Birth of the chaordic age*. Berrett-Koehler Publishers.

Hock, D. (2005). *One from many: VISA and the rise of chaordic organization*. Berrett-Koehler Publishers.

Holman, P., Devane, T., & Cady, S. (Eds.). (2007). *The change handbook: The definitive resource on today's best methods for engaging whole systems* (2nd ed.). Berrett-Koehler Publishers.

Kesler, G., & Kates, A. (2011). *Leading organization design: How to make organization design decisions to drive the results you want*. Jossey-Bass.

Livijn, M. (2019). Navigating in a hierarchy: How middle managers adapt macro design. *Journal of Organization Design, 8*(1), 1–27.

Meyer, M. W., Lu, L., Peng, J., & Tsui, A. S. (2017). Microdivisionalization: Using teams for competitive advantage. *Academy of Management Discoveries, 3*(1), 3–20.

Nadler, D. A., & Tushman, M. L. (1997). *Competing by design: The power of organizational architecture*. Oxford University Press.

Nikolova, N., & Devinney, T. (2012). The nature of client-consultant interaction: A critical review. In T. Clark & M. Kipping (Eds.), *The Oxford handbook of management consulting*. Oxford University Press.

Puranam, P., & Clement, J. (2020). The organizational analytics e-book: A guide to data driven organization design. Retrieved February 4, 2021, from https://knowledge.insead.edu/sites/www.insead.edu/files/images/org2.0ebook.pdf
Salen, K., & Zimmerman, E. (2004). *Rules of play: Game design fundamentals*. The MIT Press.
Schein, E. H. (1990). A general philosophy of helping: Process consultation. *Sloan Management Review, 31*(3), 57–64.
Schein, E. H. (1999). *Process consultation revisited: Building the helping relationship*. Addison-Wesley.
Schein, E. H. (2017). *Organizational culture and leadership* (5th ed.). John Wiley & Sons.
Stanford, N. (2018). *Organization design: The practitioner's guide* (3rd ed.). Routledge.
Van Bree, J. (2014). *Game based organization design: New tools for complex organizational systems*. Palgrave Macmillan.
Weisbord, M., & Janoff, S. (2010). *Future Search: Getting the whole system in the room for vision, commitment and action* (3rd ed.). Berrett-Koehler.
Worley, G. W., Mohrman, S. A., & Nevitt, J. A. (2011). Large group interventions: An empirical field study of their composition, process, and outcomes. *The Journal of Applied Behavioral Science, 47*(4), 404–431.
Worren, N. (2017). The matrix as a transitory form: The evolution of FMC technologies 2001–2016. *Journal of Organization Design, 6*(1), 1–14.
Worren, N. (2018). *Organization design: Simplifying complex systems* (2nd ed.). Routledge.
Worren, N., Christiansen, T., & Soldal, K. V. (2020). Using an algorithmic approach for grouping roles and sub-units. *Journal of Organization Design, 9*(1), 1–19.
Worren, N., Van Bree, J., & Zybach, W. (2019). Organization design challenges: Results from a practitioner survey. *Journal of Organization Design, 8*(1), 1–18.

How to Group the Tasks of an Organization

7

Abstract

A design project starts with the discovery stage. In this stage, the current context of the organization in question is explored. This includes the strategic objectives of the organization, its high-level value chain, the current organization design, and the strengths and weaknesses of the current way of organizing. Besides an exploration of the current context, the desired future state needs to be described as part of the discovery stage. A final aspect of the discovery stage is setting the conditions for the design process, in terms of negotiables and nonnegotiables, HR policies, and design governance. At the end of the discovery stage, the design criteria can be developed, which describe what the organization design should achieve. With the deliverables of the discovery stage, the necessary ingredients are in place for the grouping stage. In this stage, the structure of the organization is designed by creating autonomous clusters of tasks. Different grouping dimensions (activity, output, customer, or geography) can be used for this. Grouping works recursively from the macro level down to the meso level, until the lowest-level units are small enough to be allocated to one team. As a final step, the ancillary and support tasks need to be allocated.

Keywords

Organization design • Division of labor • Discovery stage • Strategy • Value chain • Design criteria • Grouping stage • Strategic design • Organizational structure • Grouping dimensions

J. van Bree, *Organization Design*, https://doi.org/10.1007/978-3-030-78679-3_7

Learning Objectives

- Understand the purpose of the discovery stage in an organization design project.
- Identify the value chain of an organization.
- Understand the conditions that need to be set for an organization design project.
- Identify the advantages and disadvantages of different options for design governance.
- Develop a set of design criteria for an organization design project.
- Identify relevant grouping dimensions for an organization.
- Generate design options by conducting grouping at the macro and meso level.
- Identify ancillary and support tasks.
- Understand the considerations for positioning support tasks inside, close to, or at a distance from the core units.

After a general discussion of the design approach in the previous chapter, we will now turn to the two core design activities: grouping (in this chapter) and linking (in the next chapter). As we saw when we reviewed Puranam's four fundamental problems of organizing (Puranam et al. 2014) in Chap. 2, solutions to two interlinked problems form the core of the organization design work: division of labor and integration of effort.[1] The tasks of an organization need to be grouped in the manner that makes most sense, and then these groups, or clusters, of tasks need to be tied back together to produce goods or services for clients (or perform any other goals the organization may have). As we have seen in Chap. 4, there are a number of important principles that need to be applied to this grouping effort. These principles have to do with creating clusters that are as autonomous as possible, by grouping tasks that have a high level of interdependence. This is not a trivial matter, but there are structured ways to go about it. A large part of this chapter is dedicated to guidelines for and examples of this process of grouping. But first, we must look at the step that precedes grouping: the discovery stage (Fig. 7.1).

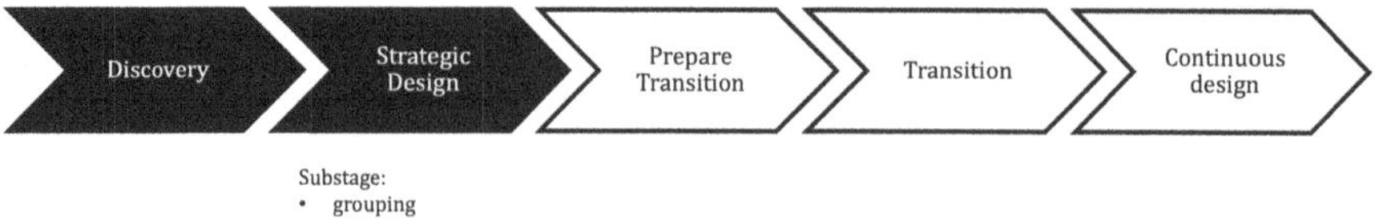

Fig. 7.1 The stages of the design approach covered in this chapter

[1] March and Simon (1958) spoke of specialization and coordination and Lawrence and Lorsch (1967) of differentiation and integration.

7.1 The Discovery Stage

As we have seen throughout this book, it is essential that there is a fit between an organization's design and its internal and external context (contingency thinking, see Chap. 3). If we follow that logic through, one of the first things to do in an organization design project is to chart that context. That is one of the aims of the discovery stage or, as practitioner Andrew Zielinski[2] calls it, the 'problem space'. A general comment about the discovery stage that we can make up front is that leadership teams tend to rush through this problem space,[3] to get to the 'solution space'.[4] The lesson Zielinski and his colleagues at Deutsche Bank learned was to force organization design teams to stay in the problem space longer, to explore it more thoroughly. This is in line with the principles of process consultation (Schein 1999), which—as we saw in the previous chapter—underlies the approach to organization design proposed in this book. We will cover three aspects that need to be addressed in the discovery stage: current context, desired outcomes, and conditions for the design process. We will then show how you can formulate design criteria as the link between the discovery stage and the grouping work.

7.1.1 Current Context

The obvious starting point of the discovery stage is a scan of the current internal and external context in which the organization design project takes place. This scan of the context should have four key deliverables, which we will cover in this section:

- The strategic objectives of the organization
- The high-level value chain
- The current organization design
- The strengths and weaknesses of the current design

Strategic objectives of the organization. As we have seen in Galbraith's Star model and—a bit more implicitly—in Puranam's four fundamental problems framework (both covered in Chap. 2), the starting point for any organization design needs to be clarity about the organization's strategy. Galbraith (2014) has summarized strategy in the form of three questions:

- What to do: the long-range goals and objectives of the organization
- How to win: the courses of action necessary to achieve these goals
- Where to play: choices with regard to customer segments, channels, and countries

[2] Zielinski was Head of Group Management Consulting for Deutsche Bank at the time of this presentation; see Zielinski (2019).

[3] Which was one of the findings of the survey of organization design practitioners discussed in the previous chapter; see Worren et al. (2019).

[4] 'Problem space' and 'solution space' are terms that come from design thinking; see Lindberg et al. (2011).

Even though answering these questions would seem fairly straightforward for an organization's leadership team, experience shows that it can be a rather painful process. Some leadership teams are so caught up in day-to-day operational details that they rarely have a chance to have strategic discussions; others have documented a three-year strategic plan that no one has looked at in months. Of course, the strategic process is not always this wanting—the bigger the organization is, the more professional it tends to be—but one should be prepared for a step back in the design process during the discovery stage. Time may need to be spent on aligning the leadership team around the organization's strategy, before an organization design project can start in earnest. This is crucial, because a lack of agreement on the strategic direction will make it virtually impossible to choose between design options down the road. A useful shorthand for strategy proposed by Jay Galbraith (Galbraith et al. 2002) is to have the organization determine their primary value discipline (Treacy and Wiersema 1993): operational excellence, customer intimacy, or product leadership. Each will result in a very different orientation when embarking on the design work.

The high-level value chain. This is the second input that the original version of the Star model (Galbraith 1977) prescribes, before basic choices about structure—what we shall refer to as grouping in this chapter—can be made. Galbraith refers to this as 'task'. Since the design approach described in this book works from the macro level down to the micro level, what we are looking for here are not detailed business process diagrams, but rather a high level of abstraction. The basic question that needs to be answered is: *which are the five to ten main activities that need to be performed well by the organization in order to achieve its strategic goals?* The focus should be on primary activities, not on support activities; the latter will be addressed later on in the design process. The focus should also be on the desired future state, not on the current state. As such, the value chain serves as one of the links between the strategy of the organization and its organization design. This is how Michael Porter (1985) positioned his conception of the value chain, which is close to the way we use the term in this chapter. Figure 7.2 shows the primary activities in Porter's generic value chain.

Similar to Galbraith, Porter saw activities as the bridge between the strategy and the implementation of that strategy (he only mentions organizational structure in passing). It shows what the organization needs to do, not necessarily what it currently does. A task that Porter relegated to the support activities—with the label of 'technology development'—is that of developing new products, services, technologies, and business models—the exploration, or changing the business, task, if you will (see Chap. 4). Contingent on the strategy of the organization in question, this can be an important task to include in the primary value chain (which is where we depart somewhat from Porter's categorization).

It can be helpful to disaggregate each of the value chain activities further, not with the aim of producing a 20- or 30-activity-long chain—10 activities is a useful maximum—but to show which activities each of the main steps in the value chain is

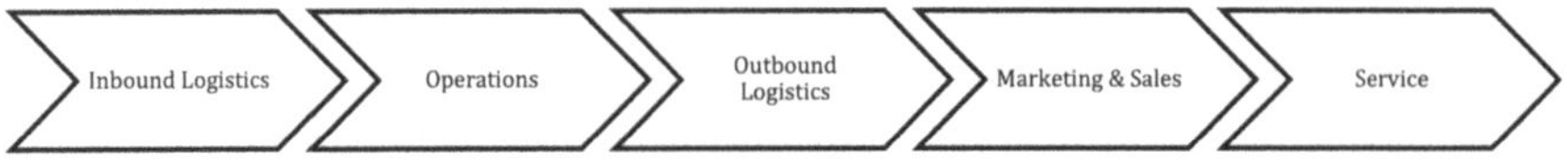

Fig. 7.2 The primary activities of Porter's generic value chain (Porter 1985)

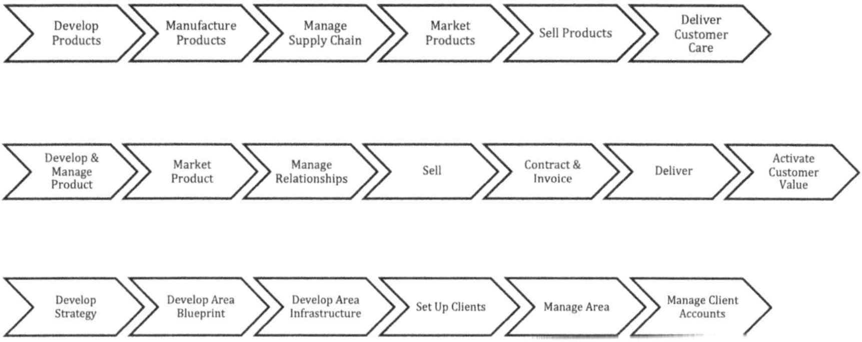

Fig. 7.3 Three examples of real-life value chains

composed of. Listing these sub-activities helps in creating clarity and in making sure no important activities are being overlooked. In Fig. 7.3, a number of examples are shown of value chains from organization design projects conducted in firms in a number of different industries. As you can see, it is helpful to state the activities in the form of verbs.

Value Chains, Value Streams, and Customer Journeys

The value chain concept we use in this section gives a macro-level view of the activities of an organization. As we will see further on in this chapter, it serves as a basis for a first allocation of these activities to units (grouping). As such, the value chain is not meant as an analytical tool in which deeper, more detailed levels of business processes can be embedded. It stands on its own as a tool to connect strategy to structure. That is what distinguishes the value chain from the value stream, as it is used in lean management and in business architecture (see Chap. 2). In lean management, value stream mapping is used to identify and eliminate 'waste' from a firm's processes. The resulting diagrams represent a much more granular view of business processes than do value chain diagrams and typically include metrics such as processing time (Rother and Shook 2003). Value streams as they are mapped in business architecture are similar to value chains, although these value streams are usually of a more granular level than the macro, enterprise level we use for the value chain. The biggest difference is that business architecture uses a number of formal requirements for mapping value streams. The representation of the value streams needs to fit into the overall meta-model that the business architect uses.[5] No such requirements are placed on the value chain we use in this chapter. Having said that, if a high-level—usually called level 0—value stream map is available as a product of an enterprise or business architecture effort, this may very well be an excellent basis for describing the value chain to be used in an organization design project.

[5] See, for example, The Open Group (2018).

Customer journeys are something entirely different, although there seems to be increasing confusion about their usefulness as a basis for organization design efforts, that is, as an alternative starting point to the value chain. Customer journeys are a series of so-called touchpoints that occur between customers and an organization that provides a service (Følstad and Kvale 2018). Mapping these customer journeys can help in identifying opportunities to improve the delivery of services and, as such, improve the customer experience. However, the customer journey map is not a replacement for the value chain. To give an example, a customer journey map for a visit to an amusement park may include touchpoints such as seeing an ad on social media, buying a ticket online, arriving by public transport, going on rides, and talking to others about the experience. These touchpoints are not the same as the main activities that this organization needs to perform well in order to achieve its strategic goals (the value chain, as we define it in this section). An analysis of the customer journey may very well provide clues as to which elements of the organization will need extra attention, which can be an important input for design criteria (covered later on in this section). But the customer journey map in itself will not tell you what the main activities are that an organization needs to perform. In the example of the amusement park, these main activities could be: develop plans, produce entertainment, build rides, market the park, sell tickets, deliver entertainment, operate rides, and maintain park. Using a customer journey map instead of a value chain will hide a large part of the activities from view and will lead to an incomplete organization design. ◀

The current organization design. The third key deliverable when mapping out the current context of the organization is a representation of the current organization design. This is not something to dwell on for too long in this stage, especially not with the design team. There is a time and place in the design process for identifying the gap between the current situation and the designed future state: when conducting the impact analysis, which we will cover in Chap. 9. The design effort should have a 'blank slate approach' as much as possible and not be constrained by the current way the organization is set up. However, if an external organization design consultant is involved in the design process, a description of the current way of organizing is crucial to fully understand the organization's context and, to some extent, its history. An organization chart may be relatively easy to come by, but may be insufficient to grasp the current organization design. Typically, a number of interviews with key informants will offer more insight into how the organization operates. A framework such as the Star model (see Chap. 2) can be useful to structure the information gathering. At a minimum, the key units in the current organization and their main tasks need to be mapped. These activities can be used as a check for completeness of the value chain that was identified for the organization. In addition, a social network analysis (Cross and Parker 2004) may show interaction patterns that are not easily discernible otherwise and may offer surprising insights. Because it requires employing a very time-consuming survey across the organization,[6] social network analysis is not considered a standard part of the discovery stage as proposed in this book.

Strengths and weaknesses of the current design. The final deliverable in a scan of the current context is an assessment of the strengths and weaknesses of the current form of organizing. Weaknesses will usually come to light fairly easily once you embark on the discovery activities—or may in fact be the trigger for the redesign effort, as we saw with the symptoms of a misfit in Chap. 3—but it is important to also be aware of the strengths: what are the characteristics of the current organization design that should not get lost when we start tinkering with it? When taking stock of both strengths and weaknesses, it is important to keep the focus on the elements that can be addressed in the organization design, elements such as roles, responsibilities, decision-making, and collaboration patterns. It is only natural that other aspects are also mentioned, such as leadership or culture. These aspects may offer valuable input for describing the desired outcomes of the design (see next section). Interviews can be used to take stock of strengths and weaknesses, but a collective effort—such as a workshop—will also be necessary. The better the understanding and recognition of these points, the broader the support for the redesign effort will be.

7.1.2 The Need for Change and Desired Outcomes of the New Design

After the current context has been charted, attention needs to shift to the desired future state: what does the organization intend to achieve with the redesign? The scan of the current context will most likely offer clues—as will the results of the contracting stage, if an external consultant has been brought in[7]—but it is necessary to build the case for change more explicitly. One way to do this is to describe the desired future state of the organization in terms of the behavior of the people in it. Behavior is an observable outcome which can be influenced by the elements of the organization design (Galbraith 2014). When this is combined with the original trigger to review the organization design—such as rapid growth or a change in strategy, see Chap. 3—the result can be a succinct 'purpose statement' (Stanford 2018) that lies at the base of the design effort. Figure 7.4 shows an example of such a purpose statement.

7.1.3 The Conditions for the Design Process

The third aspect that needs to be addressed in the discovery stage—after current context and desired outcomes—is setting the conditions for the design process. Setting the boundaries of the design effort is essential before embarking on the

[6] There are techniques available now that use an analysis of email traffic and other digital traces instead of a survey for social network analysis, but privacy regulations make the application of these types of techniques very difficult, especially in EU countries.

[7] For more on the ins and outs of the contracting stage, see Maister et al. (2000) and Block (2011).

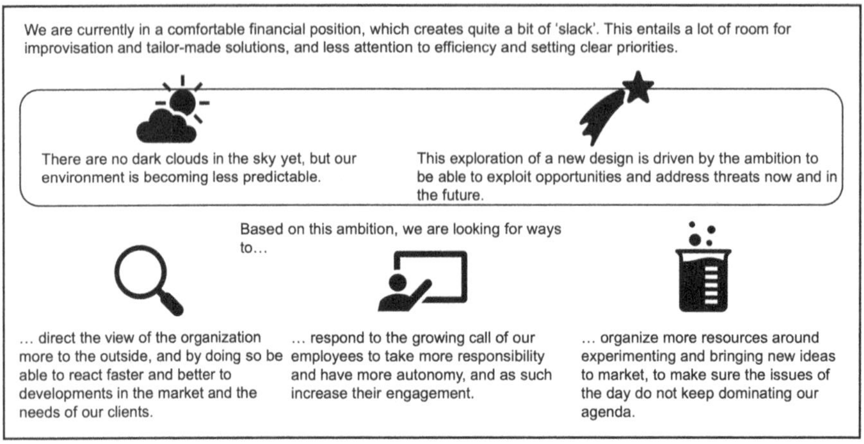

Fig. 7.4 Example of a purpose statement for a design project that addresses the need for change and desired outcomes

actual design work. All the more so because organization design work can have fundamental consequences for people's roles, the teams they work in, the manager they report to, and for the distribution of power in an organization. Although it is an illusion to think that politics can be completely eliminated from the design process, an effort should be made up front to set clear boundaries to prevent the design process from going off the rails once the pressure around these impactful topics begins to rise. These boundaries center around three aspects, which we will cover in this section:

- Negotiables and nonnegotiables
- HR policies
- Design governance

Negotiables and nonnegotiables. The first order of business is to make sure that it is as clear as possible which elements of the organization can be changed in the design work and which elements cannot. First and foremost, this is a question of scoping the design work. In most situations, it is clear what the scope is. Our assumption in the approach we describe in this book is that we have the entire organization in scope; that is, we are working at the enterprise level or at the level of an autonomous business unit in a diversified firm.[8] The approach can be applied at a lower level in the organization—for example, the department level—but it will run up against limitations. The most important limitation is the fact that both the value chain and the strategic objectives of a department are necessarily embedded in the

[8]Galbraith (2014) makes a useful distinction between multi-business unit firms with one business model (e.g., Procter & Gamble) and multi-business unit firms with several business models (e.g., General Electric). When we speak of a diversified firm here, we mean a firm exploiting several business models; the design of a multi-business unit firm with one business model should ideally be approached at the enterprise level.

larger context of the organization. This means there is less room to move and there are more links to elements outside of the control of the leadership team responsible for the design project. For now, let us assume we are working at the enterprise level. Even if that is the case, a clarification of scope can be useful. Are all support departments in scope, or is compliance exempt? Are the innovation teams in scope, or are they allowed to do their own thing? Are the offshore manufacturing plants in scope, or are they not to be disturbed? Another aspect of scope to consider at the start of the project is vertical. Is the current composition of the top management team a given, or could a change in C-level roles be a possible outcome of the redesign? When the scope has been explored and confirmed, the negotiables and nonnegotiables need to be listed. What we mean by this are those elements that stakeholders agree can or cannot be impacted by the design. The aforementioned scope is an important aspect of this. But it can be expanded to include statements about the impact on management layers, on headcount in general, the room for cost increase or the need for cost savings, or the exclusion of certain design options which have been tried or considered before. Nonnegotiables may also stem from external constraints, such as requirements that regulatory entities or a supervisory board places on the organization.

HR policies. The second important group of conditions that needs to be set during the discovery stage is around HR policies. As we have seen, organization design projects can have a fundamental impact on jobs, team structures, and leadership roles. In order to make sure that these changes do not preoccupy or inhibit those involved in the design process (the design team and the steering committee) or that they create anxiety in the organization as a whole, it is crucial to set some clear policies and communicate them frankly up front. If at all possible, this should include a statement about job security. Typically, an organization design effort as we frame it in this book is not intended to cut jobs.[9] However, that may very well be what employees expect when they hear 'redesign'. In addition, a redesign may lead to what organization design consultant Peter Turgoose calls capacity release: by removing duplication, errors, rework, and unnecessary linkages, there can be released capacity of anywhere between 10 and 20% of the current headcount.[10] An HR policy around redeployment can put people's minds at ease, including the minds of those who will be involved in the design process.

A guarantee that cannot easily be given is that no one will move to a new team or into a new position. As a matter of fact, it is quite likely that there will be these types of changes during the implementation of a new design. But this can be accompanied by an HR policy that guarantees there will be no deterioration of employment conditions. These aspects of the HR policies are usually not the biggest problem. The real challenge lies with the leadership roles. If we want to use a real 'blank slate' approach for the redesign of the organization—as proposed in this book—all of the current

[9] That is a downsizing effort; see Chap. 2, which is not compatible with a collaborative approach.

[10] Peter Turgoose (personal communication, March 2021).

leadership roles in the organization may be impacted. Depending on the vertical scope that is chosen, this may go from the frontline operational manager all the way up to the C-suite. It is crucial to have a frank discussion about this with the leadership team responsible for the design project. Are they willing to accept one of their current roles becoming obsolete as a result of the redesign? Are they prepared to put the interest of the organization in front of their own or that of their department? If there are any doubts or disagreements about this, the leadership team needs to take a step back and work out these issues first, before proceeding with the design effort. An organization design consultant can play a role in facilitating this conversation.

Design governance. A final piece of clarification that needs to be addressed up front is around who designs and who decides. As we saw in the previous chapter, the typical setup proposed in this book is one where a design team does much of the core design work, staying inside the boundaries set by a steering committee. This arrangement makes it clear who designs—the design team—but leaves room for several options as to who decides. Let us review three options, each with their merits.

The leadership team acts as design team. This situation is only possible for relatively small organizations, where the leadership team has—or has easy access to—all the information needed to perform the design work; that is, they understand how their organization operates all the way down to the lowest operational level. If this is the case, there is no need for a steering committee. All design decisions can be made by the design team. Besides some obvious advantages—clear mandate for the design team—this option has a big drawback: because only the top management team has been involved in exploring, developing, and selecting design options, they will have to guide the rest of the organization through a process of sensemaking when they present the final results of the design process.

The leadership team acts as steering committee. This is a common option, in which the leadership team empowers a design team—a 'microcosm' of the organization, see Chap. 6—to do the design work. The steering committee—equal to the leadership team in this option—sets the conditions and boundaries for the design work along the lines of the elements covered in this section. The scope and the nonnegotiables determine the size of the design space that the team can work in. The success of this mode of working depends on the willingness of the steering committee to accept any design option that the team develops inside the space made available to them. The bigger the design space, the less likely this becomes. In the previous chapter, we discussed a number of examples of situations in which this led to unanticipated and unpleasant confrontations between steering committee and design team. There are two situations in which this option can work well. The first is a leadership team that truly empowers the design team and trusts them to come up with the best design option. The second is limiting the design space using a clear scope and a set of nonnegotiables (e.g., by excluding certain design

Table 7.1 The three options for design governance, each with their advantages and disadvantages

Option	Advantages	Disadvantages
Leadership team is design team	Clear mandate for design team Confidential design process is possible	Leadership team may not have the full view of the organization The rest of the organization is confronted with design they were not involved in
Leadership team is steering committee	Design team can be a representative cross-section of the organization Design team can be truly empowered	Leadership team may not fully realize the size of the design space they are opening up
Leadership team participates in design team	Design team has broad representation as well as decision-making power	Presence of leadership may cause inhibitions for other design team members

options beforehand). To be clear, this setup with the leadership team as steering committee does not mean that the design team generates options and the steering committee chooses from those options. That is a mode of working that is doomed to fail, since the steering committee will have trouble grasping the full rationale of the options and the design team is likely to be frustrated by the committee's choices.

The leadership team participates in the design team. This is the option that Kesler and Kates (2011) describe as a 'multilevel design team'. In it, one or several members of the leadership team participate in a broader design team. They could then also form the linking pins to the steering committee, which would have a limited role or could even become redundant. This option has as a clear advantage that it combines broad representation with the necessary decision-making power in the design team. The biggest drawback is that the presence of members of the leadership team may prevent participants from freely sharing their perspectives. It may lead to a dynamic of the senior executive(s) consciously or unconsciously steering the discussions in a certain direction. A skilled organization design consultant can help prevent this dynamic from developing.

Table 7.1 summarizes the three options with their advantages and disadvantages.

It is worthwhile to document the boundaries and conditions for the design process in a project charter, which can be as brief as a one-page document. It is important for the steering committee to sign off on it and for the design team members to be aware of it before they start their design work.

7.1.4 Design Criteria

As we saw in Chap. 4, design criteria are statements that describe what the organization design should achieve (Nadler and Tushman 1997; Worren 2018; Stanford

2018). The results of the discovery stage should give you most of the sources needed to develop design criteria:

- The strategic objectives of the organization
- Factors that currently impede or facilitate organizational effectiveness
- The desired outcomes of the design project

There is one additional perspective which can be a useful source of design criteria: expectations from stakeholders that have not yet been considered. The collaborative approach proposed in this book ensures that internal stakeholders (employees and executives) will have a voice in the design process. However, there may be other groups whose expectations the steering committee wants to consider. An obvious first extension is to the organization's customers. Implicitly, their voice will have been heard in several aspects of the discovery stage. But customers can also be invited to participate more explicitly in the design process. They can be consulted as part of the discovery stage, to surface any requirements the organization may have missed. Or they can even be involved in exploring or testing design options, something not uncommon in design projects using large group interventions (see Chap. 6). A second important group of stakeholders is formed by the nonexecutive or supervisory board. It is important to ensure that expectations of the nonexecutives are not overlooked, even though their explicit involvement in the organization design project is typically limited.

Expectations of additional stakeholders may be considered, although it is up to the steering committee to decide the weight of these perspectives in developing the design criteria. The Global Reporting Initiative—an independent organization that develops standards for sustainability reporting—offers frameworks for thinking about stakeholders and the impact that an organization may have on them. Some useful categories of stakeholders they distinguish are (Global Sustainability Standards Board 2020) as follows:

- Workers who are not employees, for example, interns, apprentices, and self-employed persons
- Suppliers in the broad sense (providing services somewhere in the supply chain of the organization in question), for example, contractors, consultants, distributors, franchisees, and manufacturers
- Vulnerable groups, at risk of suffering a disproportionate burden of the impact of the organization's operations
- Local communities
- NGOs or other civil society organizations

With all this information from the discovery stage, the task at hand is now to condense these insights into a limited number of design criteria. What is a limited number? Stanford (2018) suggests a maximum of five or six items. My personal experience is that ten or fewer items is a good number to work with. If you force a leadership team to limit the list to six, what tends to happen is that they start merging criteria, which does not increase their usefulness. The idea behind a limited number is to make sure choices are made and priorities are set. Unfortunately, any design will have drawbacks as well as benefits. Design criteria are the tool that helps make the right choices in these difficult trade-offs. The more focused the set of criteria is, the sharper the tool, hence the limit on the number of design criteria.

Apart from a limited number, it is important that design criteria are "specific enough to be observable in the design options" (Kesler and Kates 2011, p. 63). Stanford (2018) warns against being too specific, to the point where it becomes the prescription of how to organize. Stanford (ibid.) also recommends that design criteria adhere to the MECE principle: mutually exclusive and collectively exhaustive. This should be seen more as a guideline than as a requirement. Complete exhaustiveness will be almost impossible to achieve, but the set of criteria should at least be "comprehensive enough collectively to represent the strategic organizational needs of the business" (Kesler and Kates 2011, p. 63). Obvious internal contradictions should be avoided, although some of these contradictions may only come to light once the work of exploring design options has begun. A useful formula for design criteria is: "'The organization design should…' (…) followed by an action verb, followed in turn by a very specific goal" (Nadler and Tushman 1997, p. 170).

Six Essential Themes in Design Criteria

Although it is possible to develop design criteria for an organization from scratch—using the information from the discovery stage—it can be useful to pay attention to a number of specific themes. Having design criteria that address these themes helps when choosing between design options in subsequent stages, because they cover some of the most difficult trade-offs that need to be made. These six themes are (partly based on Nadler and Tushman 1997; Kesler and Kates 2011) as follows:

1. How important is maximizing the utilization of resources for this organization, to lower costs through economies of scale?
2. How important is specialization and the development of expertise for this organization?
3. How important is measurement, control, and accountability for this organization?
4. How important is providing learning environments and opportunities for career progression for this organization?
5. How important is it for this organization that certain aspects of the work adhere to standards, either imposed on the organization from the environment or coming from within?
6. How important is developing new business models, products, and markets for this organization (otherwise known as exploration, see Chap. 4)? ◂

Two important points of distinction need to be made here. Design criteria are not the same as the design conditions we discussed earlier in this chapter. Design conditions—and more specifically the scope and the nonnegotiables—serve as constraints. Any design option that does not meet these constraints will not be considered, whereas design options that do not meet all of the design criteria are not automatically disqualified. The second distinction is between design criteria and the value chain. The value chain contains the core tasks of the organization that need to be allocated in the organization design. As with the constraints, any design option that does not adequately allocate all of these core tasks will not be considered.

Design criteria may be used to further qualify some of these tasks. A task such as 'manage accounts' may, for instance, be qualified by having a design criterion around 'one face to the customer for global clients'.

Although the design team can play a role in establishing design criteria, this is chiefly the prerogative of the steering committee. It is one of the most important ways for them to set the direction for the design effort. The process that can be followed is to derive a long list of criteria from the work that was done in the discovery stage. A process of elimination, prioritization, specification, and exploration (of the implications of the design criteria) will lead to the final list.

The Requirements for Good Design Criteria

- A list of no more than ten
- Specific enough to be observable
- Not prescriptions of how to organize
- Mutually exclusive and collectively exhaustive, as much as possible

The Case of NSP Insurance: Introduction and Design Criteria

In this chapter and the next, we will illustrate the organization design work of grouping and linking by using NSP Insurance[11] as a case example. NSP is a French insurance company which sells insurance to firms in the agricultural sector. They are a small niche player, founded in the 1970s, with some 700 employees and an annual turnover of 250 million Euros. Traditionally, their strong suit has been customer intimacy. Their management and sales force have been successful in building strong relationships with entrepreneurs in the agricultural sector, which has led to continued business. Now that a new generation is taking the reins in the sector (dominated by family businesses), the continued business for NSP is no longer guaranteed. The younger entrepreneurs are much more critical of cost and of a flawless online interaction with their insurer. For them, the traditional salesperson who comes by to ask how things are going, drinks a cup of coffee, and then sells or renews some insurance policies no longer works. NSP's management has realized they need to modernize if they want to survive. Furthermore, the agency supervising the financial sector has performed an audit of NSP which revealed that their systems and procedures are not up to standards. They have been given a deadline of one year to show considerable improvements. Because of this, NSP has started a sizeable project for the modernization of their IT systems. After the first steps had been taken in this IT project, NSP's management realized they needed to modernize their organization design as well.

Currently, the organization has a functional structure. The main departments are Sales, Business Development, Underwriting and Administration, Claims Management, Finance and Control, and IT. There is a separate organizational unit for Belgium, which encompasses most of these functions for the Belgian market. The value chain is shown in Fig. 7.5.

[11] This is a pseudonym for the actual company that this case description is loosely based on.

Fig. 7.5 The value chain of NSP Insurance

Table 7.2 Deliverables of the discovery stage

Deliverable	Responsible
Scan of current context	Design team or consultant team
Need for change and desired outcomes	Steering committee
Conditions for the design process	Steering committee
Design criteria	Steering committee

The main design criteria developed for NSP Insurance were as follows:

1. The organization design should make it possible to serve customers in France and Belgium and to make expansion into Germany possible.
2. The organization design should facilitate bringing ideas for new products, services, and business models to market fast.
3. The organization design should make it possible to develop and market non-insurance products and services, as well as the current insurance products.
4. The organization design should make it possible to co-create products and services with external parties (customers, partners). ◀

In Chap. 6, we distinguished between three groups who play a role in the design process: steering committee, design team, and consultant team. In Table 7.2, we summarize the main deliverables of the discovery stage and show who is responsible for each. The assumption here is that there is a steering committee and a consultant team—or some other form of support for the steering committee—at the start of the discovery stage. The design team may also have been identified already. If it has, this team can be made responsible for the scan of the current context. Based on these deliverables, the steering committee decides whether or not to proceed to the strategic design stage.

7.2 Strategic Design: The Grouping Stage

With the start of the strategic design stage, we arrive at the core of the organization design work. The first step is grouping, the purpose of which is to create a structure that adheres as closely as possible to the first design principle stated in Chap. 4: create autonomous clusters of tasks. The underlying logic for this principle is that the best structure is one where there is a limited amount of interdependence between the units. Smart grouping decisions are a way to achieve this. "[I]nformation becomes easier to process within grouping boundaries but more difficult to process between one group and another" (Nadler and Tushman 1997, p. 73).

This section offers an approach for taking the right grouping decisions when designing a structure. Keep in mind that these decisions need to be accompanied by other design activities, primarily around linking (which is the subject of the next chapter). The main ingredients needed for the grouping stage are among the deliverables of the discovery stage: the value chain and the design criteria. Working with those starting points, grouping consists of three steps, which we will cover in the course of this section:

- Determine the relevant grouping dimensions
- Determine macro-level and meso-level grouping
- Position the ancillary and support tasks

7.2.1 Determine Relevant Grouping Dimensions

The starting point for grouping is determining which grouping dimensions may be relevant for the organization in question. We are not yet looking for the preferred or dominant grouping dimension at this stage. We are simply selecting the grouping dimensions which may generate a viable design option. There are four dimensions to choose from (Nadler and Tushman 1997; Galbraith et al. 2002):

- Activity: group around major activities (manufacturing, research and development, sales, etc.) or around disciplines (product marketing, software development, user interface design, etc.)
- Output: group around the products or services that the organization provides
- Customer: group around the customer or market segments that the organization serves
- Geography: group around physical locations

The first dimension (activity) is one that can be explored in any organization. Whether or not output and customer are relevant options depends on the variety in products/services and customers. The less variety there is, the less useful it is to include that dimension for grouping. The same is true for geography: if many distinct cities, countries, or regions are served by the organization, this is a dimension that should be included when generating design options. The guideline here is: when in doubt, include the grouping dimension. You can always decide at a later stage that it does not generate any viable design options.

Once the relevant grouping dimensions have been chosen, they need to be populated with categories. If output is a relevant dimension, then product groups need to identified. If customer is a relevant dimension, we need to know which are the customer segments, and so forth. With these dimensions and their categories, we can go into the core of the grouping work.

7.2.2 Determine Macro-Level and Meso-Level Grouping

We start grouping at the highest organizational level that is in scope of the design project. Let us assume here that is the enterprise level. The first activity is to determine the macro-level grouping. This is a design activity with an iterative nature,

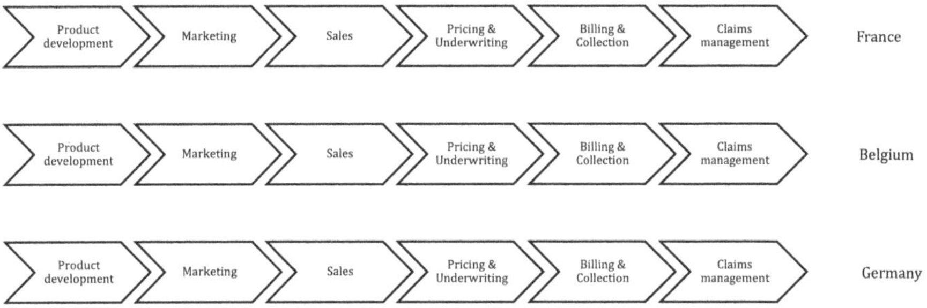

Fig. 7.6 The value chain and the geographic dimension as starting points for grouping the tasks of NSP Insurance

eminently suited for a 'prototyping' approach by a design team. The idea is to develop options, explore advantages and disadvantages, and identify the critical ingredients for the preferred design. The starting points for this exploration are the value chain and the grouping dimensions. Figure 7.6 shows what this could look like in our example of NSP Insurance, if we take geography as a grouping dimension.

As you can see in Fig. 7.6, the starting point for grouping is to assume that for each of the categories in this dimension—in this case the countries of France, Belgium, and Germany—all the activities in the value chain need to be conducted. The implication of this starting point would be that at the macro level, the organization would consist of three country units, operating entirely independently. This would largely meet our most important design principle: create autonomous clusters of tasks. However—as we saw when discussing this principle in Chap. 4—there is an important trade-off between this design principle and the benefits of economies of scale or, more accurately, between this design principle and the benefits of what Nadler and Tushman (1997) call leverage. If we go back to the design criteria for NSP, we can see that the company wants to increase its speed and impact in bringing new services to market, including noninsurance services. In order to do this effectively in all three geographic regions—including one, Germany, that is not yet a mature market for NSP—it may make sense to leverage certain capabilities across geographies. In addition to this, when exploring this grouping dimension, the design team found that the 'billing and collection' task is so similar across the three countries that it would pay to explore consolidating it in one unit. The result is a first grouping option shown in Fig. 7.7.

A similar exploration can be conducted using other grouping dimensions, such as customer segments. After all relevant dimensions have been explored, a dominant dimension at the macro level can usually be identified. The dominant dimension is the dimension that makes it possible to meet the design criteria while at the same time creating units that are as independent as possible (i.e., adhere to the first design principle). This is called 'parallelization' in Lowlands SocioTechnical Systems Design (L-STSD): dividing "the total flow of orders (including products and services) (…) into smaller 'parallel' sub-flows that are then allocated to independent business units" (Kuipers et al. 2020, p. 249). It is important to realize that any concession made to the first design principle—such as the two vertical groupings shown in Fig. 7.7—will

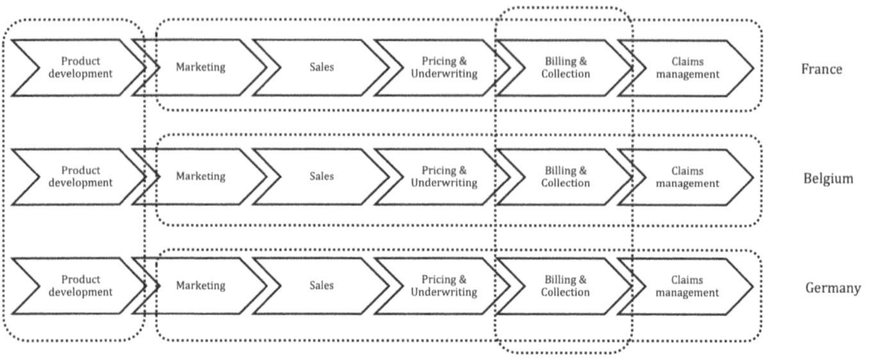

Fig. 7.7 A first grouping option for NSP Insurance

diminish the autonomy of the units that are the result of this design. Only if the design criteria or the conditions set for the design process cannot be met in another way should these concessions be considered. A condition that is sometimes difficult to meet when fully adhering to the first design principle is around cost; it can be inefficient and prohibitively expensive to duplicate tasks that are easy to standardize and pool, hence the grouping of the 'billing and collection' tasks in Fig. 7.7. Another reason to depart from the first design principle—by pooling activities—can be that one of the categories in the grouping dimension is of a much smaller size, such as the activities in Germany in the example of NSP. We will return to these types of consolidation decisions when we discuss ancillary and support tasks later in this section. Besides cost, we saw there is the broader aspect of leverage to consider, which lay at the base of the decision to group the product development tasks in Fig. 7.7. Nadler and Tushman (1997) identify three sources of leverage, leading to three design options:

- Leveraged front-end: consolidating tasks such as sales, marketing, and customer service for all products, markets, or geographies
- Leveraged back-end: consolidating and/or standardizing tasks such as product development, manufacturing, or the development of technological components
- Leveraged middle: pooling services and resources in the supply chain or processing infrastructure

Figure 7.8 shows two examples of leveraged grouping options.

Again, leveraging should only be done if it is needed to meet the design criteria. The starting point when grouping should be to strive for units that are as independent as possible (the first design principle). As you can see in Fig. 7.8, these simple examples of leveraging already create three crucial interfaces in the design (the arrows) that have to be managed by the use of linking mechanisms (which is the subject of the next chapter). Creating three separate units—one per product group or customer segment—would have eliminated these interfaces. It is these types of trade-offs that can make grouping such a complicated puzzle. The design team should take the time to explore all possible options, in the structured way described in this section. To choose among those options, it is essential to have a clear compass in the form of design criteria, in combination with boundary conditions that

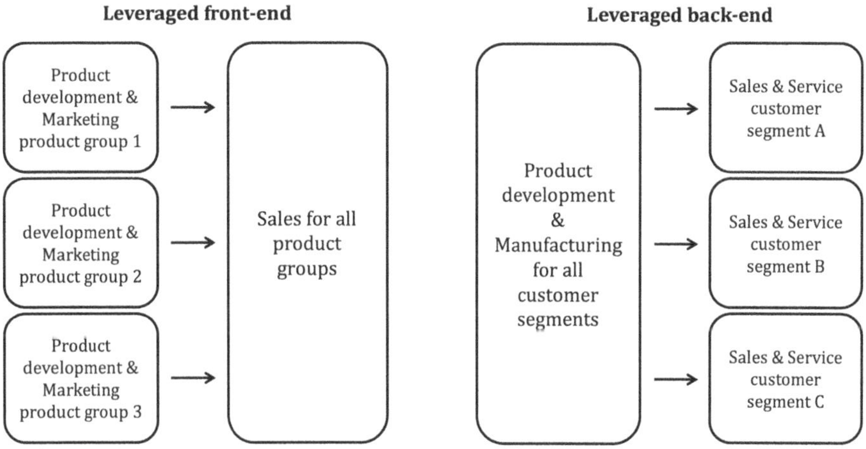

Fig. 7.8 Examples of leveraged front-end and leveraged back-end designs (based on Nadler and Tushman 1997)

circumscribe the design space. In addition, this exercise stresses the need to sometimes fight against the common tendency to consolidate and centralize, as we saw some of the trailblazers in Chap. 5 do successfully.

From Macro Level to Meso Level

In most organizational contexts, grouping is a recursive design activity. After the macro-level grouping has been completed—as described in the previous section—we usually have clusters of tasks that are too big to be allocated to one team. Lowlands SocioTechnical Systems Design gives the guideline of creating units of less than 200 people in macro design and striving for units of no more than 20 people (one team) in the next grouping step, meso design (Kuipers et al. 2020). The numbers give an indication of the size of the units we are looking for. However, these numbers should be used as a guide, not as a rule.

Typically, after the first grouping step, we have units that are too big to allocate to one team. That means we have to create sub-groups and sub-sub-groups until we reach the level of units that can be allocated to a team. In the case of NSP Insurance, we know from the discovery stage that the current organization consists of some 700 people. A macro-grouping such as the one depicted in Fig. 7.9 would create five units. So it is obvious that a sub-grouping—a meso-level grouping—is necessary to get to the required lowest unit level.

For the meso-level grouping, we follow the same logic as for the macro-level grouping. We use the relevant grouping dimensions again to explore which meso-level grouping option would create units that are as independent as possible while meeting the design criteria. The grouping dimension chosen at the meso level can be a different one than the macro-level dimension. In fact, it is quite common that dimensions differ from one level to the next. In the case of NSP Insurance, a sub-grouping is necessary of the three country units that each are tasked with marketing,

Fig. 7.9 The result of the macro-grouping of NSP Insurance

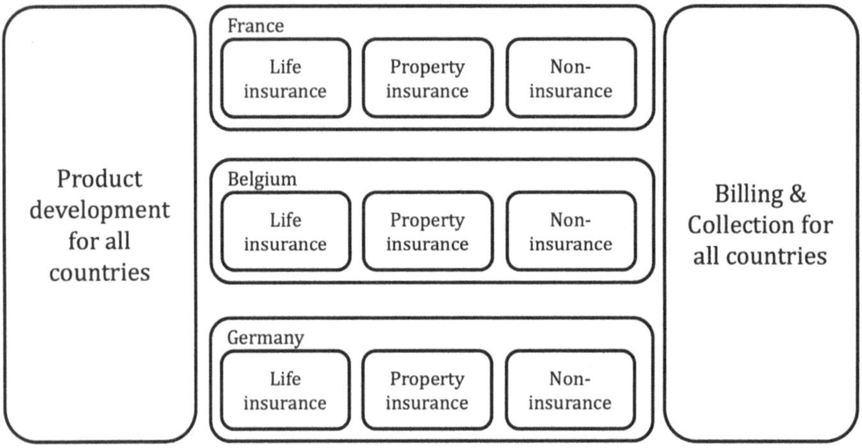

Fig. 7.10 The result of the meso-grouping of NSP Insurance

sales, pricing and underwriting, and claims management for their country. Since a further geographical sub-division did not make sense—the countries were each seen as one market—NSP explored a sub-division according to output. It turned out to be possible to create relatively autonomous sub-units that contained all tasks for one of their three main product groups: life insurance, property insurance, and noninsurance products. The result of this meso-grouping is shown in Fig. 7.10.

As you can see in Fig. 7.10, NSP could also have applied the two grouping dimensions in reverse. That is to say, they could have grouped according to products at the macro level and subsequently grouped according to countries at the meso level. However, because the differences between the countries were bigger than the differences between the product groups, it made more sense to choose geography as the dominant, macro-level grouping dimension. It may pay off to create links between the teams working on the same product group in different countries, but that is something we will return to when we discuss linking in the next chapter.

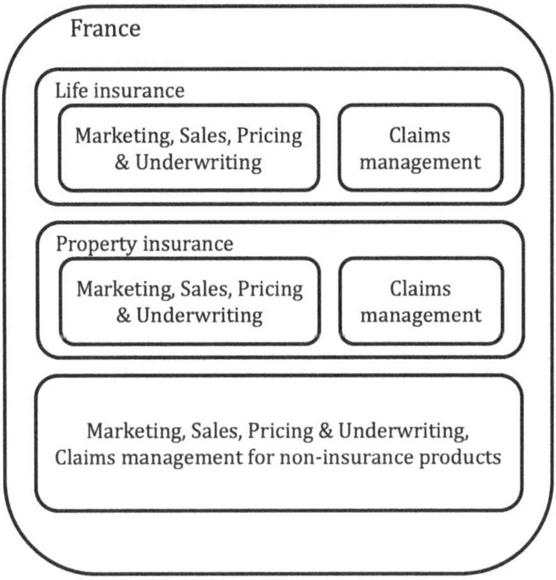

Fig. 7.11 The lowest-level grouping for NSP Insurance in France (other countries have a similar structure)

In the case of NSP, this sub-grouping according to products did not yet get the design to the level of teams (less than 20 people), so one more round of sub-grouping was necessary, specifically for the life insurance and property insurance units. At this last level, the NSP design team decided to group according to activity. There was a logical hand-off point in the flow of activities between pricing and underwriting and claims management. After pricing and underwriting had been completed, there was an intermediary product in the form of an insurance policy accepted by both NSP and the client. The next point of interaction with the client—apart from billing and collection—would occur when a claim was filed because of damage to a property or worse. Such a claim would then set in motion a separate process, which could be years from completing the accepted insurance policy (or never, if client and insurer were lucky). This natural hand-off point made it possible to create separate teams inside each product sub-group: one dealing with marketing, sales, and pricing and underwriting and the other dealing with claims management. Noninsurance products were the exception. For one, there was no sub-grouping necessary in that unit because the tasks could be handled by one team. Furthermore, the tasks were different for these noninsurance products, without a clean separation between acceptance of the policy and management of a claim. Figure 7.11 shows what the resulting sub-sub-grouping looks like for NSP in France. The other countries have a similar structure.

With this final level of grouping, NSP had reached a structure in which the lowest-level clusters of tasks could be allocated to teams of no more than 20 employees.[12] This meant the grouping activity had been completed.

More Than One Grouping Dimension at the Same Level: Hybrid Structures

In this chapter, we distinguished between four possible grouping dimensions to choose from: activity, output, customer, and geography. We also saw that it is possible to choose a different dimension at each level of grouping, that is, units grouped according to geography can for instance be further sub-divided into subunits according to output. But it is also possible that two dimensions co-exist at the same level, for instance, at the macro level. We saw a little bit of this in our example of NSP Insurance, at the macro level: product development for all countries was combined (grouping according to activity), and a number of other activities were clustered per country (grouping according to geography). The two dimensions of activity and geography are relatively easy to connect, as we will see when we cover linking in the next chapter. It is more difficult to combine the dimensions of output, customer, and geography at the same level. However, to meet the design criteria, it may be necessary to explore these design options as well. This is what Galbraith calls a "front-back hybrid structure" (Galbraith et al. 2002, p. 74). The back-end would typically be grouped by output to achieve product-related strategic objectives such as standardization or innovation. The front-end would typically be grouped according to customer or geography, to be customer-intimate or adapt to a local market. As we will see in the next chapter, this type of hybrid grouping will require sophisticated—and complicated—linking mechanisms (such as dual reporting lines, also known as matrix structures). Furthermore, with hybrid grouping it is very difficult to adhere to the first design principle: creating units that are as independent as possible. That is why this type of hybrid grouping—mixing the dimensions of output, customer, and geography at the same level—should be avoided, if at all possible. If this design option comes up, it is worthwhile to test whether the organization is not trying to realize conflicting design criteria, perhaps trying to combine product leadership with customer intimacy. Forcing a leadership team to make clearer choice when developing the design criteria could prevent this from happening. However, especially for very large multinational organizations, it may be necessary to resort to hybrid grouping to meet all design criteria. ◄

[12] We will not cover the necessary meso-level grouping for product development and for billing and collection at NSP, so as not to overcomplicate the example.

7.2.3 Positioning the Ancillary and Support Tasks

Up until this point, we have only spoken of the primary activities in the value chain. They form the basis of the grouping at the macro level as well as the meso level. Once that grouping has been completed, attention needs to be directed at the other tasks that are necessary to make the organization work. We distinguish between two types of non-primary tasks: ancillary tasks and support tasks.

Positioning Ancillary Tasks

The perspective we take here is that of the lowest level of sub-grouping, the team level. Whereas grouping has been conducted using the first design principle as the most important guideline—create units that are as independent as possible—we now need to apply the second design principle as described in Chap. 4: make teams as self-sufficient as possible. One way to do that is to make sure that the team does not just perform the primary tasks allocated to it but can also perform any ancillary tasks that are needed. There are two types of ancillary tasks: preparation and performance improvement.

Preparation. Preparation entails all the work that needs to be done before the primary tasks can be performed. The specific preparation involved will vary according to the primary activities, but typical preparatory activities are around planning and scheduling work and resources. It is essential for the team's self-sufficiency that these planning activities are performed by the team itself, not by a unit elsewhere in the organization (Kuipers et al. 2020). To be clear, this concerns planning at the team level. It may very well be that a higher-level or longer-term planning is developed elsewhere in the organization, which then forms the framework for the team's planning.

Performance improvement. This is the work that needs to be done to solve problems and improve the performance of the primary tasks performed by the team. Everything from reviewing performance data, to conducting retrospectives, and eliminating 'waste' can fall under this category. As is the case with preparation work, it benefits the self-sufficiency of the team greatly if this improvement work is performed by the team itself.

Both types of ancillary tasks need to be identified and allocated at the team level. Further micro-design will then be necessary, that is, the division of tasks and the design of jobs or roles *inside* the team, which is not among the subjects covered in this text.[13]

[13] Lowlands SocioTechnical Systems Design (De Sitter et al. 1997; Kuipers et al. 2020) and Job Characteristics Theory (Hackman and Oldham 1976; Hackman and Wageman 2005; Oldham and Hackman 2010) offer two useful starting points for design efforts at the intra-team level.

Positioning Support Tasks

Support tasks are less closely related to the primary tasks than are the ancillary tasks but are also necessary for a team to function. These tasks are characterized by their specialized and sometimes regulated nature, which makes them less suitable for allocation to the team that performs the primary tasks. Typical support tasks include those around human resources, finance, facility management, legal services, and information technology (to the extent that the latter is not part of the primary activities). Whether or not it is necessary or feasible to allocate these support tasks to the team that performs the primary activities is dependent on a number of factors. The rationale is to stretch the principle of team self-sufficiency as far as the organization is comfortable doing. As we saw with the examples in Chap. 5 (such as Haier and Vinci), this will sometimes mean actively fighting against the tendency to pool support tasks. The perfectly self-sufficient unit will be able to perform all of the support tasks needed. With Haier and Vinci, we have seen examples of models in which units come quite close to that state. However, there are limits to this, which have to do with two dimensions: specialization and standardization.

Specialization. If a support task requires highly specialized skills, we often see a combination of two phenomena: there is a scarcity of individuals possessing these skills, and one team does not have enough work for these individuals, because the tasks only occur in specific situations or specific stages of a project. In a software development environment, these tasks could be in the area of user research, IT security, or load testing. There may simply not be enough employees with these specialized skills to be able to dedicate one to each team. And even if there were, these people would have nothing to do for a large part of their time or be performing activities that do not make the best use of their skills. If this is the case, then these specialized tasks should not be added to each team, but instead be pooled in one specialized team. The implication of this design decision is that there need to be linking mechanisms in place between this specialized team and the teams performing the primary activities. These linking mechanisms deal with how this specialized support team supplies its services to the other teams. The internal market at Haier (see Chap. 5) is an example of such a linking mechanism. Linking will be dealt with in depth in the next chapter.

Standardization. For some support tasks, it is crucial that they are conducted in a standardized manner. Even in a radically decentralized organization such as BSO/Origin (see Chap. 4), its founder Eckart Wintzen stressed the need to standardize two tasks: financial reporting and corporate communication. In highly regulated industries such as financial services, there is a need to standardize processes such as risk management. In addition, these processes need to be conducted independently, which is a reason why ING left these tasks out of the squads (autonomous teams) in their implementation of the new organization model we discussed in Chap. 5 (Jacobs et al. 2017). If standardization and independence are important considerations, these tasks should not be allocated to the teams performing the primary activities. Instead, they should be allocated to dedicated teams.

When applying these two criteria to the support tasks, some choices will be obvious: tasks which are too specialized or standardized (or both) to be allocated to the primary units and thus need to be pooled in support units. But there usually are also quite a few tasks for which the choice is not so obvious, such as those having to do with personnel or financial management. The second design principle—create self-sufficient teams—guides us to allocate as many as possible of those support tasks to the primary units. Let teams manage their own quality, balance their own budgets, and hire their own people. The examples of Haier (Hamel and Zanini 2018), Nucor (Hamel and Zanini 2020), Buurtzorg (Monsen and De Blok 2013; Laloux 2014), BSO/Origin (Wintzen 2007), and many others show that this stimulates 'tactical entrepreneurship': "the search for improvements in various areas of responsibility of business operations and possibly also of commerce" (Kuipers et al. 2020, p. 287). Apart from this general consideration, it is important to take into account that in any specific design effort, there may be design criteria or conditions set by the steering committee that preclude or favor allocating these tasks to the primary units. Planned cost savings or professionalization of support tasks may steer the discussion in a certain direction.

One question remains with regard to support tasks. If the decision is taken to pool certain specialized support tasks, the new unit that is created in this way needs to be positioned in the overall structure. This can be done at one of the levels that are the result of the macro- and meso-level grouping of the primary activities. In other words, the support team can be positioned close to the primary teams, working only for a specific area of the business, or it can be placed at the enterprise level as a corporate function (or anywhere in between). The same two criteria of specialization and standardization can guide this decision. Support teams should be placed at the lowest level of grouping where the volume of specialized work can still sustain their existence. Standardized teams should be placed at the lowest level of grouping where the top management team still feels an adequate level of control over this aspect. In our example of NSP Insurance, the IT and facility management tasks were allocated to teams at the macro-level units (the countries), whereas the tasks in the areas of HR and finance were allocated one level lower, to the meso-level sub-units (grouped according to their three product lines). Only legal and risk tasks were placed at the enterprise level. The example of the resulting grouping for France is shown in Fig. 7.12.

After we have identified and allocated the ancillary and support tasks to one of the existing clusters or to a dedicated, new cluster, we have completed the grouping stage. The result is the structure of the organization, in terms of the Star model (see Chap. 2). The examples of NSP Insurance throughout this section show what the deliverable of this stage can look like visually (as you will note, the structure is not depicted in the form of an organization chart). In addition to this visual representation, each of the units and sub-units in the structure needs to be described in terms of the tasks it is responsible for (primary as well as support tasks) as well as the key decisions it has the authority to make. This information should flow logically from the grouping design work that was done. It is also helpful to have agreement on the outcomes each unit and sub-unit is accountable for. An outcome is "an end state to

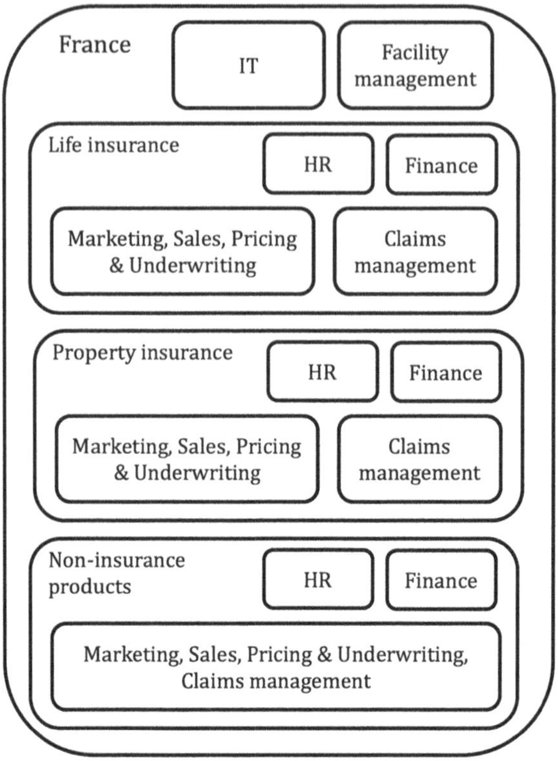

Fig. 7.12 The lowest-level grouping for NSP Insurance in France, including the support tasks (other countries have a similar structure)

be achieved (…) [or] results to be attained" (Galbraith et al. 2002, p. 84). Examples of outcomes are growth of market share, improvement of margins, reduction of cost, development of new products, retention of clients, provision of expertise, and management of risk.

With grouping, we have completed a crucial part of the design effort. However, the design is far from complete. In strategic design, the companion activity to grouping is linking. This is the subject of the next chapter.

Review Questions

1. Do you think that organizations usually do not spend enough time in the 'problem space' before they proceed to the 'solution space'? Why or why not?
2. What would you do if an organization's leadership team is not aligned on strategy, but still wants to proceed with the organization design project?
3. Do you think it is easy or difficult to capture an organization's tasks in a value chain of five to ten activities? Why so?

4. What would you do if an organization's leadership team says they do not want to spend any time on mapping out the current context ("We know how we are organized and we know what works and what does not")?
5. Do you agree that design options which have been tried unsuccessfully in the past should be excluded from the design process as nonnegotiables? Why or why not?
6. Which HR policies do you think are needed to reduce apprehension about an organization design project among employees? Can you think of situations in which these policies are not feasible?
7. What do you think is the best way for a leadership team to be involved in the design process? Why so?
8. Which stakeholders do you think should have a voice when developing the design criteria?
9. Do you see any other grouping dimensions apart from the four mentioned (activity, output, customer, geography)?
10. Can you think of a situation in which it is not a good idea to allocate the ancillary tasks (preparation and performance improvement) to the primary units?
11. Which support tasks do you think are good candidates for allocation to primary units? Why so?
12. Which support tasks do you think are good candidates for allocation at the enterprise level? Why so?
13. Do you think allocating support tasks to a team always make that team more self-sufficient? Why or why not?

References

Block, P. (2011). *Flawless consulting: A guide to getting your expertise used* (3rd ed.). San Francisco: Pfeiffer.

Cross, R., & Parker, A. (2004). *The hidden power of social networks: Understanding how work really gets done in organizations*. Boston: Harvard Business School Press.

De Sitter, L. U., Den Hertog, F., & Dankbaar, B. (1997). From complex organizations with simple jobs to simple organizations with complex jobs. *Human Relations, 50*(5), 497–534.

Følstad, A., & Kvale, K. (2018). Customer journeys: A systematic literature review. *Journal of Service Theory and Practice, 28*(2), 196–227.

Galbraith, J., Downey, D., & Kates, A. (2002). *Designing dynamic organizations: A hands-on guide for leaders at all levels*. New York: Amacom.

Galbraith, J. R. (1977). *Organization design*. Reading: Addison-Wesley.

Galbraith, J. R. (2014). *Designing organizations: Strategy, structure, and process at the business unit and enterprise levels* (3rd ed.). San Francisco: Jossey-Bass.

Global Sustainability Standards Board. (2020). *GRI standards glossary*. Retrieved March 2, 2021, from https://www.globalreporting.org/standards

Hackman, J. R., & Oldham, G. R. (1976). Motivation through the design of work: Test of a theory. *Organizational Behavior.and Human Performance, 16*(2), 250–279.

Hackman, J. R., & Wageman, R. (2005). When and how team leaders matter. *Research in Organizational Behavior, 26*, 37–74.

Hamel, G., & Zanini, M. (2018). The end of bureaucracy: How a Chinese appliance maker is reinventing management for the digital age. *Harvard Business Review, 96*(6), 50–59.

Hamel, G., & Zanini, M. (2020). *Humanocracy: Creating organizations as amazing as the people inside them*. Boston: Harvard Business Review Press.
Jacobs, P., Schlatmann, B., Mahadevan, D. (2017). *ING's agile transformation*. Retrieved January 29, 2021, from https://www.mckinsey.com/industries/financial-services/our-insights/ings-agile-transformation
Kesler, G., & Kates, A. (2011). *Leading organization design: How to make organization design decisions to drive the results you want*. San Francisco: Jossey-Bass.
Kuipers, H., Van Amelsvoort, P., & Kramer, E. (2020). *New ways of organizing: Alternatives to bureaucracy*. Den Haag: Acco Nederland.
Laloux, F. (2014). *Reinventing organizations: A guide to creating organizations inspired by the next stage of human consciousness*. Brussels: Nelson Parker.
Lawrence, P. R., & Lorsch, J. W. (1967). *Organization and environment: Managing differentiation and integration*. Boston: Harvard Business School Press.
Lindberg, T., Meinel, C., & Wagner, R. (2011). Design Thinking: A Fruitful Concept for IT Development? In C. Meinel, L. Leifer, & H. Plattner (Eds.), *Design thinking: Understanding innovation*. Berlin: Springer.
Maister, D. H., Green, C. A., & Galford, R. M. (2000). *The trusted advisor*. New York: Touchstone.
March, J. G., & Simon, H. A. (1958). *Organizations*. New York: John Wiley.
Monsen, K., & De Blok, J. (2013). Buurtzorg Nederland. *The American Journal of Nursing, 113*(8), 55–59.
Nadler, D. A., & Tushman, M. L. (1997). *Competing by design: The power of organizational architecture*. Oxford: Oxford University Press.
Oldham, G. R., & Hackman, J. R. (2010). Not what it was and not what it will be: The future of job design research. *Journal of Organizational Behavior, 31*(2/3), 463–479.
Porter, M. E. (1985). *Competitive advantage: Creating and sustaining superior performance*. New York: The Free Press.
Puranam, P., Alexy, O., & Reitzig, M. (2014). What's "new" about new forms of organizing? *The Academy of Management Review, 39*(2), 162–180.
Rother, M., & Shook, J. (2003). *Learning to see: Value-stream mapping to create value and eliminate muda*. Cambridge: The Lean Enterprise Institute.
Schein, E. H. (1999). *Process consultation revisited: Building the helping relationship*. Reading: Addison-Wesley.
Stanford, N. (2018). *Organization design: The practitioner's guide* (3rd ed.). Oxon: Routledge.
The Open Group. (2018). *TOGAF standard, version 9.2*. Retrieved January 29, 2021, from https://pubs.opengroup.org/architecture/togaf9-doc/arch/index.html
Treacy, M., & Wiersema, F. (1993). Customer intimacy and other value disciplines. *Harvard Business Review, 71*(1), 84–93.
Wintzen, E. (2007). *Eckart's notes*. Rotterdam: Lemniscaat.
Worren, N. (2018). *Organization design: Simplifying complex systems* (2nd ed.). Oxon: Routledge.
Worren, N., Van Bree, J., & Zybach, W. (2019). Organization design challenges: Results from a practitioner survey. *Journal of Organization Design, 8*(1), 1–18.
Zielinski, A. (2019). *Lessons learned from the finance sector: How Deutsche Bank is using organization design to address rapid digitalization, manage competing cycles of change, and improve customer experience*. Presented at the European Organisation Design Forum Annual Conference 2019, The Lensbury, London, October 25.

8 How to Link the Efforts of an Organization

Abstract

Linking refers to the integration of effort, which is the second of the two interlinked problems at the core of organization design (the first being the division of labor). The extent of linking necessary will depend on the design decisions made with regard to the division of labor. Linking mechanisms are needed to address interdependencies that remain in the structure that was designed. There are six types of interdependence. Goal interdependence and task interdependence are the two most important ones and will exist in almost any structure. The other types of interdependence are around sharing and leveraging resources (funding, support services, brand names, etc.), sharing knowledge, working according to standards, and delivering to the same market. Interdependencies in a structure can be identified using these six categories. Only the most critical interdependencies should be addressed in the organization design. The linking mechanisms available to organizations are authority, rewards, management processes, tacit coordinating mechanisms, and lateral roles and teams. These linking mechanisms differ in terms of complexity and cost and in terms of their formalization. The least expensive linking mechanism that adequately addresses the critical interdependence in question should be chosen. Remaining interdependencies can be addressed by informal means of coordinating.

Keywords

Organization design • Integration of effort • Linking stage • Coordinating mechanisms • Coordination • Collaboration • Rewards • Authority • Interdependence • Management processes

J. van Bree, *Organization Design*, https://doi.org/10.1007/978-3-030-78679-3_8

Learning Objectives

- Identify interdependencies in a structure that was designed.
- Understand and recognize the six types of interdependence.
- Assess interdependencies according to their criticality.
- List the linking mechanisms available to the organization designer.
- Understand the different roles that authority can play in an organization.
- Distinguish between a hierarchy in the design of a structure and a hierarchy of authority.
- Understand the relative cost and complexity associated with the different linking mechanisms.
- Recommend a linking mechanism that is suited to address a specific interdependence.
- Understand the role of informal means of coordinating.

The previous chapter discussed grouping as the way to design the structure of the organization and explained the steps necessary in this stage. Grouping covers the first of the two interlinked problems at the core of organization design (Puranam et al., 2014): division of labor. This chapter deals with the second of these two interlinked problems: integration of effort, quite simply referred to here as linking (Fig. 8.1). How do we make sure the units we created through grouping coordinate their efforts to jointly deliver products or services to clients?

8.1 The Starting Points for the Linking Stage

The result of the grouping stage is a design of the structure of the organization. Figure 8.2 shows this structure for NSP Insurance, the example we used to go through the grouping steps in the previous chapter.[1]

By looking at the structure of NSP Insurance in Fig. 8.2, we may already see three starting points for the linking effort:

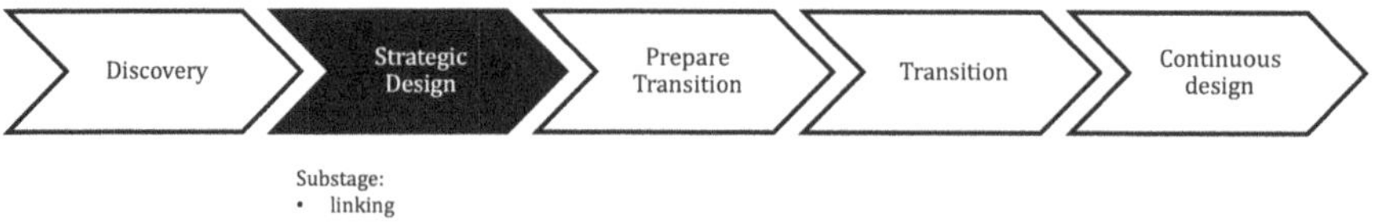

Fig. 8.1 The stage of the design approach covered in this chapter

[1] Normally, this visual representation would be supplemented by a description of the tasks, key decisions, and outcomes of each of the units; we have left this out to simplify the example.

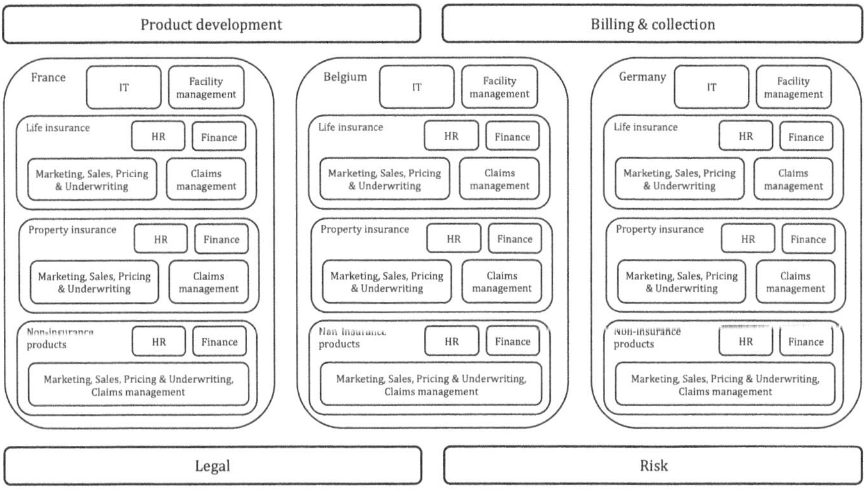

Fig. 8.2 The result of the grouping stage: design of the structure of NSP Insurance

1. The value chain of NSP is not contained in one unit, which means the units that together cover the end-to-end value chain need to be linked.
2. Some tasks are duplicated for different countries and product groups (such as claims management and HR), which may give rise to a need for coordination, and the exchange of knowledge and resources across countries or product groups.
3. Some units, such as product development and IT, serve more than one other unit, which may require a linking mechanism to properly prioritize resources.

As this example shows, the extent and type of linking that is necessary is dependent on the design decisions made in the grouping stage. As you will recall, the intent with grouping is to design a structure that has a minimal amount of interdependence between the units (the first design principle from Chap. 4). Minimal interdependence would mean minimal linking requirements. But as we saw, the context, value chain, and design criteria of the organization in question will usually make some compromises to this first design principle necessary. Each of these compromises will create a need for linking. If the extent of linking necessary seems excessive, it can be worthwhile to go back to the grouping stage to see if a different design of the structure would not be possible.

A final point about the example of NSP Insurance is that we can see a hierarchy in the organization's structure. Not in the sense of levels of authority (we will get to that later in this chapter), but in the sense of an inclusive clustering. Smaller (product) units are contained in larger (country) units. These hierarchical groups are a useful starting point for our linking effort, because they show at least two levels at which efforts can be linked: at the product group level, which holds four units, and at the country level, which holds five units (see Fig. 8.3). Whether or not linking is needed at these levels, and which mechanisms we will use for it, is a question we will return to in the course of this chapter. For now, it is important to note that these two hierarchical levels in the structure do not necessarily need to translate to two management layers.

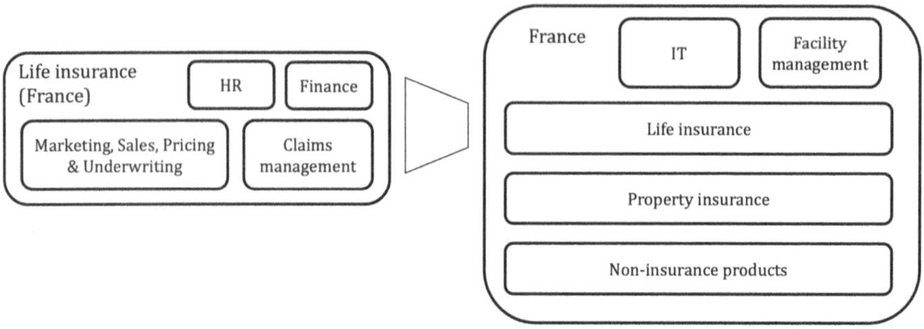

Fig. 8.3 The structure of NSP Insurance at the product group and country levels

Fig. 8.4 The three-part structure of this chapter

Our discussion of linking in this chapter will consist of three parts. First, we will discuss the different types of interdependence that can exist in an organization design. Then we will discuss the different linking mechanisms available to the organization designer. And finally, we will offer some guidance for matching the right linking mechanism to a specific type of interdependence. Figure 8.4 shows the three parts of this chapter. We will start by discussing different types of interdependencies.

8.2 Types of Interdependence

Throughout this book, we have stressed the need to create organizational units that are as autonomous as possible. The first two design principles in Chap. 4 offer a theoretical rationale for why this is necessary. The examples in Chap. 5 show contemporary organizations which have been successful—to a larger or lesser extent—in creating these autonomous units. And the approach to grouping presented in the previous chapter shows the practical steps necessary to design a structure that meets this requirement as much as possible. The example of NSP Insurance (used in this chapter and the previous one) shows that there will be compromises and trade-offs along the way, stemming from the specific context of the organization and from the design criteria that were chosen. But let us put that practical example to the side for a moment and assume we have been successful in creating autonomous units. We have a structure similar to that of Buurtzorg Nederland (Monsen & De Blok, 2013;

Laloux, 2014) or BSO/Origin of years past (see Chap. 4): completely self-sufficient teams. With this extent of autonomy, is there anything left to be managed at a higher level in the organization? Well yes, there is. These units are *conditionally* autonomous (Thompson, 1967) and form a *nearly* decomposable system (Simon, 1996), because otherwise they would no longer be part of the same organization. This leads us to the first type of interdependence.

Goal interdependence. If we see the organization as a system which has "system level goals, towards which (…) the constituent agent's efforts make a contribution" (Puranam, 2018, p. 4), the minimum critical interdependence lies with these system-level goals: the strategic goals of the organization as a whole. There needs to be a process in place for the development and adjustment of these goals, their translation down to the lowest unit level, and the reporting of each unit's contribution to them. This is the first and minimal source of interdependence in any organization: each unit's contribution to the organization's goals. This interdependence may seem self-evident, because in a lot of organizations it is taken for granted that this is managed through the 'chain of command' in the hierarchy, with strategic goals cascading down to the operational level. But at this stage of our design effort—after we have completed the grouping—all we have is a structure. We do not yet have a hierarchy of graded authority, and we may choose not to include that in our design, following some of the trailblazers we saw in Chap. 5. That is why we need to be aware of this interdependence and adequately address it.

Task interdependence. The second important source of interdependence is task interdependence: the situation in which the performance of one task in an organization is affected by the performance of other tasks (McCann & Ferry, 1979; Kumar et al., 2009; Puranam et al., 2012). In the design of the structure (through grouping, see previous chapter), we should have contained as much as possible of this task interdependence inside units. Where the interdependence crosses unit boundaries, it will need to be identified and addressed. The most important task interdependence is that between tasks in the value chain that are not contained in the same unit. In the example of NSP, we see that the value chain for each product group is split in two: one unit deals with marketing, sales, and pricing and underwriting, while another deals with claims management. In addition, there are two central units at the enterprise level that deal with product development and billing and collection for all countries and all product groups. This creates three points of task interdependence that need to be addressed in our linking efforts for NSP Insurance (see Fig. 8.5).

Resource interdependence. A third source of interdependence that will likely occur, even if the units that were designed are highly autonomous, is around sharing

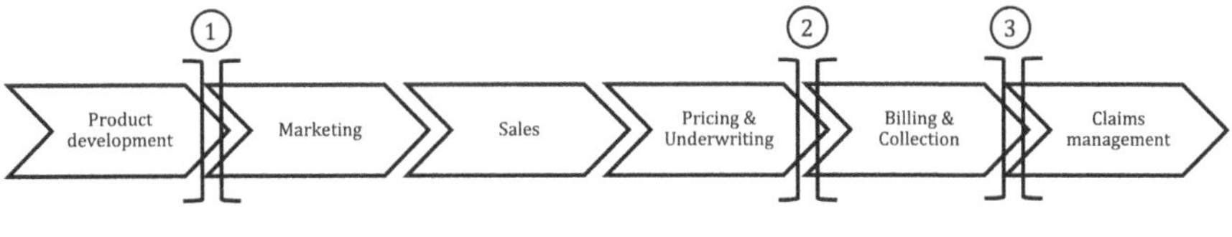

Fig. 8.5 The three points of task interdependence created by the structure of NSP Insurance

resources. It is rare that the lowest-level units in an organization—teams of less than 20 people, according to the guidelines we used in the previous chapter—have all the resources at their disposal to perform the tasks allocated to them. They may need funding, specialized expertise, support functions such as IT or HR, shared equipment or infrastructure, or access to a joint client base, operating license, or brand name. This is the third common source of interdependence: sharing and leveraging resources.

Knowledge interdependence. A fourth source of interdependence is the sharing of knowledge and know-how. While it is not a universal requirement, in most situations the organization will benefit greatly from sharing knowledge between units, especially between units that perform similar tasks, such as those conducting claims management in the NSP Insurance example. There may also be a benefit to connecting professionals that work in different units but share a certain field of expertise, such as marketeers, software engineers, or data scientists. Even radically decentralized organizations such as Haier or Buurtzorg ensure that this exchange of knowledge is facilitated. Haier has their 'platforms' that bring together microenterprises (Hamel & Zanini, 2018), and Buurtzorg has their BuurtzorgWeb intranet (see Laloux, 2014). This need for knowledge sharing is something that needs to be made explicit in the design criteria for the organization design project in question (see Chap. 7).

Standards interdependence. The fifth source of interdependence is not universal, but quite common nonetheless. This is the need to standardize certain work processes. Since it is not universal, this need should also be made explicit in the design criteria or the conditions set for the design project. The need for standardization can stem from stakeholders outside the organization, such as the requirement to comply with certain tax and labor laws. It may also originate inside the organization, because a standardized way of working is believed to increase efficiency or the quality of the work.

Front-end interdependence. The final source of interdependence—which we will label front-end interdependence—can arise if the organization has several distinct products or services that are delivered to the same market. A market in this case can be a customer segment or a geographic region. This is the case for NSP, where we can see that three product categories (life insurance, property insurance, and noninsurance products) are delivered to the same national market (either France, Belgium, or Germany). From a customer experience perspective—but also from the perspective of leveraging marketing and sales efforts—this can produce an interdependence that the organization would like to manage (see Fig. 8.6). Again, the importance of managing this interdependence will depend on the context of the organization and the specific design criteria (e.g., to what extent are the products related? How important is customer intimacy in the organization's strategy?). This final source of interdependence also implies there can be interdependencies even if the entire value chain is contained in one unit per product group (so without a break in the value chain such as the one shown in Fig. 8.5). If several or all of these product groups are delivered to the same market, there is still a possible interdependence between the units that the organization would then need to manage.

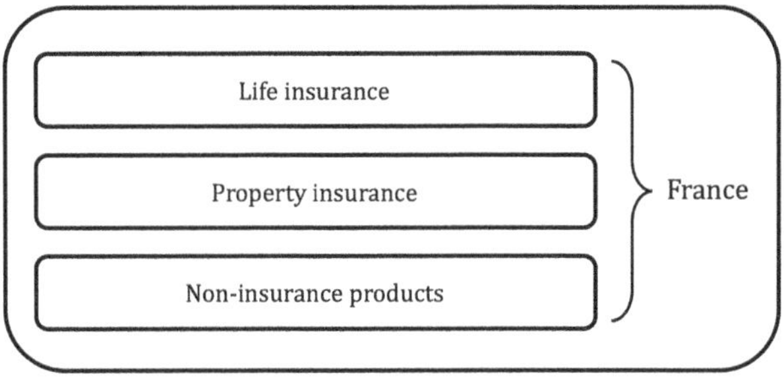

Fig. 8.6 The potential source of front-end interdependence created by the structure of NSP Insurance

Table 8.1 Six types of interdependence and examples of each

Category	Examples of interdependence
1. Goal interdependence	Units each have an interrelated part to play in achieving the organization's goals It is hard to combine two goals which are both important for the organization's survival (such as exploration and exploitation; see Chap. 4)
2. Task interdependence	Several units jointly conduct the core work in the end-to-end value chain
3. Resource interdependence	Allocating or redistributing funds Using shared support services such as HR or finance Making joint use of a client base or a brand name Making joint use of an indivisible infrastructure (such as a rail network, a telecommunications network, a museum's art collection, or a network of stores) Making joint use of consolidated back-end resources, such as product development, manufacturing, or supply chain Making joint use of expensive equipment Pooling negotiating power
4. Knowledge interdependence	Sharing best practices among units Sharing expertise among professionals in the same field
5. Standards interdependence	Enforcing safety standards Ensuring risks are consistently managed Making sure labor laws are applied Ensuring financial management follows reporting standards Safeguarding one corporate image
6. Front-end interdependence	Several units serve related products to the same customer base

Based on the structure (the result of the grouping activity) and using the design criteria, the main interdependencies in the organization design can be identified by systematically investigating each of these six categories. The categories are summarized in Table 8.1, including some examples of interdependencies for each.

This investigation of interdependencies can produce quite an extensive list, although it will become apparent that some interdependencies are more critical than others. An interdependence is critical if the actions taken by one unit *affect important outcomes* of other units (Worren, 2018). The design criteria can guide this assessment of the interdependencies and the selection of the most critical ones that need to be addressed in the organization design.

Keeping in mind our principle of preventing overdesign (see Chap. 4), it is important to focus only on the critical interdependencies when we start designing linking mechanisms. Some of the more minor interdependencies can be left to employees to manage themselves through what has been called feedback (March & Simon, 1958), mutual adjustment (Thompson, 1967), or ongoing communication (Srikanth & Puranam, 2011). In other words, by quite simply picking up the phone, writing an email, or scheduling a meeting to deal with an issue that comes up for which the help of another unit is needed.

The identification of a large number of critical interdependencies may lead the design team to reconsider the structure that was designed. Is there not a different grouping option possible that would reduce or attenuate the interdependencies? Going through another iteration of grouping (see previous chapter) can prove worthwhile. It is important that the design team stays in this mode of iterating and prototyping until the close of the strategic design stage. The strategic design is not complete until the best configuration of the communicating vessels of grouping and linking has been chosen.

To close out this section, Table 8.2 lists the ten most critical interdependencies in the structure of NSP Insurance, our example in this and the previous chapter.

Table 8.2 The ten critical interdependencies in the structure of NSP Insurance

Perspective	Critical interdependencies
1. Goal interdependence	The three country units need to contribute to the corporate strategy of the organization
2. Task interdependence	Product development needs the product group units to get information about client needs and to bring new products to market For each of the product groups, the 'marketing, sales, and pricing and underwriting' teams need the 'claims management' teams to complete the service they deliver to clients
3. Resource interdependence	The IT and facility management support teams each need to support three product group units The HR and finance experts in each product group each need to support two teams The teams that supply noninsurance products want to leverage the client base of the life insurance and property insurance teams
4. Knowledge interdependence	Marketing and sales professionals in the product group units want to exchange best practices
5. Standards interdependence	There need to be common HR practices across the organization Risk needs to be managed uniformly across the organization
6. Front-end interdependence	There needs to be one face to the customer per country for life insurance and property insurance.

8.3 Linking Mechanisms

Now that we have identified the interdependencies in the structure that was designed—and have potentially gone through another iteration of grouping to design a structure with fewer or lighter interdependencies—we can start designing the linking mechanisms needed to address these interdependencies. In this section of the chapter, we will cover the array of linking mechanisms that are available to the organization designer (Fig. 8.7).

Figure 8.8 gives an overview of the linking mechanisms we will cover in this section. As you can see, we will not just cover what is traditionally referred to as coordinating mechanisms. We will also look at the role of rewards as a linking mechanism, as well as a topic we have been putting aside—one could say, willfully ignoring—until now: the role of authority in organizations.

Fig. 8.7 The focus of this section: the linking mechanisms that are available

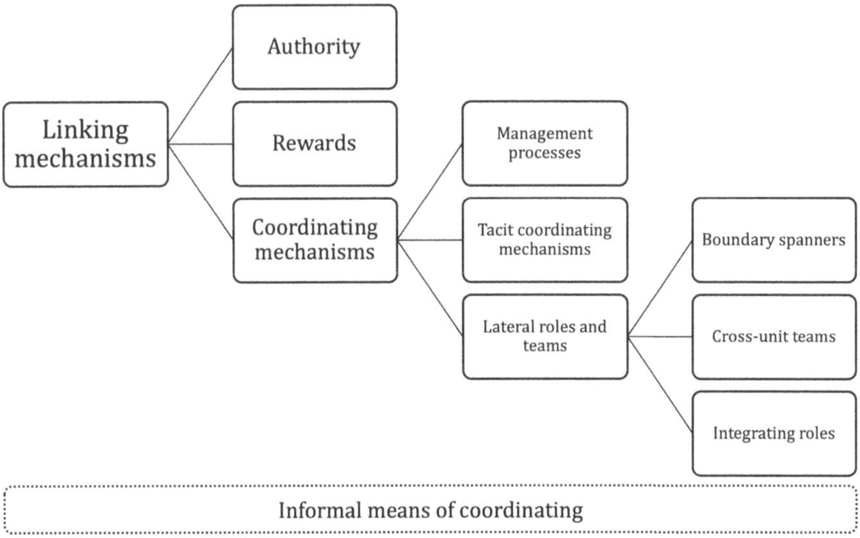

Fig. 8.8 An overview of the available linking mechanisms we will cover in this section

8.3.1 Authority

Although the current zeitgeist makes it almost a dirty word, authority is still an essential feature of any organization. No matter how eagerly we discuss busting bureaucracies, rebelling against corporate frustration, or empowering frontline workers, authority will still need to be addressed as part of an organization design effort. What role will managers, directors, and executives play in the organization?

Phanish Puranam has conceptualized authority in relation to his four fundamental problems of organizing (Puranam et al., 2014), which we discussed in Chap. 2: task division, task allocation, provision of information, and provision of rewards. Puranam sees three roles for authority (Puranam, 2018).

- The authority to *design*: selecting and enforcing the solutions chosen to the fundamental problems of organizing, that is, selecting and enforcing the organization design
- The authority to *direct* subordinates: using authority as a solution to one or more of the fundamental problems of organizing, by having an authority figure who "may monitor, hold accountable, sanction, and instruct employees to ensure their efforts are integrated" (ibid., p. 93)
- Authority as *dispute resolution*: handling exceptions that arise from imperfections in the organization design (which cannot be managed by mutual adjustment)

Let us start by addressing the third role of authority: dispute resolution or exception management. Although there are other ways to resolve disputes—such as decision-making with the 'consent principle' (The Sociocracy Group, 2021) or the 'advice process' described by Laloux (2014)—authority can be a very effective method. If two employees or two managers cannot reach a joint decision, they can refer the decision up to a common superior. The source of the dispute may lie in any one of the six forms of interdependence that were covered in the previous section (except for knowledge interdependence). Alternatively, it may be a flaw in the design of the structure, where we inadvertently created overlapping responsibilities. If that is the case, the problem should be addressed in the design or redesign of the structure.

Let us now extend our discussion to the second role of authority, that of directing subordinates. In this role, authority can also be used to address any of the six types of interdependence (again with the exception of knowledge interdependence). More so than in the case of dispute resolution, using authority to manage interdependencies in this way—by directing subordinates—is a choice. There may be other linking mechanisms available that better meet the design criteria, are less expensive, or require less effort. We will cover these alternative linking mechanisms in the course of this chapter.

Based on these two roles of authority (dispute resolution and direction), a useful first step in the design of linking mechanisms is to see how the hierarchy that is present in the structure could translate to a hierarchy of authority. In the example of NSP Insurance, we can see there are four layers in the hierarchy at which authority could be placed:

1. The lowest-level units, such as claims management
2. The product group units (comprising the lowest-level units)
3. The country units (comprising the product group units)
4. The organization as a whole

We can also see that placing authority at levels 2, 3, and 4 could be a way to address quite a few of the interdependencies that were identified for NSP, such as aligning the goals of the country units, connecting teams that together need to deliver a service to clients, and leveraging the client base across product groups. But as we will see in our further discussion of linking mechanisms, there are other ways to address these interdependencies. Using authority may be considered a default option in many organizations, but in the context of this book, we consider it to be a choice—a choice that should be considered carefully. For now, it suffices to conclude that the four hierarchical levels in the structure of NSP can be used to create four graded levels of authority, shown in a simplified form in Fig. 8.9. Furthermore, we see potential in a hierarchy of authority as a multifaceted linking mechanism (addressing several critical dependencies), but we will not yet commit ourselves to that choice at this point in the design.

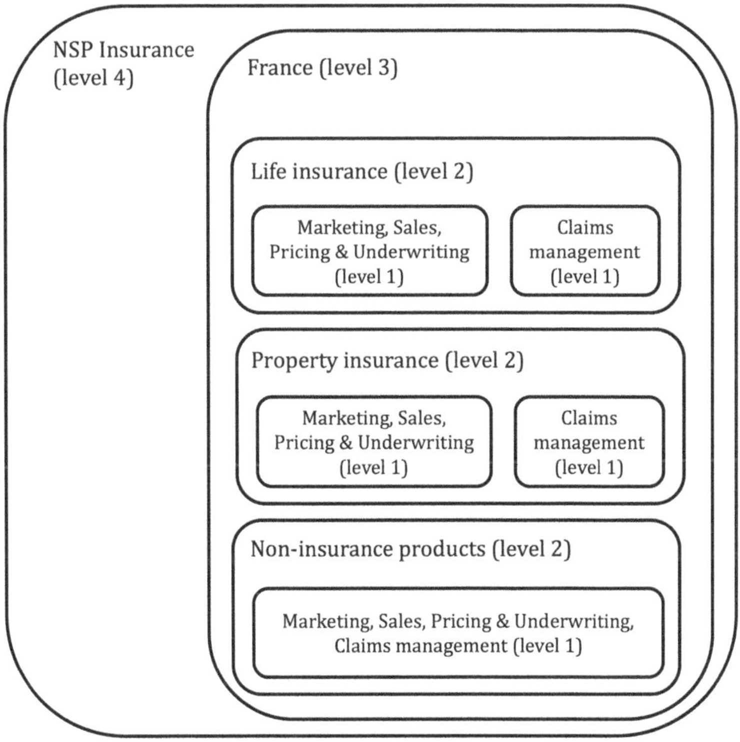

Fig. 8.9 The four potential levels of graded authority which can be derived from the structure of NSP Insurance

Expanding our view on authority still further, we can include its first role: designing solutions to the fundamental problems of organizing and enforcing them. Especially this latter part of enforcing solutions or rules is a common aspect of authority. As you may recall from Chap. 7, it is important to express the need for control and standardization that the organization in question has, in the design criteria. This will guide discussions about this enforcing role of authority. What we have called 'standards interdependence' in the previous section would typically be addressed by authority. This could be done by creating a staff unit at the enterprise level to which the specific authority is delegated to enforce standards in areas such as HR, finance, or risk. Note that this is distinct from a support unit which supplies services to a number of other units (such as the HR, finance, IT, and facility management units we see in the structure of NSP Insurance). A support unit does not have any authority over the units it supplies its services to.

8.3.2 Rewards

An important second topic we need to address when it comes to linking is that of rewards and incentives. Provision of rewards is one of the four fundamental problems of organizing in Puranam's framework (Puranam et al., 2014). According to Puranam, the provision of rewards is intended to address the challenges to the integration of effort in an organization that arise from motivational causes. These are cooperation problems, as opposed to coordination problems. Cooperation problems "occur when interdependent individuals lack the motivation to achieve the best collective outcome" (Puranam, 2018, p. 67). In other words, the goals of the organization are not aligned with the goals of the units or individuals. The intervention of an authority figure—the role of authority to direct—can be used to solve this cooperation problem. But the solution can also be sought in designing a reward structure that aligns the efforts of individuals or units in the organization. A prerequisite for this solution is unambiguous metrics to measure performance, cascading down from the strategic goals of the organization.[2] If these are in place, compensation can be based to some extent on either individual or group performance, to address these motivational challenges.[3] Of course, rewards do not have to be monetary. In fact, some of the most powerful rewards are those that instill the motivation to contribute to the organization based on its purpose alone, as we saw in the example of Hyperloop Transportation Technology (see Chap. 5). Unfortunately, not all organizations have the luxury of working on an inspiring technology such as hyperloop transportation.

---

[2] Chapter 5 of Galbraith et al. (2002) contains an extensive description of how to develop these types of metrics.

[3] Chapter 4 of Puranam (2018) offers a good review of the supporting literature for performance-based compensation.

We will not cover the design of performance management or compensation and benefit systems in this book. We will briefly return to this topic in the next chapter, because it may have a place in the operational design or transition plan. For our current discussion, it is important to acknowledge that the provision of rewards is one of the linking mechanisms available to organizations, particularly when it comes to managing goal interdependence and task interdependence.

8.3.3 Coordinating Mechanisms

Now that we have broadened our perspective on linking mechanisms to include authority and rewards, we can direct our attention to the narrower and more traditional view of linking as coordinating: using mechanisms and processes to achieve coordinated action between the interdependent units of an organization (Thompson, 1967; Nadler & Tushman, 1997; Kretschmer & Puranam, 2008). So, what is the toolkit we have on offer for this?

Management Processes

The first and most formalized coordinating mechanism is to define management processes that govern the coordination between interdependent units. Some authors have called this an organizational interface: a description of how organizational units interact with each other (Srikanth & Puranam, 2011). This encompasses what was referred to as procedures, plans, and rules in some of the foundational works of organization design (March & Simon, 1958; Thompson, 1967; Galbraith, 1973). Nadler and Tushman (1997) offer a distinction between three types of management processes: strategic management processes (such as strategic planning, resource allocation, and budgeting and forecasting), business management processes (such as product development, customer management, and new business acquisition), and support management processes (such as talent management, information security, and public relations). Galbraith gives the guideline of only formalizing and documenting the three to five management processes that are the most critical to the business (Galbraith et al., 2002). Again, the design criteria in combination with the critical interdependencies can help in identifying what those critical management processes should be.[4] A specific type of management process we should highlight is that of creating an internal customer-supplier relationship, which we saw at Haier (see Chap. 5). Based on a case study of a multinational engineering firm, Worren (2017) shows how such an internal customer-supplier link can be an alternative to dual reporting relationships (i.e., to a matrix structure) for combining several grouping dimensions.

[4] Chapter 4 of Galbraith et al. (2002) gives a detailed instruction on how to document these management processes.

It seems obvious that ongoing communication between the units needs to be facilitated on top of these management processes (March & Simon, 1958; Thompson, 1967; Gittell, 2002). This is where three important other categories of coordinating mechanisms come in, which facilitate interaction between the organizational units.

Tacit Coordinating Mechanisms

The first category is that of tacit coordinating mechanisms (Srikanth & Puranam, 2011), a term which I expand slightly to denote any means to communicate large amounts of information efficiently (March & Simon, 1958). One example of this is given by Argyres (1999) in his description of the development of the B-2 stealth bomber. He talks about how a highly standardized 'technical grammar' was established, which allowed for a very efficient information exchange between engineers from different companies. In a very different context, Gittell (2002) found that clinical pathways in hospitals enhanced participants' understanding of their role in the overall process, which facilitated their interactions. So, standardized language and codified routines are two examples of tacit coordinating mechanisms. The other broad way to communicate a large amount of information efficiently—in the context of coordinating—is "through enhancing observability (…) of context, actions, and outcomes" (Srikanth & Puranam, 2011, p. 855). Any way to share the work status falls under this category, whether mediated by technology (Slack, Teams, Salesforce, SAP) or by using objects such as Kanban boards and prototypes (Okhuysen & Bechky, 2009).

Lateral Roles and Teams

A final main category of coordinating mechanisms is that of establishing formal groups or roles to facilitate lateral relations between organizational units (Galbraith, 1973). We can distinguish between three types of lateral roles and groups.

Boundary spanners. Boundary spanners are team members specifically tasked with liaising with one or more other units, to make sure there is not unbridled communication between team members on all kinds of issues (Gittell, 2002; Lanaj et al., 2013). This is "not usually a full-time responsibility but rather is done in conjunction with other activities" (Nadler & Tushman, 1997, p. 96).

Cross-unit teams. These are teams composed of members from different units, also referred to as task forces (Maltz & Kohli, 2000; Martin & Eisenhardt, 2010). These teams can be permanent or flexible and can address any issue or opportunity that crosses unit boundaries (Nadler & Tushman, 1997; Galbraith et al., 2002). Typically, these teams are needed to integrate efforts on a dimension that was not used as the grouping dimension. As an example, if grouping of tasks was done according to output (resulting in product group units), then cross-unit teams may be needed to integrate efforts for specific customers, to which several product group units are delivering. If formal decision-making is necessary, these teams can be supplemented by a cross-unit committee (Brown, 1999; Galbraith, 2010).

Integrating roles. In contrast to the boundary spanner, the integrating role is a full-time responsibility, usually accompanied by some formal authority and sometimes supported by a team. Typical integrating roles in organizations are program managers, account managers, and product managers (Nadler & Tushman, 1997; Stan & Puranam, 2017). Similar to cross-unit teams, integrating roles are often used to offset negatives of the grouping choices made. If several customer-oriented units use similar products, a product manager can cut across those units to coordinate on the product dimension. The extent of formal authority that an integrator has can vary. Typically, integrators have a 'dotted-line relationship' to the units they coordinate. This means they do not have formal authority over those units, but will have to use other means to achieve their coordinating objectives. Galbraith (2014) mentions means such as their position in the organization (i.e., who they report to), their interpersonal and networking skills, and their access to data. If the integrator has full authority over the units she coordinates (the dotted line has become a solid line), we speak of dual authority relations, otherwise known as a matrix structure.

Matrix Structures: Reviled and Admired

The matrix structure is not so much a structure, as it is a coordinating mechanism in which an integrator is given formal authority. It is a way to combine two or more dimensions (activity, output, customer, geography) at the same level of the organization. One is used as the grouping dimension; the other is assigned to an integrator. For example, an employee may have to report to a country manager of the country unit they are in as well as a product manager for the product they are delivering. In this way, the matrix—or dual reporting relation—does away with one of the few design principles from scientific management (see Chap. 3) which is still considered common sense: unity of command. When using a matrix, there are people who have two bosses (although this usually is a small minority of the organization). This has shown to be a potential source of conflict (between managers), insecurity (on the part of employees), an overload of meetings, and bogged-down decision-making. Those are some of the reasons why matrix structures fell into disrepute in the 1990s after their 'invention' and initial success in the 1960s and 1970s at organizations such as NASA, Xerox, 3M, and Citibank. However, for some multinational organizations with a broad product portfolio, it is still an attractive option. And some of these big multinational firms have been successfully running a matrix for parts of their business for some time now. Important work has been done by Galbraith (2009), as well as Kesler and Kates (2016), in providing executives tools to successfully design and operate a matrix organization. The message here is that it should not be taken lightly. It requires management capabilities that may take years to develop. "Given its complexity and its inherent instability, a matrix structure should be reserved for situations in which no other linking alternative is workable" (Nadler & Tushman, 1997, p. 101). ◂

8.3.4 Informal Means of Coordinating

Several authors have pointed out that an important condition for achieving coordinated action is common understanding (Okhuysen & Bechky, 2009; Srikanth & Puranam, 2011; Pine & Mazmanian, 2017). Although the evidence about their effectiveness is mixed, informal means of coordinating can play an important role in achieving this common understanding, in concert with the other—more formal—linking mechanisms. They can be seen as the necessary organizational groundwork on top of which a design of linking mechanisms can be built. We can distinguish between three informal means of coordinating:

- Physical colocation of employees (Brown, 1999; Maltz & Kohli, 2000; Okhuysen & Bechky, 2009)
- Interpersonal/interdepartmental networking (Ghoshal et al., 1994; Jansen et al., 2009)
- Job rotations (Brown, 1999; Weigelt & Miller, 2013)

Why Not Simply Schedule a Meeting or Pick Up the Phone?

You may wonder why the default coordinating mechanism of a lot of organizations is not covered in this chapter: the meeting. Quite a few managers spend a large part of their day in meetings. An overload of meetings can be a clear sign of a design flaw in either grouping (too many interdependencies) or linking. Using the meeting as a linking mechanism "is a time-intensive solution that frequently crowds-out other work in the organization, pushing it to the evenings, weekends, or transactional space between meetings" (Schmitz, 2020, section The payoff of coordination). That is why simply scheduling a weekly meeting between two departments that have an interdependence is not the way to approach linking. A deliberate design effort is needed to choose the right linking mechanism for the most critical interdependencies. It may very well be that some of those mechanisms require meetings: a management process such as budgeting requires them, a cross-unit committee will want to meet, and an account manager will want to speak regularly with those dealing with 'her' clients in the product units she oversees. But all of these meetings are conducted within the framework of a specific linking mechanism, which means the goals of the meeting should be clear, as well as the responsibilities and authority of those present.

A second element you may be missing in this overview is what has been called mutual adjustment (Thompson, 1967), direct contact (Galbraith, 1977), or ongoing communication (Srikanth & Puranam, 2011). In other words, simply picking up the phone if two units experience an interdependence. Obviously, we assume that channels of communication are open in the organization in question. That is usually not the problem. The problem lies rather with an overload of communication—and meetings—to try to tie the efforts of an organization together. That is why well-designed linking mechanisms are needed as a framework inside which this communication—or relational coordination (Gittell, 2002)—can take place. Apart from these formal frameworks, informal means of coordinating (networking, job rotation, etc.) are also important foundations for effective communication: if I was in a training session with that fellow unit manager last month, it lowers to threshold to approach her about an issue that needs to be coordinated between our two units. ◀

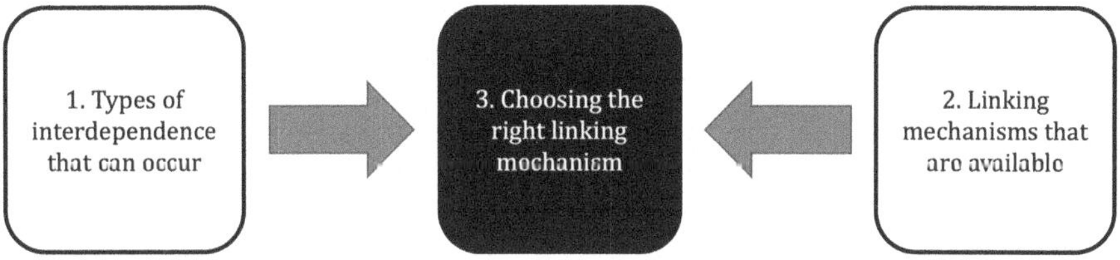

Fig. 8.10 The focus of this section: choosing the right linking mechanism

8.4 Choosing the Right Linking Mechanisms

Now that we have investigated interdependencies and linking mechanisms, it is time to connect the two: which linking mechanism should be used for which interdependence? (Fig. 8.10)

Two important considerations for this choice are mentioned in the literature:

- Linking mechanisms differ in terms of complexity and cost (time and energy spent on them); choose the least costly option that still adequately addresses the interdependence (Tushman & Nadler, 1978; Nadler & Tushman, 1997; Galbraith et al., 2002; Galbraith, 2014).
- Linking mechanisms differ in the extent to which they are formalized or prespecified; the higher the uncertainty is for a specific interdependence, the less formalized the linking mechanism should be (Argote, 1982; Daft & Lengel, 1986; Gittell, 2002).

So, the first thing we need is an ordering of the linking mechanisms according to their cost and their formality. These two dimensions lead to the graph shown in Fig. 8.11.

Three points about the graph in Fig. 8.11 are important. The first is that this mapping of linking mechanisms assumes there is already a foundation of informal means of coordinating present in the organization. We assume that this is out of scope of our linking design effort. The second point is that 'authority' is qualified as expensive here because the assumption at this point in the design is that there is no hierarchy of graded authority yet. Instituting this is a design choice, which has a relatively high cost associated with it (hiring managers and directors who are paid to perform noncore work). The third point is that this graph shows important limitations to the linking mechanisms we have available to us: most of them are relatively formal (hence less suited for high uncertainty interdependencies), and some of them are also quite expensive. This shows us again how important it is to design a

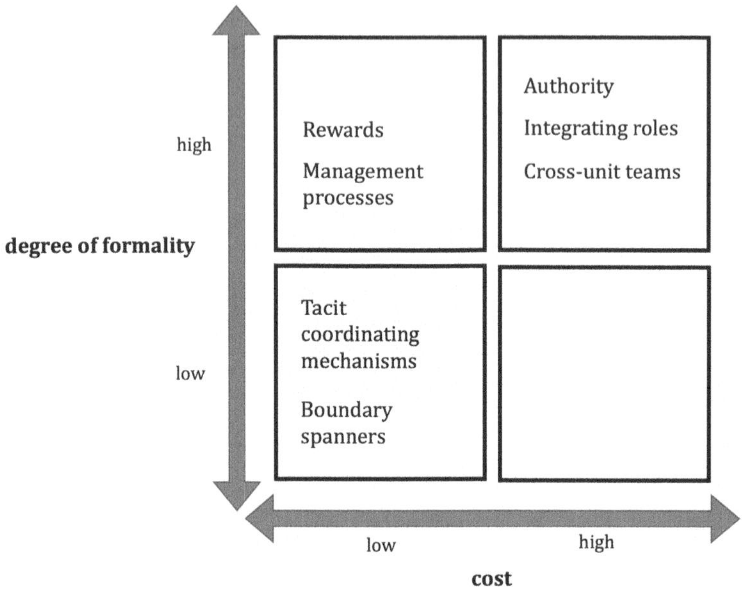

Fig. 8.11 The linking mechanisms mapped according to their relative formality and cost

structure (through grouping, see previous chapter) that reduces the amount of interdependencies between units. We have also seen that this will never completely eliminate the need for linking. So, linking mechanisms, despite their cost, are still a necessity.

We will now discuss the appropriate application of the various linking mechanism. It is important to realize that this discussion can only supply general guidance. The design choices for linking will have to be made based on the design criteria, the specific context of the organization, and the way in which the linking mechanism will be operationalized (one management process can be more formal than the other). In addition, it is not uncommon to use more than one linking mechanism to address a particular interdependence.

8.4.1 Using Authority and Rewards as Linking Mechanisms

As we have seen earlier on in this chapter, authority can be a useful linking mechanism that may be able to address some of the critical interdependencies in an organization. Let us unpack what using authority as a linking mechanism looks like in practice. First of all, we can take as a given that the owners or supervisors of the organization have placed formal authority in one or more actors at the top of the organization, typically the Chief Executive Officer (CEO), perhaps flanked by a Chief Financial Officer (CFO). Let us also assume that the lowest-level units in the structure of the organization are self-sufficient (as the result of a successful grouping design). With regard to linking, we are then left with two questions:

- Which authority will the CEO delegate to other C-level roles or corporate staff units?
- At which hierarchical layers in the structure that was designed—if there are any—will the organization introduce a management layer?

To answer these questions from the perspective of linking, we have to look first at the extent of 'standards interdependence' we have identified (see Table 8.1). Critical interdependencies in that category will likely require authority. If we look at our example of NSP Insurance, we see that there are two interdependencies which will likely require authority: common HR practices and managing risks. Having a Chief Human Resources Officer (CHRO) and Chief Risk Officer (CRO) report to the CEO—each potentially supported by a team—is a possible solution to address these interdependencies.

Rewards as a linking mechanism often work in concert with authority; both can be based on the hierarchical structure present in the design. Rewards are particularly suited to address goal interdependence. In the example of NSP, we have a structure with three country units that each have to contribute to the corporate strategy of the organization. One way to address this goal interdependence is to specify how the contribution of each country unit can be measured and to then create three leadership roles (e.g., Country Directors) whose incentives are tied to this contribution. By choosing this solution, we have created an additional management layer for NSP Insurance at the country unit level. This layer of Country Directors can then be made responsible for translating the country-level goals down to the units below and addressing any goal interdependencies that may exist at that lower level.

Other types of interdependence can also be addressed by authority, but it is worthwhile to explore less costly and less formalized linking mechanisms first. The extent to which instilling authority and creating management layers is a preferred solution differs greatly from one organization to the next. For some it is a given that the hierarchical levels in the structure will translate to management layers, while other organizations are allergic to management hierarchies and try to avoid layers at all cost. The approach in this book is meant to structure and objectivize this discussion as much as possible. An important compass in the discussion is a specification of the need for control and oversight in the design criteria.

Reporting Lines and Spans of Control

If an organization uses authority as a linking mechanism, this link will take the form of a reporting line: in our example of NSP, the Country Directors, the CHRO, and the CRO all report to the CEO; in other words: they are her direct reports. That means we could finally draw an organization chart with boxes connected by lines (Fig. 8.12, one of the very few organization charts you will encounter in this book). However, as the reader will by now be aware, that diagram will tell us precious little. If authority is installed, the role and extent of that authority needs to be made explicit. The minimum of what Fig. 8.12 implies is that the CEO handles dispute resolution for her direct reports. If the CRO and one of the Country Directors cannot come to an agreement, it is the CEO who has the final call. The organization chart also implies that the CHRO and CRO are authorized to issue and enforce standards on behalf of the CEO. From those starting points, there is still a wide spectrum of autonomy available to the country directors: from highly autonomous, with the CEO only monitoring quarterly figures, to low autonomy, with a CEO involved in their daily operations. What exactly is delegated down the reporting line, and how that impacts the authority instilled in the various leadership roles, needs to be made explicit as part of the operational design (see Chap. 9). It cannot be read from an organization chart. Elliott Jaques' Stratified Systems Theory (see Chap. 4) offers a guideline for designing these levels of authority: make sure that each has a distinct time span.

Reporting lines also bring us to one of the eternal questions in organization design: what is the right span of control (number of direct reports) for this manager? The only right answer is of course: it depends. It depends on how much direction or coaching the direct reports need, how many disputes and exceptions need to be resolved, how good the metrics to measure the performance of the direct reports are, and how much time the manager has available to manage besides their other tasks: the CEO may have responsibilities toward external stakeholders, and some managers may also be individual contributors ('player-coaches') or be involved in cross-unit task forces. All of these factors, combined with the manager's own experience in the role, determine whether a given span of control is realistic.[5] ◄

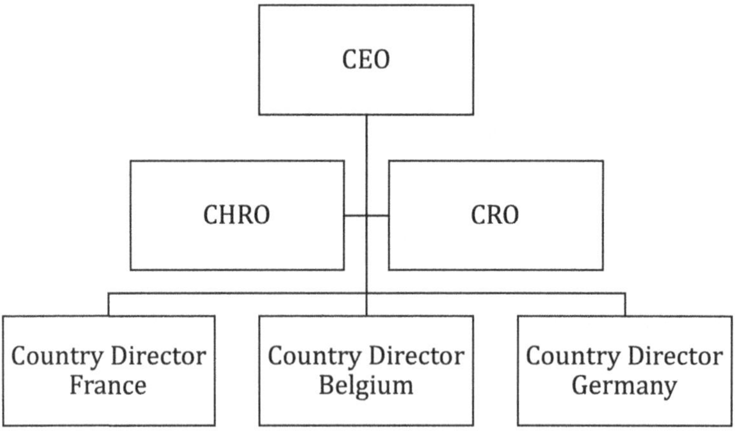

Fig. 8.12 Partial organization chart for NSP Insurance

[5] See Khaddamallah (2017) for a context-sensitive framework to assess and discuss spans of control.

8.4.2 Using Management Processes as Linking Mechanisms

Management processes are essential as the glue or cement—pick your metaphor—that holds an organization together. It is hard to imagine an organization that does not have management processes, even though other terms may be used to refer to them. Even the most radically decentralized organizations we have seen in Chap. 5—such as Haier and Hyperloop Transportation Technologies—have some management processes in place to make sure the right connections are made between the teams. Even though we classified management processes as formal in Fig. 8.11, that does not mean they cannot be used in environments that require flexibility. The formality pertains to the pre-specified steps that need to be taken. The content and actors involved, however, can be highly flexible. Haier has predefined rules that facilitate the internal contracting between microenterprises (MEs), but does not prescribe which services or which MEs to contract. The quarterly business review meetings at ING are conducted according to a prescribed format, but there is room for a large variety of participants, content, and outcomes in the discussion. At one of the consulting firms I worked for, we had a management process in place to screen every lead or request for proposal and to make sure it landed with the right unit and was not appropriated by the manager who happened to receive it. The process was prescribed, but it was highly flexible in dealing with all types of client requests.

As we see in these examples, management processes can be a good alternative to authority to address several types of interdependencies: goal interdependence (the quarterly business review at ING), resource interdependence and task interdependence (internal contracting at Haier), and front-end interdependence (the screening process at the consulting firm). At our NSP Insurance example, a management process was put in place to make sure the IT and facility management teams are able to adequately prioritize and allocate their support for the three product group units. In addition, a client management process was put in place to make sure the teams delivering noninsurance products are able to leverage the client base of the insurance products teams.

8.4.3 Using Tacit Coordinating Mechanisms and Boundary Spanners as Linking Mechanisms

We classified tacit coordinating mechanisms as low on cost and low on formality. Low on formality does not mean that nothing is documented. As a matter of fact, codified routines or standardized technical language can lie at the base of tacit coordinating mechanisms, as we have seen, as can using technology to register and convey the work status. But only to the extent that they economize on the need for communication between the interdependent units. Tacit coordinating mechanisms can be a good way to address task interdependence. Because of its relatively low cost and high flexibility, addressing task interdependence through tacit coordinating mechanisms should always be explored as an option. Where more extensive communication is necessary between the interdependent units in question, the tacit coordinating mechanism can be supplemented by boundary spanners. In our example of NSP Insurance, the use of an integrated IT system was enough to manage the task interdependence between the 'marketing, sales, and pricing and underwriting' teams and the 'claims management' teams. Each team had a member who took the role of boundary spanner, to periodically liaise with the other team about issues that arose and performance improvements that the two units needed to collaborate on. Operational problems were of course handled by simply picking up the phone or walking over to the other team.

8.4.4 Using Cross-Unit Teams and Integrating Roles as Linking Mechanisms

A relatively expensive, but very common, way to manage interdependencies is to create cross-unit teams or integrating roles. These linking mechanisms are particularly suited for task interdependence, resource interdependence, and front-end interdependence. But they should only be used if the lower-cost alternatives—management processes, tacit coordinating mechanisms, and boundary spanners—are not sufficient to address the interdependencies in question.

The example of ING (see Chap. 5) shows that it is sometimes difficult to distinguish between the teams that are a result of the grouping choices made (i.e., the structure) and the teams that are used as a linking mechanism. Following Mintzberg's conceptualization of the adhocracy and Galbraith's conceptualization of the multi-dimensional organization (see Chap. 5), it is the 'home base' of employees that indicates the structure. In the case of ING, that would make the 'chapter'—which represents a discipline such as product development or software engineering—the result of grouping (by the activity dimension) and the squad the result of linking. But as this example shows, in some cases the linking mechanism of creating cross-unit teams—especially when they have a semipermanent nature—can become a prominent feature of the organization design and can mitigate the negatives of choices made in the design of the structure.[6]

At our example of NSP Insurance, cross-unit teams were seen as a good way to address the task interdependence between the central product development unit and the product group units in the different countries. The product development unit needed the intelligence about client requirements and other environmental factors that these local units had, in order to decide which new products or services to investigate and test. In addition, members of the product development unit knew that they could never successfully implement new products if they would not involve the local product units in their development work. That is why cross-unit teams were set

[6] It is of course also possible to turn this around. If we group according to output—say, according to the different modules of a software product that the company sells—the result would likely be units that are to some extent cross-functional. The remaining interdependence would then be a knowledge interdependence, with developers in different units wanting to exchange best practices.

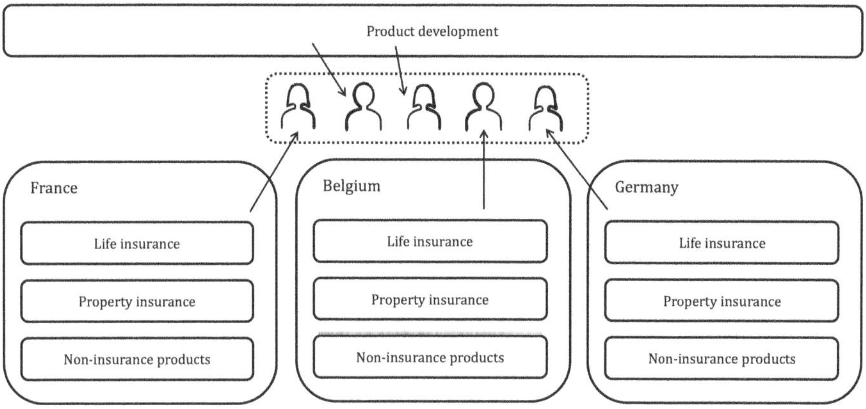

Fig. 8.13 A simplified representation of a cross-unit team at NSP Insurance (icons by Ralf Schmitzer from the Noun Project)

up to address specific opportunities, composed of employees who had local customer and product knowledge—and who contributed part of their time to these teams while remaining based in their local product unit—combined with experts from the product development group (see Fig. 8.13). Sometimes these teams would be supplemented by representatives of customers or partners, to bring in fresh perspectives and potential sources of collaboration.

Running Versus Changing the Business

Throughout the grouping and linking work, attention should be paid to how the tension between running and changing the business (Nieto-Rodriguez, 2014) plays out in the design, otherwise referred to as exploitation versus exploration (Lavie et al., 2010). Like any aspect of the design, the importance of addressing this tension should be expressed in the design criteria. As we saw in Chap. 4, there are two fundamental options for managing this tension. One is to separate the two tasks. We can do this by acknowledging the exploration task as part of the value chain that forms the basis for the grouping work (see Chap. 7) and subsequently allocating it in the most fitting way. The second option is to combine both orientations (exploration and exploitation) inside the same organizational unit. If this second option is chosen, the tension needs to be managed by using linking mechanisms. Typical linking mechanisms would be a combination of management processes and cross-unit teams (as in the NSP Insurance example described in this section). ◀

At NSP Insurance, no integrating roles were necessary. The front-end interdependence that existed between the life insurance and property insurance units in each of the countries—the wish to have one face to the customer—was managed by a committee (a specific form of cross-unit team). This committee consisted of the Country Director and an (elected) representative from each of the two product units. Any issues that arose between the product units with regard to this front-end interdependence were discussed and decided upon in this forum. If needed, the Country Director made the final call.

8.4.5 Addressing the Interdependencies That Remain

You may have noticed that we have not yet said much about how to address knowledge interdependencies. That is because the linking mechanisms discussed in this chapter are ill-suited to address knowledge interdependencies: "the problem of knowledge transfer and that of ongoing coordination are quite distinct and require different solutions" (Srikanth & Puranam, 2011, p. 865). It is of course possible to create an integrating role that addresses knowledge interdependencies such as an Engineering Leader or a Chief Knowledge Officer. However, if developing and bundling expertise is such an important design criterion for the organization, should that not have been reflected in the grouping choices made? Grouping units according to activity bundles expertise in a much more effective way than an integrating role—or a matrix structure—ever could. That is the reason why Apple—rather counterintuitively—has structured itself along the activity dimension (Podolny & Hansen, 2020).

The best way to address any knowledge interdependencies that remain—and any of the other interdependencies that were not deemed critical—is to rely on the informal means of coordinating. Facilitating interpersonal networking, job rotations, and, where possible, physical colocation will serve as a necessary foundation for any of the other linking mechanisms.

Informal Means of Coordinating While Working from Home

The COVID-19 pandemic has meant that a lot of organizations have reconsidered the extent to which physical presence at the office is necessary for their employees. While this forced time away from the office showed many people that a lot more could be done remotely than they had thought possible, it also showed some clear limitations. In the context of this chapter, the good news is that none of the linking mechanisms described are particularly impacted by remote working. All of them can be applied in remote settings. One might even say that deliberately designing linking mechanisms—rather than leaving coordination to be resolved in ad hoc communication and meetings—makes an organization less dependent on where its employees are physically located. The bad news is that the important foundation of informal means of coordinating suffers from remote working, because it benefits so from physical proximity. Networking, getting to know each other, and chance encounters are more difficult with everyone working from home or in a home/office hybrid setting. Organizations that have had extensive pre-COVID experience working remotely may offer clues as to how the informal aspects can be addressed in a remote setting. GitLab is such a firm, which has therefore recently been the subject of scholarly attention (Choudhury et al., 2020). ◄

This concludes our discussion of the core of the strategic design work: grouping (previous chapter) and linking (this chapter). The next and final chapter of the book talks about the work that remains, once the core of the design work has been completed.

Review Questions

1. Can you think of an organization that does not have any goal interdependence? What does such an organization look like?
2. Can you think of an organization that does not have any task interdependence? What does such an organization look like?
3. If front-end interdependence exists, do you think there is also such a thing as back-end interdependence? Why or why not?
4. Take an organization you are familiar with in mind. Which type of interdependence (of the six categories mentioned in this chapter) do you think is most prevalent? Why do think that is?
5. Do you think the use of authority is the best way to resolve disputes? Why or why not?
6. What would some of the advantages be of placing a level of authority on each level of the structural hierarchy (see Fig. 8.9)? What would some of the disadvantages be?
7. Take an organization you are familiar with in mind. What are some of the things you think need to be enforced by authority in this organization?
8. Do you consider authority to be an expensive linking mechanism? Why or why not?
9. Do you see any downsides to using rewards as a way to resolve cooperation problems in an organization? If so, what are they?
10. Name some of the management processes you think are important in an organization.
11. Do you consider management processes to be a formal linking mechanism? Why or why not?
12. Explain how codified routines could be considered a tacit coordinating mechanism.
13. What are some of the advantages of giving an integrating role extensive formal authority? And what are the downsides?

References

Argote, L. (1982). Input uncertainty and organizational coordination in hospital emergency units. *Administrative Science Quarterly, 27*(3), 420–434.

Argyres, N. S. (1999). The impact of information technology on coordination: Evidence from the B-2 "Stealth" Bomber. *Organization Science, 10*(2), 162–180.

Brown, C. V. (1999). Horizontal mechanisms under differing IS organization contexts. *MIS Quarterly, 23*(3), 421–454.

Choudhury, P., Crowston, K., Dahlander, L., Minervini, M. S., & Raghuram, S. (2020). GitLab: work where you want, when you want. *Journal of Organization Design, 9*(1), 1–17.

Daft, R. L., & Lengel, R. H. (1986). Organizational information requirements, media richness and structural design. *Management Science, 32*(5), 554–571.

Galbraith, J., Downey, D., & Kates, A. (2002). *Designing dynamic organizations: A hands-on guide for leaders at all levels*. Amacom.

Galbraith, J. R. (1973). *Designing complex organizations*. Addison-Wesley.

Galbraith, J. R. (1977). *Organization design*. Addison-Wesley.

Galbraith, J. R. (2009). *Designing matrix organizations that actually work*. Jossey-Bass.

Galbraith, J. R. (2010). The multi-dimensional and reconfigurable organization. *Organizational Dynamics, 39*(2), 115–125.

Galbraith, J. R. (2014). *Designing organizations: Strategy, structure, and process at the business unit and enterprise levels* (3rd ed.). Jossey-Bass.

Ghoshal, S., Korine, H., & Szulanski, G. (1994). Interunit communication in multinational corporations. *Management Science, 40*(1), 96–110.

Gittell, J. H. (2002). Coordinating mechanisms in care provider groups: Relational coordination as a mediator and input uncertainty as a moderator of performance effects. *Management Science, 48*(11), 1408–1426.

Hamel, G., & Zanini, M. (2018). The end of bureaucracy: How a Chinese appliance maker is reinventing management for the digital age. *Harvard Business Review, 96*(6), 50–59.

Jansen, J. J. P., Tempelaar, M. P., Van den Bosch, F. A. J., & Volberda, H. W. (2009). Structural differentiation and ambidexterity: The mediating role of integration mechanisms. *Organization Science, 20*(4), 797–811.

Kesler, G., & Kates, A. (2016). *Bridging organization design and performance: 5 ways to activate a global operating model*. John Wiley & Sons.

Khaddamallah, A. (2017). *What about my span of control? Assessing a supervisor's span of control using its determinants and quality indicators*. Rotterdam School of Management. http://hdl.handle.net/2105/40127.

Kretschmer, T., & Puranam, P. (2008). Integration through incentives within differentiated organizations. *Organization Science, 19*(6), 860–875.

Kumar, K., Van Fenema, P. C., & Von Glinow, M. A. (2009). Offshoring and the global distribution of work: Implications for task interdependence theory and practice. *Journal of International Business Studies, 40*(4), 642–667.

Laloux, F. (2014). *Reinventing organizations: A guide to creating organizations inspired by the next stage of human consciousness*. Nelson Parker.

Lanaj, K., Hollenbeck, J. R., Ilgen, D. R., Barnes, C. M., & Harmon, S. J. (2013). The double-edged sword of decentralized planning in multiteam systems. *The Academy of Management Journal, 56*(3), 735–757.

Lavie, D., Stettner, U., & Tushman, M. L. (2010). Exploration and exploitation within and across organizations. *The Academy of Management Annals, 4*(1), 109–155.

Maltz, E., & Kohli, A. K. (2000). Reducing marketing's conflict with other functions: The differential effects of integrating mechanisms. *Journal of the Academy of Marketing Science, 28*(4), 479–492.

March, J. G., & Simon, H. A. (1958). *Organizations*. John Wiley.

Martin, J. A., & Eisenhardt, K. M. (2010). Rewiring: Cross-business-unit collaborations in multi-business organizations. *The Academy of Management Journal, 53*(2), 265–301.

McCann, J. E., & Ferry, D. L. (1979). An approach for assessing and managing inter-unit interdependence. *The Academy of Management Review, 4*(1), 113–119.

Monsen, K., & De Blok, J. (2013). Buurtzorg Nederland. *The American Journal of Nursing, 113*(8), 55–59.

Nadler, D. A., & Tushman, M. L. (1997). *Competing by design: The power of organizational architecture*. Oxford University Press.

Nieto-Rodriguez, A. (2014). Ambidexterity Inc. *Business Strategy Review, 25*(3), 34–39.

Okhuysen, G. A., & Bechky, B. A. (2009). Coordination in organizations: An integrative perspective. *The Academy of Management Annals, 3*(1), 463–502.

Pine, K. H., & Mazmanian, M. (2017). Artful and contorted coordinating: The ramifications of imposing formal logics of task jurisdiction on situated practice. *Academy of Management Journal, 60*(2), 720–742.

Podolny, J. M., & Hansen, M. T. (2020). How Apple is organized for innovation. *Harvard Business Review, 98*(6), 86–95.

Puranam, P. (2018). *The microstructure of organizations*. Oxford University Press.

Puranam, P., Alexy, O., & Reitzig, M. (2014). What's "new" about new forms of organizing? *The Academy of Management Review, 39*(2), 162–180.

Puranam, P., Raveendran, M., & Knudsen, T. (2012). Organization design: The epistemic interdependence perspective. *Academy of Management Review, 37*(3), 419–440.

Schmitz, D. (2020). *How task uncertainty plays into the social and technical coordination of work*. Retrieved March 26, 2021, from https://blog.on-the-mark.com/blog/social-and-technical-coordination-of-work

Simon, H. A. (1996). *The sciences of the artificial* (3rd ed.). The MIT Press.

Srikanth, K., & Puranam, P. (2011). Integrating distributed work: comparing task design, communication, and tacit coordination mechanisms. *Strategic Management Journal, 32*(8), 849–875.

Stan, M., & Puranam, P. (2017). Organizational adaptation to interdependence shifts: The role of integrator structures. *Strategic Management Journal, 38*(5), 1041–1061.

The Sociocracy Group. (2021). *4 principles*. Retrieved January 31, 2021, from https://thesociocracygroup.com/4-principles/

Thompson, J. D. (1967). *Organizations in action: Social science bases of administrative theory*. McGraw-Hill.

Tushman, M. L., & Nadler, D. A. (1978). Information processing as an integrating concept in organizational design. *The Academy of Management Review, 3*(3), 613–624.

Weigelt, C., & Miller, D. J. (2013). Implications of internal organization structure for firm boundaries. *Strategic Management Journal, 34*(12), 1411–1434.

Worren, N. (2017). The matrix as a transitory form: The evolution of FMC technologies 2001-2016. *Journal of Organization Design, 6*(1), 1–14.

Worren, N. (2018). *Organization design: Simplifying complex systems* (2nd ed.). Routledge.

How to Prepare for the Transition 9

Abstract

Once the strategic design has been completed, it should be submitted to an impact assessment. The outputs of the impact assessment will be points of refinement for the strategic design and the issues to be addressed in the detailed operational design and transition plan. The impact assessment consists of a theoretical test and a practical test of the organization design. The latter takes the form of a 'stress test' in which business scenarios are used to explore the consequences and potential shortcomings of the design. If, based on the results of the impact assessment, the steering committee decides to take the strategic design forward, a detailed operational design needs to be produced. Two important elements of the operational design are the size and composition of the teams that will populate the structure and the governance model; the latter pertains to leadership roles and management processes. In addition to the operational design, the second deliverable of the 'prepare transition' stage is the transition plan. In it, the transition strategy needs to be described in terms of the choices for staging, pacing, sequencing, and governing the transition. In addition, the people processes that are associated with the transition need to be laid out.

Keywords

Organization design • Impact assessment • Operational design • Transition plan • Stress test • Governance model • People processes

J. van Bree, *Organization Design*, https://doi.org/10.1007/978-3-030-78679-3_9

Learning Objectives

- Perform an impact assessment of an organization design.
- Understand the role of an impact assessment in the organization design approach.
- List the major components of an operational design.
- Understand the nature and extent of design work needed to produce an operational design.
- Identify the necessary management and leadership roles in an organization design.
- Make recommendations with regard to the choices for staging, pacing, sequencing, and governing the transition to a new organization design.
- Identify the people processes which should be addressed in the transition to a new organization design.
- Compare and contrast project design with continuous design.

In the previous two chapters, we covered the core of the organization design work: grouping and linking. The result is a strategic design, which addresses all the major features of the future state of the organization: the way it is structured and the way in which the units in that structure will be linked. In terms of Galbraith's Star model (see Chap. 2), we have now covered task, structure, information and decision processes, and—depending on the linking mechanisms chosen—an outline of reward systems. The strategic design is an important milestone, but it is not the end of the organization design effort. Before this design can be implemented, three activities remain:

- Performing an impact assessment on the strategic design
- Designing the necessary operational details
- Planning the transition

These activities will be the main focus of this chapter. To close out this chapter and this book, we will look at what needs to happen after the transition to a new organization design has been completed. Figure 9.1 shows the stages of the design approach covered in this chapter.

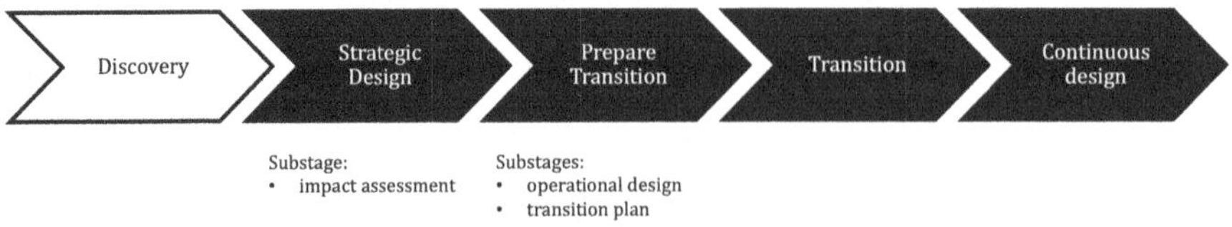

Fig. 9.1 The stages of the design approach covered in this chapter

9.1 Impact Assessment of the Strategic Design

Once the strategic design has been completed, it is necessary to assess what the impact on the organization will be of transitioning to this desired future state. The intent here is not to evaluate several design options in order to make a choice between them. In the approach described in this book, generating, evaluating, and eliminating design options is done throughout the strategic design stage. As the design team goes through the grouping and linking stages, they will use the compass of the design criteria and the boundaries of the design conditions to explore and refine options, in an iterative process. By the end of the strategic design stage, they will have landed on the optimal design. Because the design team forms a representative cross-section of the organization (see Chap. 6), many implicit impact assessments will have been made by that time, in the context of their design workshops. Still, a more explicit impact assessment is necessary to close of the strategic design work and to form a bridge to operational design and transition planning. The impact assessment will have three outputs (Nadler & Tushman, 1997):

1. Points of refinement for the strategic design, if appropriate
2. Issues to be addressed in the detailed operational design
3. Issues to be considered in planning for transition

Although it is highly unlikely at this stage—if the design work was conducted diligently—the option of outright rejection of the organization design should not be ruled out. It is possible that the design team or the steering committee had a blind spot that comes to light in the impact assessment as a distinct downside of the design. What is a slightly more likely option is that the design itself is not the problem, but the impact of transitioning to this new design is deemed too big in relation to the expected benefits. In both cases—rejection of the design or rejection of the transition—the steering committee can either ask the design team to go through another iteration of design work, or they can bring the project to a close. Because it is such an important go/no-go moment, the impact assessment work should be conducted with care. It consists of two parts: a theoretical test and a practical test.

9.1.1 Theoretical Test of the Organization Design

The first test of the organization design is against the design criteria. As we saw, the design criteria should be part of the discussion throughout the grouping and linking stages. Even so, it is helpful to do a formal evaluation against the design criteria, once the strategic design has been completed. The design team can do this by awarding a score to each of the design criteria, to indicate how well the design meets this requirement, and supplementing this with a brief justification of the score. It is a way for the design team to document how close they came to fulfilling the design goals that were set by the steering committee. It may raise issues that can be addressed in the detailed operational design. In addition, it may offer a basis for documenting the rationale of the design, in order to be able to communicate it to stakeholders who were not involved in the design process.

Table 9.1 Key questions for the impact assessment (based on Nadler & Tushman, 1997; Galbraith et al., 2002)

Aspect	Questions
People	What will the impact of the design be on the fit between the requirements of the work and the capacities of individuals? What are the leadership skills, talent, and experience that are required to run this design?
Behavior	To what extent does the design facilitate or motivate needed behavior? What will the impact of the design be on the organizational culture (values and beliefs)? What will the impact of the design be on communication and influence patterns?
Stakeholders	Will the design create significant power shifts inside the organization? To what extent will the design raise issues with external stakeholders?
Cost	To what extent will the design require additions or reallocations of people, capital, technology, or other resources? How extensive will the (direct or indirect) implementation costs of the design be?

The second part of the theoretical test is to subject the organization design to a list of questions that address its potential consequences (positive or negative). Some key questions are listed in Table 9.1. This list should be seen as a starting point; other questions may be relevant for a specific organization. Much like the test against the design criteria, the answers to these questions will show issues to be addressed in the operational design or transition planning. In addition, the combined answers to these questions will give an indication of how easy or hard it will be to implement the new design, in other words: how big is the gap between current situation and desired future state?

9.1.2 Practical Test of the Organization Design: The Stress Test

As we saw in Chap. 6, including a form of prototyping improves the quality of the organization design process. This prototyping will be conducted informally throughout the grouping and linking stages, but especially in the early stages of grouping when different grouping dimensions and different options for grouping are being explored by the design team. During the impact assessment, a more structured way of prototyping needs to be conducted: the stress test. This is loosely based on what game designers describe as 'playtesting' (Van Bree, 2014). Game designers do their first rounds of playtesting as they are designing the rules of the game, much like the small-scale prototyping done by the organization design team during grouping. Later in the game design process, a paper prototype of the game is produced that can be playtested independently by players, without close supervision by the game designers. A similar stage should be reached by the time the strategic organization design is finished: people who have not been involved in the design process should be able to comprehend the organization design and be able to test it by letting

Table 9.2 The steps in preparation and facilitation of an organization design stress test

Stage	Activity	Responsible
Preparation	Decide which stakeholders to invite (can be up to a hundred participants or more, with the right facilitation)	Steering committee
	Invite participants, explain the intent of the session, and ask them to submit (short, several-sentence) business scenarios they would like to use for the stress test	Design team or consultant team
	Select the ten business scenarios to use in the stress test, a good mix of day-to-day situations and exceptions, as broadly across the value chain of the organization as possible	Design team
Facilitation	Present the strategic design, stressing the scenarios will be run against this new design, not against the current situation	Design team
	Split the participants up into small breakout groups, each joined by a member of the design team to answer any questions about the design	Consultant team
	Supply a format for a structured walk-through of the scenarios: for example, answering the questions 'who does what?', 'who decides what?', and 'who talks to whom?'	Consultant team
	Have each breakout group go through the same scenarios and have them document their findings	Consultant team
	Have a brief plenary report back by each breakout group, and identify the main threads in the vulnerabilities that were found in the design	Consultant team
	Optional: do a second round of breakouts with the focus on ways to address the vulnerabilities found	Consultant team

workflows, customer journeys, or business scenarios run through it. This stress test is the ideal moment to start familiarizing a larger group of stakeholders with the organization design than just the design team (and the people the design team members have spoken with). Table 9.2 lists the steps for conducting an effective stress test. Responsibilities for the steps are shared among the three groups identified in the approach of this book (see Chap. 6): the steering committee, the design team, and the (internal or external) consultant team.

With all the information collected in the theoretical and practical tests of the organization design, the design team should be able to produce an impact assessment report for the steering committee.

▶ **The Impact Assessment Report Should Contain Answers to a Number of Questions**

- To what extent will the organization design achieve what was intended?
- What will the impact of implementing the design be on people, behavior, stakeholders, and cost?
- Is any refinement of the strategic design necessary before the project can proceed to the next stage?
- Which issues need to be addressed in the detailed operational design?
- Which issues need to be considered in planning for transition?

Based on this report, the steering committee can decide to stay in the strategic design stage a little longer (for another design iteration), to proceed to the next stage (prepare transition), or to shelve the organization design, because they consider the negative impacts to exceed the potential benefits. Again, this latter option is unlikely if the design process was conducted carefully. But it should not be ruled out.

9.2 The Operational Design

If the steering committee decides to take the strategic design forward, the design project proceeds into the 'prepare transition' stage. This is the stage in which the high-level decisions that were made as part of the strategic design need to be translated to a more detailed, operational design. These details are necessary to be able to make the transition. We need to know which activities go where in the new situation, who will be responsible for what, how teams are composed, and what accountabilities new leadership roles will have, to name but a few aspects. Even though we warned against 'overdesign' in Chap. 4, these are key aspects of the design that need to be documented in this stage, to prevent confusion or even chaos during the transition.

Because the major design decisions were made during the strategic design stage, the operational design work will have a different nature. The framework has been established, and now each element of that framework (structure, teams, roles, processes, etc.) needs to be operationalized. This work is less creative in nature than the strategic design work, and it will also require more effort. While a design team can develop a high-level structure in one or several sessions, specifying all the teams in this structure, their size, and the roles involved will be a lot more work. Because the framework has been set, this detailed work is suited for a divergent approach, where several work groups are formed that work independently and in parallel on specific aspects of the operational design. A typical way to divide the work between these work groups is to have each work on the operational design of a specific part of the organization, for example, one of the macro-level or meso-level groups identified in the grouping stage. Similar to the design team—as we saw in Chap. 6—these work groups need to form a representative cross-section of the part of the organization they are designing. Furthermore, as is the case with the design team, work group participants are asked to take a constructive and future-oriented mindset and to place the interests of the organization above their own (or those of their department).

The connection between these work groups and the design team that conducted the strategic design stage is essential. In some cases, the design team will be discharged and disbanded at the end of the strategic design stage. If that is the case, an extensive briefing of the work groups by representatives of the design team is necessary at the start of the operational design work. If members of the design team are available to continue their work into the prepare transition stage, it can be beneficial to have a representative of the design team in each of the work groups. The consultant team could also play a role in making sure the strategic design framework is

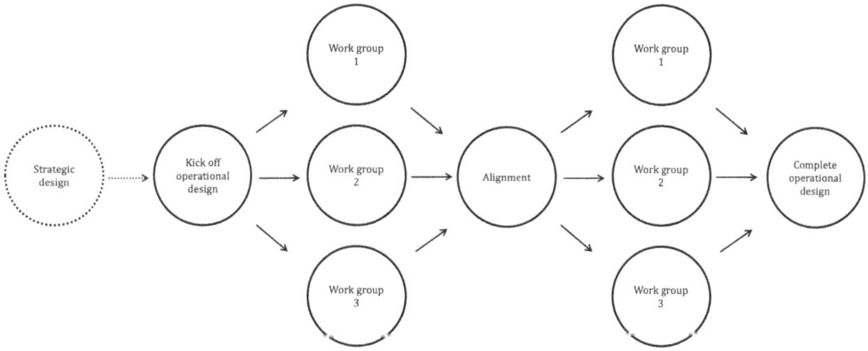

Fig. 9.2 The divergence-convergence approach in working on the operational design

interpreted and carried forward in the right way. Either way, the steering committee needs to ensure there is some form of design governance during the operational design work, to keep the operational design inside the boundaries set by the strategic design and to keep the work groups connected. In addition, a moment of convergence at the end of the operational design work is important to fit the deliverables of the work groups back together, perform the necessary alignment, and come to a collective decision about the complete operational design. It may be beneficial to have one or more additional moments of convergence, depending on the extent and planning of the operational design work. Fig. 9.2 shows this divergence-convergence approach in the operational design stage.

While the exact topics and depth of the operational design are dependent on the appetite for detail that the organization in question has, it should contain at least two important elements, which we will cover in the sections to follow. They are the necessary specifications of the results of the grouping stage and the linking stage, respectively:

- The size and composition of the teams
- The governance model

9.2.1 Size and Composition of the Teams

The grouping stage (see Chap. 7) resulted in the design of the structure of the organization. The structure was documented in the form of a diagram that showed the units and sub-units that the organization is composed of, a listing of the tasks each of these (sub-)units is responsible for, the outcomes it is accountable for, and the key decisions it is authorized to make. The way of working during the grouping stage was that we kept sub-dividing units until we reached a level where the sub-units—as a collection of tasks—could be assigned to one team (of less than 20 employees). In the operational design, the teams that will be populating this structure need to be specified in terms of their composition—which roles are part of the team—and in terms of their size.

Team composition. Typically, designing the composition of each team will be a combination of moving existing roles into the team, adapting some existing roles, and creating new roles. The responsibilities—including ancillary tasks—and

Does Each Team Need a Team Lead?

Special attention is required for management jobs. The need for a formal management job in the team—a team lead or operational manager—depends on elements such as the size of the team, their type of work and type of expertise, and the guidelines for the organization design as expressed in the design criteria or other design conditions. If the principles and approach of this book are followed, the resultant teams should be self-sufficient and thus should be able to manage themselves (as we saw in Chap. 7). However, even though it can be a costly solution, there may be valid reasons to add a management role to the team:

- Organizations may require operational oversight or direction of (some of) their teams.
- Organizations may not want to allocate the ancillary tasks—such as planning and scheduling work and doing performance reviews—to the core team members, because that is not considered the best use of their time.
- Organizations may want to make sure team members receive adequate coaching in their work.
- Organizations may feel there is a need for someone to make the final call if a team cannot reach a decision.

The latter two reasons do not necessarily require a formal management role. There are alternatives such as a 'player-coach' (a team member who is responsible for core work but also takes on team lead responsibilities), a team coach who helps several teams where needed (such as an Agile coach at ING or a regional coach at Buurtzorg), or a leadership role placed at a distance from the teams, to handle disputes and exceptions.

It is important to note that a team management role is not necessary to represent the team to a higher level in the management hierarchy. This can be done by an elected delegate, as is common in Sociocracy and Holacracy (see Chap. 5). Nor is a team lead necessary to represent the team laterally, to other teams. Any team member can take this linking role of 'boundary spanner' (see Chap. 8). But as noted with the ancillary tasks above, an organization may decide that this (vertical and horizontal) linking work is not the best use of the team members' time, which may warrant a separate management role. ◄

[1] This text does not offer specific guidance for job design. Lowlands SocioTechnical Systems Design (De Sitter et al., 1997; Kuipers et al., 2020) and Job Characteristics Theory (Hackman & Oldham, 1976; Hackman & Wageman, 2005; Oldham & Hackman, 2010) offer great resources for designing roles and jobs, in line with the design philosophy of this book.

outcomes of the unit form the starting point for moving, adapting, or designing the roles that will make up the team.[1]

Size of the team. Determining the right size of the teams that constitute the structure can be a difficult task. In some rare cases, there is a clearly quantifiable flow of work that a team needs to handle, such as orders processed or calls answered. In those situations, it is possible to calculate the size of the team based on the projected quantity of work and assumed productivity per team member. However, these situations are the exception. A typical starting point for sizing is the collection of roles that the team is made up of (see previous step). Based on the scope of work that the team takes on (e.g., which region, product, or customer segment they focus on), an attempt can be made to quantify each role in terms of full-time equivalents (fte's) and add this up to a total team size. Often, an organization can use current headcount numbers or benchmark data as a reference, although close attention should be paid to the changes in responsibilities. Roles may look quite different after a redesign, especially if ancillary or support tasks are allocated to the team, whereas they may have been the responsibility of dedicated departments in the previous design.

Although downsizing efforts are not suited for the collaborative organization design approach presented in this book, there may be conditions set by the steering committee with regard to the leeway for headcount numbers in the new design. This people cost aspect of the new design will have been investigated and addressed as part of the impact assessment, but these conditions should continue to be watched over during the operational design.

In the NSP Insurance example that was used in the previous chapters, we identified core teams that needed to handle the tasks of marketing, sales, and pricing and underwriting. Each of the teams performed these tasks for one product group (life insurance or property insurance) in one country. During the operational design, a generic set of roles was designed to perform these tasks. Then, based on the scope of work of each team, the size in terms of fte's was determined. The French market turned out to need a larger life insurance team than the comparable team in Germany, because the existing customer base in France was much bigger.

A different way to approach team sizes is to take them as a given and to only let the amount of work flow through them that the team can handle (with a rule of thumb for this amount). Cross-functional Agile teams often operate this way, with work being prioritized and time-boxed before the team takes it on. The neighborhood nursing teams at Buurtzorg work in a similar manner. Teams do not grow beyond the size of 12. If the number of patients in their neighborhood starts to exceed what they can handle, the team is split into two. The rule of thumb is 50 patients per team (Laloux, 2014). We saw a similar way of dealing with unit sizes—splitting when they become too big—with the cell philosophy at BSO/Origin (see Chap. 4) and at Vinci (see Chap. 5).

9.2.2 Governance Model

Whereas the size and composition of the teams is the necessary specification of the grouping work, the governance model forms the necessary specification of the linking work. The governance model flows from three specific linking mechanisms (see Chap. 8): authority, management processes, and integrating roles. The operational design of these linking mechanisms leads to two main deliverables: leadership roles and teams and a specification of the management processes required.

Leadership roles and leadership teams. As part of the linking stage of the strategic design, the extent and position of authority in the future organization was determined. Based on this, the organization chart can be drawn. In the example of NSP Insurance used in the previous chapters, we saw that at the highest level there were three Country Directors, a Chief Risk Officer, and a Chief HR Officer, who all report to the CEO. As part of the operational design, these leadership roles need to be specified in terms of their accountabilities (what outputs or results are they held accountable for) and responsibilities (which decisions are they authorized to make). Both accountabilities and responsibilities should flow from the description of the unit the leadership role is made responsible for. However, there may be specific responsibilities which have been allocated to staff units—such as HR or risk—or which fall to an integrating role, such as a product manager. Some responsibility charting (Galbraith et al., 2002) will be necessary to avoid any overlaps or conflicts. In addition, some responsibilities may fall to a leadership team rather than an individual leadership role. In the example of NSP Insurance, the CEO and her five direct reports form the executive team, which has a joint responsibility for far-reaching decisions such as investments over a certain threshold or entering new markets. These leadership teams—or decision-making forums, if they are reconfigurable (Galbraith, 2010)—need to be specified in the operational design, in terms of their participants and mandate.[2] A common problem in organizations is that the leadership team—the top executive and her direct reports—do not form a team, because they have no joint responsibilities. Every leader sees themselves as responsible for their part of the business, and the leadership team meetings become a forum for exchanging views and updating each other, but not for taking decisions and jointly moving the organization forward. Only if the organization has a highly diversified nature—with leaders being responsible for independent companies, exploiting separate business models—would this type of dynamic be acceptable for a leadership team. Placing joint responsibilities and the associated metrics in the leadership team is a good place to start moving beyond this.

Management processes required. An important linking mechanism—present in pretty much any organization—is that of management processes. As part of the strategic design, the required management processes were identified and outlined.

[2] For a more extensive description of the design of this 'vertical structure' of management layers, see Chap. 6 of Worren (2018).

In the operational design stage, these management processes need to be specified further. They may also need to be populated with metrics. If a quarterly meeting is designed as a management process to review and align the objectives and results of teams, then the metrics that teams can use to measure their performance—their key performance indicators (kpi's), if you will—need to be defined as part of the operational design. In the NSP Insurance example, the strategic design included a client management process to make sure the teams delivering noninsurance products are able to leverage the client base of the insurance products teams. In the operational design stage, a number of representatives from each of the teams involved formed a work group to design this management process in more detail. When it comes to management processes, the danger of overdesign looms large. As we saw in the chapter on linking (Chap. 8), a maximum of three to five key management processes should be specified as part of the organization design. The rest can be left to the organization to deal with during and after transition to the new design.

9.3 The Transition Plan

With the completion of the operational design, the new organization design has been specified to a level that makes it ready for implementation. But before the steering committee can decide whether or not they want to give the go-ahead for the transition to this new design—a crucial stage gate in an organization design project—the transition itself needs to be planned and prepared. This results in the transition plan, which is the second key deliverable of the 'prepare transition' stage. The transition plan consists of two key elements, which we will cover in this section:

- The transition strategy: how to bridge the gap between current state and future organization design
- The people processes: the HR practices of hiring, developing, and promoting the right talent to successfully run the organizational model that was designed.

9.3.1 Transition Strategy

An important first point to make when it comes to the transition to a new design is that it does not start in the transition stage. The approach proposed in this book is one where a representative cross-section of the organization—the design team—is doing the design work and acts as ambassadors and key conduits for the design process to the rest of the organization. This means a relatively large time investment is made by the organization to develop the strategic and operational design. This investment should start to pay off in the transition stage. Compared to a more expert-driven design process that involves a small group, the approach proposed here ensures that a large group of employees and managers have had a voice in the design, are aware of the rationale and the trade-offs that are inherent in it, and understand why other design options were discarded. Transitioning to a new organization design is very much a process of collaborative sensemaking (Jelinek et al., 2008):

the description of the design does not come to life until people start imagining and talking about what occupying it means for them. This is a process that takes time. The sooner this process of collaborative sensemaking starts, the easier the transition will be. If the kickoff of the transition is the first time anyone beyond the C-suite is exposed to the new design, the transition itself can be a long and costly road with rework, gaps being filled by middle managers (Livijn, 2019), and a great potential for resistance. These costs and delays during transition are what Dan Schmitz and his colleagues call 'making resistance payments', as opposed to 'making commitment payments' upfront by employing a collaborative design approach (Schmitz, 2021). Even when sufficient commitment payments have been made, a deliberate transition strategy will of course still be necessary. There are four dimensions of the transition that need to be considered: staging, pacing, sequencing, and governing.

Change Management

This is a book about organization design, not about organizational change. Please do not take the relatively limited attention to implementation and transition in this book as an indication of the importance that should be given to these topics. In fact, "even the most sophisticated and elegant designs are doomed if management fumbles the implementation" (Nadler & Tushman, 1997). However, since we will not be able to do the topic of organizational change justice here, and since there are many excellent resources on organizational change available,[3] the discussion in this chapter is limited to those aspects specific for transitioning to a new organization design. ◀

Staging the Transition

Staging refers to the question whether the desired future state—the result of the design work—can be achieved in one step, with a 'big bang'. This question can be answered by considering the results of the impact assessment: how big is the gap that needs to be bridged? If an organization wants to move from a highly centralized, functional design to a design with decentralized, self-sufficient micro-enterprises, this gap may be too big to bridge in one step. If that is the case, a staged approach should be chosen. This means that one or more intermediary stages—or plateaus—are defined. Such a plateau will require a separate design effort, because it needs to be a self-contained organization design that can act as the end state, if

[3] The work of John Kotter (1996, 2014) is a popular entry point to change management for practitioners. For a review of Kotter's and other models, and an integration with scholarly research, see Stouten et al. (2018).

needed. The transition plan will then cover the road to the first plateau in detail, and the organization will revisit the end state design once that first plateau has been reached.

Is Piloting a New Organization Design a Good Idea?

It is important to stress here that an intermediary stage or plateau is not the same as a pilot. A pilot for a new organization design is only useful "when there is a contained unit that is composed of all or most of the elements of the larger system" (Kesler & Kates, 2011, p. 212). That condition is rarely met. In all other cases, a pilot will give a distorted view of the impact and outcomes of the new design. For instance, piloting two autonomous teams in the context of an organization that has not yet adapted its centralized support functions and management processes will likely show low effectiveness and high frustration for these teams. That is not the result of a design flaw, but of the fact that the design has only been partially implemented. If a comprehensive test of the design is needed, the stress test described in this chapter—which can be made as large-scale and sophisticated as the steering committee wants—is generally a better idea than a pilot. ◀

Generally speaking, it is rare to see a steering committee give the go-ahead for transitioning to a design that needs an intermediary plateau. The results of the impact assessment—at the end of the strategic design stage—should produce enough information to assess the feasibility of implementing the design. If the gap is considered too big, the design would typically be sent back to the design team for another iteration. In fact, if the right conditions and design criteria were set and adhered to during the design process, the design team would not produce an infeasible design.

Pacing the Transition

In general, a high pace for the transition is to be preferred, for a number of reasons. First of all, the trigger for the redesign typically and preferably has some urgency behind it: a new strategy, new competitors, or rapid growth (see Chap. 3). The faster the fit between context and organization design can be restored, the better. If the organization waits too long, the context may have shifted substantially again. Second, a transition that takes too long loses momentum and creates prolonged insecurity for employees (Galbraith et al., 2002). Of course, going fast also comes with risks, such as leaving people behind or causing confusion. But this is where the time investment of the collaborative approach proposed in this book pays off. Since a lot of communication and sensemaking has already taken place in the course of the design process, it is much easier and less risky to go fast during implementation.

Sequencing the Transition

A third dimension of the transition strategy is that of sequencing: in what order will the changes take place? Depending on the scope of the new organization design, changes can pertain to any of the elements of the Star model. A general principle to use is to start with high-visibility changes (Galbraith et al., 2002). This will likely include structural changes, such as changes to the composition and responsibilities of the leadership team of the organization and of their direct reports. Other highly visible changes include major shifts in accountabilities, responsibilities, and the associated metrics and rewards: if a team's rewards change from being based on revenue to being based on the profit they generate, that will likely have an immediate impact on their priorities and the way they work. In general, one of the most visible changes and the one with the biggest personal impact is the staffing process: employees move into new roles, join new teams, or may decide the new organization design is not for them. We will discuss the staffing process further in the section on people processes.

Governing the Transition

A final point to address as part of the transition strategy is how the process will be governed. It is crucial that there is continuity between the governance of the stages that came before and the transition stage. That means the same steering committee will still have a central role to play. They need to be at the steering wheel of the transition, the same as they were for the design. Appointing a transition manager and a transition team will be a first step. In addition, there may be a role in the transition for members of the design team—responsible for the strategic design—and of the work groups, who produced the operational design. Members of the design team should take a role in continuing a form of design governance: making sure that the inevitable changes to the design which will arise during implementation are addressed in a way that is consistent with the strategic design and that the implications of these changes for other parts of the design are carefully thought through. This can take the form of a 'design board'—consisting of one or more members of the steering committee, some members of the original design team, and the transition manager—that has the final say on any major changes in the design. Members of the working groups can be a valuable addition to the broader transition team, since they are already intimately familiar with some specific aspects of the design. The sociotechnical principles of Albert Cherns eloquently emphasize the important role of the transition team.

> As we are engaged in change from a traditional to a new organization, from a traditional to a new philosophy of management, from an old to a new system of values, we need to see the design team and its process as a vehicle of transition. Its design process embodies the new values, its membership constitutes a cadre for diffusing those new values through the organization. Its role in selecting and socializing the new leadership is vital. (Cherns, 1987, p. 159)

9.3.2 People Processes

Once the major decisions about staging, pacing, sequencing, and governing the transition have been taken, the transition plan can be developed by the transition team. This plan will include all the activities necessary to implement the changes to all aspects of the Star model: task, structure, information and decision processes, and reward systems. The element of the Star model we have not touched upon so far is that of people processes. In any transition plan to a new organization design, people processes will need to have a place.

At the very least, there will be a staffing process to transition people into new roles and to attract new talent as the new organization design is populated. The transition to a new organization design is "a window of opportunity to bring more or different talent into the business" (Kesler & Kates, 2011, p. 190). When the CEO of a medium-sized, internationally operating firm looked back recently on the transition his organization went through in moving to a new design, he highlighted this aspect. By promoting people into new roles and attracting new external talent, there had been this big influx of energy and renewal. It made the staffing process a very positive one. To get this energy flowing, a number of principles should form the basis of the staffing process as part of the transition to a new organization design (based on Galbraith et al., 2002; Kesler & Kates, 2011):

- *Fill senior positions first*: this is a highly visible change that puts the end-responsibility for the subsequent transition steps in the right hands.
- *Conduct the staffing process quickly*: dragging the process out will create prolonged and unnecessary insecurity and anxiety for employees.
- *Make the process transparent*: there need to be clear criteria and requirements for new or changed jobs and a transparent process for how candidates are assessed; this process needs to refer back to the HR policies that were set during the discovery stage (see Chap. 7).
- *Be rigorous in the assessment of candidates*: if the organization truly wants to seize the opportunity the transition offers to get the right talent in the right places, employees should not be moved into new jobs without a thorough evaluation of their fitness for the role; furthermore, the organization should not shy away from looking externally if a suitable candidate is not found among their current staff.

Besides the staffing process, the new organization design may have an impact on other people processes as well. Performance feedback is a process that is frequently impacted. If an organization moves from a traditional model of a manager with a team of direct reports for which he conducts the performance evaluation to a model in which teams are more autonomous and managers are placed at a distance, this will impact how performance feedback can and should be done. As we saw in Chap. 5, this was one of the necessary changes in the people processes of ING as they moved to their new model with 'squads' and 'chapters'.

---

[1] I refer the interested reader to Boxall and Purcell (2016) and Heneman et al. (2018).

People processes form a topic we cannot do full justice to in this book. We have highlighted some important aspects here that are linked to the transition to a new organization design. Luckily, there are many excellent resources available for the reader interested in the field of human resource management.[4]

The transition plan together with the operational design forms the deliverables of the prepare transition stage. Based on this, the steering committee can decide to give the go-ahead for the transition. This is the third, and most important, go/no-go moment of the design approach as proposed in this book. A positive decision will move the project into the transition stage. That is where the guidance that this book offers ends, and more general resources on project management and change management will prove valuable.[5] The issue that remains for us to discuss here is that of continuous design.

9.4 Continuous Design

In her work on organization design, Naomi Stanford makes a distinction between project design and continuous design (Stanford, 2021). The approach we have proposed in this book would belong in the category of project design, or what Marianne Livijn called 'macro design'. In accordance with contingency theory—see Chap. 3—macro design assumes an organization has the ability "to create and maintain fit through episodic sequences of static organization (re)design" (Livijn, 2019, p. 4), and that this design project "takes place isolated from the day-to-day activities of the organization" (ibid., p. 4).

So, what is meant by continuous design or 'micro design' (Livijn, 2019)? This complementary view assumes that a deliberate, project-based design effort—such as one that follows the approach proposed in this book—is not always necessary or feasible. Small changes in the context of an organization are constantly taking place, which may influence the fitness of an organization design at the micro level. Customer demands may change, local regulations may be adapted, new competitors may enter the field, and technology may offer new possibilities. Not every change justifies the expense associated with a full-fledged redesign project. It pays to have organization design ability embedded in the organization, not in the form of a central pool of organization design consultants—although that may also be a good idea for larger organizations—but in the form of some level of organization design skills and competences for all employees and for managers in particular. We may again turn to Albert Cherns' sociotechnical principles for guidance.

> Redesign is not the task of a special design team; it is the function of self-regulating operating teams provided with the techniques of analysis, the appropriate criteria and the principles of design. (Cherns, 1987, p. 160)

---

[5] Chapter 14 of Kesler and Kates (2011) and Chap. 7 of Stanford (2018) offer guidance on aspects of project and change management as they specifically apply to organization design transitions.

Performing a systematic evaluation of the organization design—whether that design was implemented last year or has been there since the organization was founded—forms an important input for continuous design. The design criteria and the purpose statement of the design effort (see Chap. 7) can be used as a basis to answer the question whether or not the design achieved its intended outcomes. If no design criteria were drawn up for the current organization design, they can usually be reverse engineered by making a reconstruction of the context at the time the design was initiated. I once had to go deep into the archives and had to track down former employees to help an organization reverse engineer the design criteria for their current organization. In doing this, it is important to be aware of the fact that evaluations are not always welcomed by those responsible for the organization design (Worren et al., 2019).

In building continuous design ability, employees and (middle) managers will have an important role to play. They are the ones that can most accurately perceive changes in the external environment, and they should be equipped to make micro-design changes. Typically, these changes will be in the area of linking mechanisms: adding or refining a management process, improving ways to share the work status among teams, or forming a new cross-unit team. With the help of HR, changes to roles could also be implemented, and reward systems could be enhanced. At some point, however, the limits of what can be achieved by micro design will be reached, and an organization (macro) redesign project will need to be initiated. In keeping with the design principle of creating flexibility (see Chap. 4), good macro-designs are the ones that offer ample room for micro-level adaptations.

Calls for the manager as designer have been heard frequently over the past two decades (Romme, 2003; Boland & Collopy, 2004; Brown, 2008; Garud et al., 2008; Van Bree, 2014; Puranam, 2018; Livijn, 2019). I am not seeing a lot of that design ability materializing yet in the organizations that I come across. But as the traditional role of middle managers comes increasingly under threat with the emergence of new organization models such as those we saw in Chap. 5, it seems the pressure is building. It is my hope that this book is not just a resource for those undertaking project design, but that its frameworks, principles, and approaches are also of value to employees and managers building their abilities for continuous organization design.

Review Questions

1. Which of the key questions for the impact assessment mentioned in Table 9.1 are the three most important ones, in your opinion? Why so?
2. What are some of the challenges you see of doing a stress test as part of the impact assessment?
3. If the steering committee decides not to go ahead with the design based on the impact assessment, does that mean something went wrong during the design process? Why or why not?

4. The steering committee asks you to go ahead with the implementation based on the strategic design. They want to avoid 'overdesign', so they propose to skip the detailed operational design. What would you do?
5. What are some of the differences you see between the design team in the strategic design stage and the work groups that produce the operational design?
6. What do you consider to be the default option: give each team a team lead, or assume teams can be self-managing? Why so?
7. What do you prefer: considering the amount of work a given and basing the team size on that amount? Or vice versa, considering the size of the team a given and basing the amount of work for the team on that size? Why so?
8. Do you think defining leadership roles is a challenging part of the design process? Why or why not?
9. Can you give an example of a situation in which piloting a new organization design is a good idea?
10. What are some indicators that the gap from current to future organization design is too big to bridge in one step?
11. Which downsides do you see of choosing a high pace for the transition?
12. What are some of the risks associated with the staffing process during an organization design transition?
13. Which do you think is the more important competence for an organization to have: project design (macro-design) ability or continuous design (micro-design) ability? Why so?

References

Boland, R. J., & Collopy, F. (2004). Design matters for management. In R. J. Boland & F. Collopy (Eds.), *Managing as designing*. Stanford University Press.

Boxall, P., & Purcell, J. (2016). *Strategy and human resource management* (4th ed.). Palgrave.

Brown, T. (2008). Design thinking. *Harvard Business Review, 86*(6), 84–92.

Cherns, A. (1987). Principles of sociotechnical design revisited. *Human Relations, 40*(3), 153–162.

De Sitter, L. U., Den Hertog, F., & Dankbaar, B. (1997). From complex organizations with simple jobs to simple organizations with complex jobs. *Human Relations, 50*(5), 497–534.

Galbraith, J., Downey, D., & Kates, A. (2002). *Designing dynamic organizations: A hands-on guide for leaders at all levels*. Amacom.

Galbraith, J. R. (2010). The multi-dimensional and reconfigurable organization. *Organizational Dynamics, 39*(2), 115–125.

Garud, R., Jain, S., & Tuertscher, P. R. (2008). Incomplete by design and designing for incompleteness. *Organization Studies, 29*(3), 351–371.

Hackman, J. R., & Oldham, G. R. (1976). Motivation through the design of work: Test of a theory. *Organizational Behavior and Human Performance, 16*(2), 250–279.

Hackman, J. R., & Wageman, R. (2005). When and how team leaders matter. *Research in Organizational Behavior, 26*, 37–74.

Heneman, H. G., Judge, T. A., & Kammeyer-Mueller, J. D. (2018). *Staffing organizations* (9th ed.). McGraw-Hill Education.

Jelinek, M., Romme, A. G. L., & Boland, R. J. (2008). Introduction to the special issue organization studies as a science for design: Creating collaborative artifacts and research. *Organization Studies, 29*(3), 317–329.

Kesler, G., & Kates, A. (2011). *Leading organization design: How to make organization design decisions to drive the results you want*. Jossey-Bass.
Kotter, J. P. (1996). *Leading change*. Harvard Business School Press.
Kotter, J. P. (2014). *Accelerate: building strategic agility for a faster-moving world*. Harvard Business Review Press.
Kuipers, H., Van Amelsvoort, P., & Kramer, E. (2020). *New ways of organizing: Alternatives to bureaucracy*. Acco Nederland.
Laloux, F. (2014). *Reinventing organizations: A guide to creating organizations inspired by the next stage of human consciousness*. Nelson Parker.
Livijn, M. (2019). Navigating in a hierarchy: How middle managers adapt macro design. *Journal of Organization Design, 8*(1), 1–27.
Nadler, D. A., & Tushman, M. L. (1997). *Competing by design: The power of organizational architecture*. Oxford University Press.
Oldham, G. R., & Hackman, J. R. (2010). Not what it was and not what it will be: The future of job design research. *Journal of Organizational Behavior, 31*(2/3), 463–479.
Puranam, P. (2018). *The microstructure of organizations*. Oxford University Press.
Romme, A. G. L. (2003). Making a difference: Organization as design. *Organization Science, 14*(5), 558–573.
Schmitz, D. (2021). *Complex change needs more than change management*. Retrieved April 22, 2021, from https://blog.on-the-mark.com/blog/complex-change-needs-more-than-change-management
Stanford, N. (2018). *Organization design: the practitioner's guide* (3rd ed.). Routledge.
Stanford, N. (2021). *Continuous organization design*. Retrieved April 22, 2021, from https://naomistanford.com/2021/03/08/continuous-organisation-design/
Stouten, J., Rousseau, D. M., & De Cremer, D. (2018). Successful organizational change: Integrating the management practice and scholarly literatures. *Academy of Management Annals, 12*(2), 752–788.
Van Bree, J. (2014). *Game based organization design: New tools for complex organizational systems*. Palgrave Macmillan.
Worren, N. (2018). *Organization design: Simplifying complex systems* (2nd ed.). Routledge.
Worren, N., Van Bree, J., & Zybach, W. (2019). Organization design challenges: Results from a practitioner survey. *Journal of Organization Design, 8*(1), 1–18.

Index

J. van Bree, *Organization Design*, https://doi.org/10.1007/978-3-030-78679-3

The manufacturer's authorised representative in the EU is Springer Nature Customer Service Centre GmbH, Europaplatz 3, 69115 Heidelberg, Germany. If you have any concerns regarding our products, please contact ProductSafety@springernature.com

Printed and bound by CPI Group (UK) Ltd, Croydon, CR0 4YY
30/09/2026
02225439-0015